"Lee Warren opens himself up entirely to being seen, and he ministers to readers in the process."

—TRACI RHOADES, author of *Not All Who Wander (Spiritually) Are Lost*

"Grief isn't tame, something Dr. Lee Warren knows as a follower of Jesus, a husband, a father, and a neurosurgeon. Get ready to laugh and cry. But even more—get ready for a massive dose of hope!"

—MARK VROEGOP, pastor and author of *Dark Clouds, Deep Mercy*

"Dr. Lee Warren not only helps diagnose what we're feeling and experiencing in dark times, but also, like any good doctor, he educates us on what we need to do to move forward on a path to healing. This book is a prescription for hope."

—JARRETT STEPHENS, pastor and author of *The Always God*

"In a time that truly tries the depth of our humanity, Dr. Lee Warren's work lifts us to higher ground."

—PAUL SAMUEL DOLMAN, author of *Hitchhiking with Larry David* and host of the *What Matters Most* podcast

"As a hospital chaplain, I walk into rooms saturated with the pain of The Massive Thing. When that first shock of pain and the following numbness fades, the intentional choices toward hope that Lee demonstrates will guide my conversations with others—and with myself."

—JON SWANSON, PhD, hospital chaplain, professor, and author of *This Is Hard*

"World-renowned neurosurgeon Lee Warren has experienced severe tragedy in his own life and witnessed more of it in his patients. With his characteristic honesty and grace, he lays out a step-by-step, battle-tested self-treatment plan that combines scientific and biblical truths."

—MICHAEL GUILLEN, PhD, author and former *ABC News* science editor

"When hard things knock you out, you can't stay out. Dr. Lee Warren prescribes a treatment plan that will help you rise again so you can discover hope in hardship."

—JOHN BEVERE, bestselling author, minister, and co-founder of Messenger International

"If you're tired of books that promise in the title that you'll feel better and be happier—but don't actually deliver a plan to get and live better—then *Hope Is the First Dose* is the book you've been waiting for. It is the blessing and blueprint the world needs right now."

—KRISTIN SMEDLEY, TEDx speaker and bestselling author

"*Hope Is the First Dose* teaches and enables the reader to find healing and hope after major trauma."

—SCOTTY SMILEY, MAJ (RET), U.S. Army, author of *Hope Unseen*

"Neurosurgeon Dr. Lee Warren's rediscovery of the need for faith, family, and friends is a prescription for all of us to recall in times of severe adversity."

—JOSEPH C. MAROON, MD, FACS, neurosurgical
consultant for the Pittsburgh Steelers

"This book opens us up to the depths of human experience. The brave and vulnerable stories, including the author's own, touch the sacred places of pain and loss in each of us to bring hope and healing."

—CATRINA HENDERSON, teacher, pastor, and director
of undergraduate studies at Alphacrucis College

"With beautiful prose and intimate insights, these pages take you where you need to go before life forces you to go there. And if you're already 'there,' I have good news for you: You've found your book."

—ADDISON BEVERE, author of *Saints* and COO of Messenger International

"When you stare into the abyss of loss that stands between you and the life you lived before, grasp hands with Dr. Lee Warren and hold on tight. Warren's bedside manner is honest and kind, companionable and direct. Bring your heartache to these pages and find healing and abundant life again."

—CLARISSA MOLL, author of *Beyond the Darkness*

"Dr. Warren provides a treasure chest of life experience about how he deals with the hard knocks of life. That a man and his family can go through so much, be so low and near the bottom, and then, through God's miraculous grace, fly so high! It's utterly amazing, Jack!"

—UNCLE SI ROBERTSON, *Duck Dynasty*

"Dr. Lee Warren has personally gone through the devastating school of loss and come out stronger on the other side of what he calls The Massive Thing—or TMT. No matter what your TMT is, you will walk away from this book with a deep infusion of God's healing hope!"

—TOMMY WALKER, singer-songwriter and worship leader

"Lee Warren is not a rocket scientist, but he is a brain surgeon. He is also a brother who understands both suffering and God's grace and kindness in the deepest trials. I love Lee's tender heart and warm wisdom, and they are fully evident in *Hope Is the First Dose*."

—RANDY ALCORN, director of Eternal Perspective Ministries
and author of *Heaven*

"Lee takes us on a journey through his personal heartbreak to his scriptural and scientific discoveries about the power of changing your mind. His 'treatment plan' may be just what you need to find happiness and hope again."

—JIM DALY, president of Focus on the Family

HOPE IS THE FIRST DOSE

HOPE IS THE FIRST DOSE

A Treatment Plan for Recovering from Trauma,

Tragedy, and Other Massive Things

W. Lee Warren, MD

WATERBROOK

All Scripture quotations, unless otherwise indicated, are taken from the Holy Bible, New International Version®, NIV®. Copyright © 1973, 1978, 1984, 2011 by Biblica Inc.™ Used by permission of Zondervan. All rights reserved worldwide. (www.zondervan.com). The "NIV" and "New International Version" are trademarks registered in the United States Patent and Trademark Office by Biblica Inc.™ Scripture quotations marked (AMP) are taken from the Amplified® Bible, copyright © 2015 by the Lockman Foundation. Used by permission. (www.lockman.org). Scripture quotations marked (BSB) are taken from the Holy Bible, Berean Study Bible, BSB. Copyright © 2016, 2020 by Bible Hub. Used by permission. All rights reserved worldwide. Scripture quotations marked (ESV) are taken from the ESV® Bible (The Holy Bible, English Standard Version®), copyright © 2001 by Crossway, a publishing ministry of Good News Publishers. Used by permission. All rights reserved. Scripture quotations marked (MSG) are taken from The Message, copyright © 1993, 2002, 2018 by Eugene H. Peterson. Used by permission of NavPress. All rights reserved. Represented by Tyndale House Publishers. Scripture quotations marked (NASB) are taken from the (NASB®) New American Standard Bible®, copyright © 1960, 1971, 1977, 1995, 2020 by the Lockman Foundation. Used by permission. All rights reserved. (www.lockman.org). Scripture quotations marked (NCV) are taken from the New Century Version®. Copyright © 2005 by Thomas Nelson. Used by permission. All rights reserved. Scripture quotations marked (NLT) are taken from the Holy Bible, New Living Translation, copyright © 1996, 2004, 2015 by Tyndale House Foundation. Used by permission of Tyndale House Publishers, Carol Stream, Illinois 60188. All rights reserved. Scripture quotations marked (TPT) are taken from The Passion Translation®. Copyright © 2017, 2018, 2020 by Passion & Fire Ministries Inc. Used by permission. All rights reserved. (ThePassionTranslation.com). Scripture quotations marked (Voice) are taken from The Voice™. Copyright © 2012 by Ecclesia Bible Society. Used by permission. All rights reserved. Scripture quotations marked (YLT) are taken from Young's Literal Translation. Public domain.

Published in the United States by WaterBrook, an imprint of Random House, a division of Penguin Random House LLC.

WATERBROOK and colophon are registered trademarks of Penguin Random House LLC.

Library of Congress Cataloging-in-Publication Data
Names: Warren, W. Lee, author.
Title: Hope is the first dose: a treatment plan for recovering from trauma, tragedy, and other massive things / W. Lee Warren, MD.
Description: First edition. | Colorado Springs: WaterBrook, [2023] | Includes bibliographical references.
Identifiers: LCCN 2022042519 | ISBN 9780593445396 (hardcover) | ISBN 9780593445402 (ebook)
Subjects: LCSH: Psychic trauma—Religious aspects—Christianity.
Classification: LCC BF175.5.P75 W37 2023 | DDC 155.9/3—dc23/eng/20221228
LC record available at https://lccn.loc.gov/2022042519

Printed in Canada on acid-free paper

waterbrookmultnomah.com

2 4 6 8 9 7 5 3

Book design by Caroline Cunningham

Branch image variations based on the original image by AdobeStock/Kirill

Most WaterBrook books are available at special quantity discounts for bulk purchase for premiums, fundraising, corporate and educational needs by organizations, churches, and businesses. Special books or book excerpts also can be created to fit specific needs. For details, contact specialmarketscms@penguinrandomhouse.com.

To Josh, my son and my friend: you're stronger than you know

Lisa, for loving Mitch as your own, and for catching all my tears

Dale and Joyce Margritz, friends who became
family in the furnace of suffering

And to all those looking for the light again

Dum spiro spero (While I breathe, I hope)

Contents

Author's Note

The stories in this book are true. Names and some identifying details have been changed to protect the privacy of individuals. Conversations are reproduced from memory, and the dialogue is true to the spirit of the conversations, even if the actual words I use have been changed. Drs. Win Lyle, Michael Roberts, Jonna Cubin, and Eric Cubin graciously allowed me to use their names and the shared parts of our stories.

MEDICAL DISCLAIMER

This is a book about how to deal with the hardest things in life and still find your way back to hopefulness, faith, peace, and happiness—even if that happiness may look different from what you knew before. In the following pages, I talk a lot about something I call "self–brain surgery," and I lay out my treatment plan for *the parts of healing that we can do ourselves with God's help*. However, there are times and situations when we need professional help to process and recover from trauma, abuse, loss, and other serious life events, and even anxiety, depression, and other mood and thought disorders. *Do not substitute my advice for the advice of your physician or therapist!* Please, if you're struggling, seek professional help.

Prologue

It's Coming for You, but There's a Plan

Shatter them with double destruction.

—Jeremiah 17:18, BSB

Awake, O sleeper,
    and arise from the dead,
and Christ will shine on you.

—Ephesians 5:14, ESV

Once, when I was a student at the United States Air Force School of Aerospace Medicine, I received a ride in a T-37 jet trainer aircraft so I could learn about the gravitational forces that pilots' bodies are exposed to. This experience would help me be a better flight surgeon, a better air force physician.

Prior to the flight, the crew chief responsible for the airplane gave me a briefing on the things I needed to know for a safe flight. He walked me to the plane, helped me get settled into the cockpit, fastened my safety harnesses around me, and then directed my attention to the floor under my feet.

"Sir," he said in a deep Texas drawl, "keep your feet off them pedals 'less you want to turn this into a real short trip, understand?"

I nodded. "Yes, Sergeant."

"Good," he said. "And, Lieutenant, you see that yellow handle there?"

I noticed the U-shaped metal handle just in front of my seat. It was labeled **EJECTION SEAT! CAUTION!**

"Yes, Sergeant, I see it," I said.

He leaned closer and said in a louder voice, "There ain't no rocket in this seat; only one like it in the whole air force. Just a big ol' spring. If you should pull that handle before you've reached one thousand feet of altitude, sir, you will be killed. Do you understand, Lieutenant?"

"I do. I won't touch it," I said.

He smiled, straightened, and gave a crisp salute. I returned the salute and he said, "You have yourself a nice flight, then, Lieutenant. Keep your feet still, though."

He walked away, the pilot climbed into the cockpit, and we had an amazing and uneventful flight, outside of a little vomiting and a lot of prayer while he introduced me to aerobatics.

———— // ————

This book is about what happens when *life* pulls the yellow handle before you've reached a safe altitude: You get ejected from everything you know and launched onto a dangerous and seemingly impossible trajectory that feels completely out of your control and unsurvivable. There's no rocket in the seat; you're going to fall.

When the handle gets pulled and we get launched, the inciting event is what I call The Massive Thing, or TMT. These life traumas cause tremendous pain and invoke in us a sense of being lost or out of control. They trigger emotional and even physical problems that reach into every area of our lives and are, in every way, massive things.

Although I'll be sharing a lot about my own TMT in the pages to come, the reason I wrote this book is because you have some massive thing in your life, too, friend. Whatever it is, it's *your* massive thing: someone left, someone cheated, the biopsy was bad, the baby didn't have a heartbeat, somebody died, you've suffered abuse, a global pandemic destroyed your business . . . there's something.

And I hate to break it to you, but if you don't have that massive thing yet, you will. Some of us feel like our whole lives are a series of less-massive-but-still-troubling traumas, which you could call "mini-massive things," but the truth is, your trauma is your trauma.

The bad news? TMT is impossible to survive without a treatment plan—just as it's impossible for the T-37's ejection seat to deploy its parachute in time to save your life if there's not enough altitude.

The good news? I've spent more than twenty years studying the best way to doctor people when I can't save them with surgery or medicine. And my family has been in graduate school for human suffering since 2013, after our TMT, and I've been taking notes. What I've learned is that it's not impossible to live again. Somehow, God can deploy the chute and you can survive—find your feet, find your faith, and even find your happiness again. It won't look the same, but you *can* find it.

When TMT comes for you, you'll feel overwhelmed, desperate, and crushed. To make it worse, TMT will eject you from your life, just as pulling that handle will shoot you off into space, and you can never go back to your old life. It's a double destruction: Your body will ache, your faith will plummet, and you won't know what to do.

TMT is the gift that never stops giving. You'll have post-traumatic stress (and its involuntary intrusions in your least expected moments) and an insatiable desire to purposefully revisit in your mind the thing that hurts you so much. These undesired flashbacks and compulsive ruminations threaten your sanity, and there's a real danger of getting lost in them.

But you're not crazy, and your feelings are normal and natural.

I know because I'm living what I've described. It's been almost ten years, and I've learned a lot about the natural course of TMT and the treatment plan to manage it.

And that, my friend, is why I'm writing this book. Because once you have a treatment plan, you'll start to see the light again.

If you're in the depths of your own TMT, rediscovering hope might seem impossible. But I promise that it *is* possible, and in the pages ahead I'll show you how.

I'll share the story of our family's experience with TMT in part 1. You'll see that TMT happens to everyone, and it's largely out of your control. But in part 2, you will learn that you aren't doomed to be a victim of TMT forever. The Massive Thing will change you, but you have the power to choose how some of those changes affect your life

XIV   PROLOGUE

going forward. After my TMT, I started noticing how other people responded to their traumas and tragedies, and I realized that it's not our experience of trauma that defines our quality of life but rather the choices we make afterward. In part 3, I share stories of patients as they encountered their TMTs and how I made the breakthrough discovery that changed everything for me: *There is a reliable, repeatable method* we can use to find hope when all seems lost. In parts 4 and 5, I present the treatment plan that I discovered and applied to my own broken heart after TMT came uninvited into my life on a Tuesday night in 2013. The treatment plan helped me find happiness again, and helped my wife, Lisa, and our family learn to live again, and it will help you too.

If you're one of those people who skip epilogues when you read, please don't skip this one. Why? Because in the epilogue, you will see how all these stories come together to make sense of two things Jesus said that seem impossible to align:

- In John 16:33, he promised that in this world we would have trouble.
- In John 10:10, he promised that he came to the world to enable us to have abundant lives.

The treatment plan helps you square up these two verses. It helps you know that when the yellow handle gets pulled, the ejection seat's parachute is going to open, even though there's not nearly enough sky below you.

> When TMT comes for you, you'll feel overwhelmed, desperate, and crushed. But there *is* a treatment plan.

As a warning, like in all those drug commercials in which a smiling actor tells you all the side effects of the new drug they're promoting, I must disclose this: The treatment plan is not a vaccine to prevent TMT, and it is not a cure that eradicates TMT and all its harmful effects. It is maintenance chemotherapy to keep us alive and as well as possible in the post-TMT life we must live.

TMT is coming for everyone. It may have already come for you. But as I always tell my patients: It's going to be okay. It's going to take some self–brain surgery. It's going to take some soul surgery. It's going to hurt. It's going to leave a scar.

But there *is* a treatment plan, and the first dose is hope.

PART ONE

When the Thing Happens That You Never Get Over

Look long and hard. Brace yourself for a shock.

Something's about to take place

and you're going to find it hard to believe.

—Habakkuk 1:5, MSG

1

Where on Earth Is Hope?

The thief comes only to steal and kill and destroy. I
came that they may have life and have it abundantly.

—Jesus, John 10:10, ESV

*On Tuesday, August 20, 2013, my nineteen-year-old son Mitchell
died of multiple stab wounds to his neck.*

*His best friend also died in the same way that night but with
only one wound.*

*Whether the knife that was used to kill Mitch was in his hand
or someone else's, whether he was at fault or a victim, we will
never know. It's impossible for us to know. The official story is so
far removed from what we know our gentle son to have been
capable of, we cannot believe it.*

APRIL 2021
NORTH PLATTE, NEBRASKA

"How many kids do you have?" you ask.

I grit my teeth—a little carefully because I've cracked two molars in
the eight years since my son Mitchell died.

It's the worst question you can ask bereaved parents because we immediately go into a private conversation with ourselves. I ask myself, *Five? Or four?*

If I say four, it's with an asterisk, but at least I don't have to go down the waterslide this question is going to take me on if I answer truthfully.

You didn't mean for the question to hurt me, obviously, but there we are.

Here's how this plays out: If I say four, then the whole time we're talking I'm emotionally flogging myself for ignoring the entire life of my beautiful son, just for the sake of sparing myself your inevitable apologies and your prying questions into what happened. I'm Peter at the foot of the cross, in shame about not owning up to who I really am.

If I say five, I'm doing so in hopes that you'll be like most people; you'll nod and say, "That's great! We have three." But it never works out that way for me. There is a 367 percent chance that you're going to respond by saying, "Wow! Tell me about them!"

This is where I deploy tactics. I'll go into great detail about Josh and his wife, Amber, and our amazing new grandson, Ryker. I'll gush over Caity and Nate and their perfect angels, Scarlett and George. Then I'll overshare about Kimber and her special-forces husband, Bryce, and their brilliant son, Jase, and about Kalyn in graduate school and-did-I-tell-you-about-her-research? And, oh boy, our grandkids are destined to be a bunch of world-class athletes and future CEOs, I tell ya!

I'll then try to change the subject, but of course, you're an actuary or a CPA or some sort of math genius, and you stop me.

"Wait, that's only four."

So then it's go time. Let's do this. "We lost Mitch in 2013."

And you never ever just say "I'm so sorry" and move on with the conversation.

Nope. You have to say it.

"What happened?"

I want to lie. "He died saving seventeen nuns, two kittens, and six puppies from a house fire. But he got them all out!"

Unfortunately, my brain stops me. The internet is forever. It's too easy for you to look it up, and for some reason people always do.

So I tell the truth, at least as far as I understand it. "He was stabbed in the neck."

And that's when, every single time, I realize that everyone else in the room has stopped talking, so my words hit everyone's ears like I am speaking directly into them.

Great way to bring a party to a screeching halt.

And then I can't stop myself. I tell you that he and his best friend both died. There were three knives. Multiple stab wounds and blood everywhere. The police in this small Deep South town spent a nanosecond in the house and said Mitch killed his friend and then himself. However, the other boy had only one wound and Mitch had eight. Mitch had a cast on his arm, and all the knives had blood on them, yet the police didn't even check for fingerprints or call for detectives to investigate. It was an open-and-shut case for them—nothing to see here; clean up the scene, put it in the papers as fact, and move on.

But it was not so for us. Mitch was not a fighter. His drug-and-alcohol screen was negative. He loved this other boy. And he hated violence, so the idea of him killing someone and then himself is impossible for me to even contemplate.

Knowing another family was also devastated that night, and being unable to ever know what actually happened, is unbearable. It's impossible. Choose which is more palatable: Your son killed his best friend and then himself, or the two lifelong buddies fought and both died, or some unknown third person got away with murder. None of those provide answers, clarity, or any hope of healing.

By now your mouth is open, you're kicking yourself for asking, and you're trying to find an excuse to go talk to someone else.

Make a mental note to not invite me next time.

———————//———————

So I'm sitting in the dark by the fire, with my two seven-month-old German shorthaired pointers, Harvey and Louis, at my side, trying to find the words to tell you what happened between the Phone Call—the moment life pulled the yellow handle on us—and now, and how we managed to not die but to actually live again. My wife, Lisa, is sleeping down the hall, and I'm battling with myself, deciding whether I love you enough to tell you this story or whether I should just have another cup of coffee and look at funny memes on Instagram until she wakes up. Because giving you the story isn't going to be easy, but I keep hearing a voice—God's, I believe—saying you need my story and that the telling will help more than it hurts.

If you've read my last book, *I've Seen the End of You,* then you already know about Mitch and about how, as a neurosurgeon, I work with a lot of people who are dealing with hard things: brain tumors, head injuries, cancer. I told you in that book that the three things that saved me were: (1) realizing that hopelessness is deadlier than cancer or anything else that can happen to us, (2) that God's promises are all true, and (3) that you can't change your life until you change your mind.

What I didn't tell you was that losing a son made me infinitely sad, hopeless, tormented, lost, and faithless for a while. Your massive thing will likely do the same to you.

Lisa and I had sat on a bench of misery and talked about what needed to happen next: Would we live in the darkness, or would we find a way to walk toward the light again? Then some well-meaning friend asked me to read a book by Dan Harris with the minimally optimistic title *10% Happier.* I did, but it just made me realize that 10 percent happier than infinitely miserable would not move my misery needle enough to help me at all.

So this is the story of the most painful surgery I've ever had: the self–brain surgery I learned how to perform when I needed to transplant into my own head Jesus's promise in John 10:10—that he came here so we could have abundant life—because I felt dead inside.

I don't need to tell you the whole story of losing my son since this is not a book about grief and I've told you a lot already, both here and in *I've Seen the End of You.* But I'm blessed/cursed with writing books that are about multiple things at once: a war memoir (*No Place to Hide*), which was really about control, PTSD, and God's faithfulness, and a book about brain tumors and loss (*I've Seen the End of You*), which was really about doubt, faith, and hope. So here we go again: a book about pain that's really about happiness.

If the human nervous system obeyed classical physics, then an infinitely crushed, sad, or hopeless person could reach emotional equipoise only by obtaining an infinite amount of happiness. But it doesn't work like that. Grief and pain put us into a paradoxical world in which Jesus told us that we will have trouble but also that he came to give us abundant life[1]—and you *can* have both.

But just like the line from the old Sinatra song "Love and Marriage": "You can't have one without the other."

> Losing a son made me infinitely sad, hopeless, tormented,
> lost, and faithless for a while. Your massive thing
> will likely do the same to you.

My research into how people handle the hardest things life can throw at them had shown me that some of those people *were* able to find a path to happiness and abundance eventually. And somehow in our darkest days our family found it, too, by "the awful grace of God."[2]

I wrote this book because Lisa and I realized it wouldn't be fair to tell you only *that* we found a path; I have to tell you *how*. I need to give you the treatment plan because I do love you enough.

But to get to the treatment plan, it's important to start at the place where the trauma of losing our son took us: down a dark mental staircase to the furnace of suffering, the depths of life's worst moments. If you trust me enough to go there briefly, then I'll show you how God pulled me and my family out of the miry clay, out of the horrible pit, how he set our feet on the rock again,[3] and how he can do the same for you when you face your version of The Massive Thing (TMT).

If you'll go down this mental staircase with me, I'll show you how I came to discover the treatment plan, and then you'll be ready for me to share it with you.

In the following pages, I'm going to be talking a lot about things you can do to try to live again after TMT turns the lights out in your world. But in all the talk about changing our minds, self-brain surgery, and fighting for faith, do not think it's all up to you. Because TMT will take your strength and your resolve, and you'll soon despair if you miss this one important point: Just as you have to actually walk into the cancer center to receive the radiation beams you did not invent and cannot administer to yourself, there is some work to be done in learning to live again. But you don't do it alone. I already told you that the first dose is hope—but it comes in a syringe of grace from the skilled hands of the Great Physician.

2

Un-Holy Week

Right now I'm having amnesia and déjà vu at the same time. I think I've forgotten this before.

—Steven Wright, comedian

The Massive Thing arrives in the form of my telephone ringing.

We're already in bed when the Phone Call comes: my ex-wife, desperate, devastated, crying. "Mitchell is dead!"

My memories are patchy; renowned psychiatrist Elisabeth Kübler-Ross did not deal with sudden traumatic losses when she wrote of the five stages of grief. If she had, surely she would have added a sixth: amnesia. It's the most memorable day of my life, and I can't remember most of it.

It's so vague: We wake up our sixteen-year-old daughter, Kalyn, call our other kids and our parents, and make the one-hour drive from Auburn to Prattville, Alabama. I know these things, but they're unknowns. I don't remember, but I know it; I think I've forgotten this before.

We're standing on the street outside the home in which lie the bodies of two teenage boys. We are not allowed to enter. Lisa has held on to me, held me up, held Kalyn's hand since the Phone Call.

> I know these things, but they're unknowns. I don't
> remember, but I know it; I think I've forgotten this before.

We're watching the coroner roll two stretchers to an ambulance. The police say we need to leave. We can get Mitch's belongings and talk to them tomorrow, or whenever they finish their reports. No one tells us what happened, except my ex keeps talking about there being blood everywhere.

I'm too much of a doctor to not notice my own physiology happening at that moment: heart racing, acid taste in my mouth, pacing like a caged animal, feeling fear. But the danger is not here in the street. Whatever happened inside that house has been over for several hours, but my body is acting like I'm in great peril. *This can't be real. Maybe it's a mistake and it's not really Mitch. God, can this be happening? I feel like I'm going to explode!*

My phone rings. It's a patient calling. I don't answer. Instead, I call Dr. Win Lyle, an orthopedic surgeon colleague and friend in Auburn, and he tells me he'll take care of it. Later, I will learn that Win told the hospital operator to call him with everything until further notice.

I remember making one other phone call that desperate evening. After speaking to Win, I realize that I have a patient in the hospital, so I call my friend Dr. Michael Roberts, an internal medicine hospitalist who I know is working tonight. Mike agrees to discharge the patient for me and to handle any issues in the hospital.

We're all just standing in the street as the ambulance carrying Mitch and his friend rolls past, no lights and sirens blaring for what is the worst emergency of our lives. Just silence. A police officer walks over and again says, "Sir, y'all need to go home now. Sorry for your troubles."

Somehow, we get back home safely, and we sit on Kalyn's bed to try to help her go to sleep. She says, "Lisa, Dad, what are we supposed to do now?"

I didn't know. I still don't know.

That is all I remember from that night.

—————— // ——————

My friend Henk-Jan, who lost his beautiful wife, Ineke, to glioblastoma, says of the early days of his grief, "Each day had its own color." For me, for my family, Tuesday's color was black. And I'm grateful for the grace of amnesia, because the parts I do remember are worse than anything else I've encountered in my fifty-three years: worse than war with its firebombed babies and blown-up teenage troops, worse than divorce, worse than PTSD. Although this situation is worse than the PTSD from the war, it has caused a recurrence of it. Nice.

And yet despite the lack of concrete memories for most of those awful first hours, one memory is burned into my brain: I had a deep, absolute knowledge that we were watching the birth of a new life for our family, the beginning of a permanent differentness that would change every one of us forever.

The first day of our very un-holy week: Black Tuesday.

We were living a new creation story. Except in ours, God said, "Let there be darkness." And so it was.

"And there was evening, and there was morning—the first day."[1]

3

What Color Is Today?

This is the curse of time. Alas!
In grief I am not all unlearn'd;
Once thro' mine own doors Death did pass;
One went, who never hath return'd.

—Alfred, Lord Tennyson, "To J. S."

Day breaks in Alabama, somehow.

I don't know how or how long we slept, but I see the sun rising through the bedroom window and a clear thought forms: *How can there be light when everything feels so dark?*

Lisa says, "We need to check on Kalyn."

We go downstairs to her room, and the lights are already on. She is in her bathroom, fully dressed, fixing her sandy blond hair. I've never seen my baby girl look that distant, that washed out. Her eyes, blue like mine, are even more remarkable framed in red.

Lisa takes her hand. "Honey, why are you getting dressed?"

"I have to go to prayer time. What else should I be doing? Anna Grace is coming to get me."

Anna Grace is Kalyn's best friend. She's part of our family. These two are inseparable, BFFs, always together. Of course she's coming. But going to church today?

Our church is in the middle of its biannual 21 Days of Prayer event. On top of the horror of losing Mitch the previous night, the prayer focus earlier that day was to seek God's blessing on our children. Lisa and I spent the whole time praying for all five of ours, including Mitch. So his death felt especially cruel on the day a whole church had been praying for its young folks. I don't want anything to do with the prayer event today.

"I think you should stay home" is all I can manage.

Kalyn looks right through me. "Dad, I have to go. I sure can't be here; there will be lots of people, and I . . . I can't. I need my routine. I'm going to school too. Mr. Smith and Anna Grace say they'll make it safe for me."

Kalyn is a force of nature, and I am an empty shell in that moment. I have no fight in me and neither does Lisa.

We call her choir director, Mr. Smith. He's already heard, and he promises to look out for Kalyn. When she sings, it's like all the songbirds and all the angels have worked together to design her voice. Choir and theater people are her community, so it makes sense to us, somehow, to let her go.

Anna Grace arrives; we all cry and hug. Lisa, miraculously, summons the ability to make breakfast, but none of us are able to eat. The girls go to school after prayer time at the church, and we later receive texts from Mr. Smith and Anna Grace that Kalyn is huddled in the choir room, surrounded by people who care for her, let her be, and support her. This will be Kalyn's daily life for several weeks.

Patty and Dennis, known to all as Nannie and Tata, are Lisa's parents who live up the street from us. They have lost two children of their own and are at our sides before Kalyn leaves for school. Our middle daughter, Kimber, a fine arts major in her junior year at Auburn University, and her then-boyfriend, Bryce, arrive next. Bryce is holding on to Kimber, who looks as numb and distant as Kalyn does—as we all do. I hold Kimber, who last night stood on the street outside the awful house and waited with us, and we don't say anything. We can't say anything.

I want to tell her it's going to be okay—which my kids have heard me say every time something bad has ever happened in any moment of their lives—but I cannot. Because this time, it's not going to be okay.

Our son Josh, who lives in San Antonio, had surgery on Tuesday morning to fix broken bones in his wrist. He's in a lot of pain, and now not just in his arm. He's medicated, suffering, and needs to be here with us. Lisa calls our friend Huda, who works for American Express, and explains what has happened. Huda does the rest: flights, a car service from the airport in Atlanta. Josh and his then-girlfriend, Amber, will be here tonight, Huda says.

Lisa's best friend, also named Lisa, comes and takes over. She is Greek and, like my Lisa, a designer and a chef. No one will go hungry, and no need of ours will go unmet. Her husband, Hans, my best friend in Auburn, is in Holland attending the funeral of his longtime dear friend who died by suicide a few days before. We speak on the phone but mostly just hear each other breathe.

People who love you, as my friend Jon Swanson says, "show up and shut up." They come, sit, and stay. Zane, my longtime friend and operating-room nurse, arrives, holds on to us, and simply says, "I'm going to sit here and wait. When you need something, I will do it." I cannot remember how many days in a row he comes, but it is many.

The fog of pain clouds most of their faces now: Dear friends, like Christy and Heather, our office staff, friends from church and the hospital, colleagues. All day long, people ring the doorbell, hug us, cry with us, drop off food, sit in our living room and sing worship songs, hold us up against the irresistible gravity of pain.

Relatives from other states, friends of Mitch and ours from every place he had ever lived—Pittsburgh, San Antonio, Montgomery—arrive as evening comes. Everyone on planet Earth, it seems, who has ever loved Mitch or us, pauses their lives and travels to Alabama to stand with us, sit with us, scream and cry with us.

Josh and Amber walk in, and the tears start all over. We sit on the couch and sob, and Josh shares a random memory of saving Mitch in the ocean in Florida a few years before, when Mitch got caught in a riptide and wasn't strong enough to swim through it. "I should have been with him yesterday," Josh says. "I could have saved him again."

Much grace is dispensed this day, most of which we could not appreciate for a few weeks. (Two neighbors, Karen and Samantha, bring an ice chest and leave it in our garage. It is filled with bottled waters, soft drinks, and ice, and there is a bag full of napkins, paper plates, toilet paper, and plastic silverware. Every time we will go into our garage for the next few days, we will find that they have refilled these items. Our friend Rob Brooks, a man of few words, keeps bringing grilled and smoked meat and feeds us for weeks. The hands and feet of Jesus. Someone takes care of our business. Patients with appointments are called, surgeries are postponed, vendors are notified. I have no idea when Lisa makes these arrangements or who actually does all that work, but we never have to think about it.)

Many times, Lisa and I find ourselves crashing together for a moment, wondering if this is all real, if maybe Mitch is okay after all and it's just a crazy nightmare we're both having at the same time.

I remember none of it and all of it simultaneously. Little moments that are clear mix in with vast stretches of black space in my mind.

But two things I can recall perfectly.

A phone call that comes midmorning. My caller ID shows it's a local number, but it's not in my contacts. We've had many such calls already today: "We're praying for you," "Is there anything I can do?" So I don't think twice about answering this one.

"Hello?"

"Lee, this is Cindy Richards. I'm so sorry to hear about your son Mitch."

"Thank you," I say. "But do I know you?"

"No, but I'm praying for you," she says. "I'm a reporter for a TV station in Montgomery. I'm sure you know that lots of people are wondering what really happened last night. It's getting a lot of gossip on social media, so I'd just like to give you a chance to go on record, to tell us your side, to get ahead of it. An exclusive."

This may surprise you, but neurosurgeons are known for being control freaks. But this day, this moment, I let that go. I am not proud of what I say to her.

"You're trying to get a *story* out of us right now? How can you live with yourself?" is the kindest thing I say. The rest would disqualify this book from the Christian section of the bookstore.

Wednesday's color? Red.

The other perfectly stored memory is later, after everyone but family has left.

Lisa and I are standing on our back porch that evening, watching the sun set over the pine trees. The kids are all downstairs huddled together, reminiscing about their brother. Lisa goes into the bedroom to answer a phone call, and I'm alone for the first time since we lost our son.

I look down into the yard, and my mind sees the kids in earlier times, running around in the August heat. Our backyard was the scene of countless moments of great joy as the kids grew up: pool parties, barbecues, laughter. I look out and see the lawn furniture Mitch helped us assemble a few years earlier, and the giant swan float he always lay on in the pool. I feel dizzy, unsteady, nauseated, and there's a vague pain in my right shoulder blade.

I become aware that I'm angry: I hate that I know what's happening physiologically because I've been explaining these things to patients for years. But *knowing it* doesn't make it easier to *feel it*. And it hits me how useless it must have been when I tried to comfort people by saying things like, "Oh, that racing heart is just your amygdala and sympathetic nervous system processing your grief. There's nothing wrong with your heart. It's just your body's response to emotional pain. It will get better." My words were a doctor's version of the Christian platitudes I am already sick of hearing for the past days: "He's in a better place now." Just as impotent, just as offensive. And now I am saying these same useless things to myself. I actually feel like my heart *is* exploding, and knowing the neurochemistry of why it feels that way does not make it better.

I look down from our balcony, and for a moment I feel like I might fall over the railing. Death has passed through my door.

I try to pray, but all I can muster is a thought: *"My God, my God, why have you forsaken me?"*[1]

Lisa returns. "That was the funeral home. We can see Mitch at ten-thirty tomorrow morning."

"And there was evening, and there was morning—the second day."[2]

4

Can It Get Any Worse?

Unless I see the nail marks in his hands and put my finger where the nails were, and put my hand into his side, I will not believe.

—Doubting Thomas, John 20:25

I've swiped my credit card thousands of times. It's such a simple thing; the clerk says the groceries are $43.14, I hand her my American Express, and seconds later I'm out the door with the bags.

But today is different.

"Your total is $3,784.36, sir," the funeral director says.

I watch my hands pull out my wallet like they belong to someone else. I extend my credit card across the desk, and then I see his face clench slightly. "I'm sorry, Doctor. We don't take AmEx. Do you have Visa, Mastercard, or Discover? Or we offer a cash discount."

He's wearing a cheap chocolate-colored suit, and I notice the shoulders are too wide for his scrawny frame. His shirt collar, white with brown vertical stripes, is a good two sizes too big for his tiny neck, and his green tie with a yellow diamond pattern clashes with the whole thing.

I retract my black AmEx—the Centurion card with no spending limit—and a thought barges into my mind: *I could buy this mortuary with this card as long as I could pay it off at the end of the month. But I can't cremate my son with it.*

He takes my Visa and swipes it.

The receipt—I kid you not—actually has **ANDERSON FUNERAL HOME WISHES YOU A NICE DAY** printed on the bottom.

As I put my card away, he leans forward and says, "Is there anything else I can do for you?" He's close enough for me to smell the perfect combination of coffee, Krispy Kreme, and cigarette smoke on his breath.

Anything else you can do? Let me give you a list:

Bring my son back, you moron.
Let all this be just a horrible nightmare, and I'll wake up in San
    Antonio where our daughter is giving birth to my first grandchild
    any day now.
Don't make a dad choose which urn to buy three days after his son died.

He interrupts my thoughts. "Is there anything else, sir?"

It's not his fault; it's just business. I tell him there's nothing else, and then I step out into the hall.

Grief and fury mix like oxygen and fire, lighting a neurotransmitter storm in my limbic brain. *Skin feels clammy, mouth is dry, stomach is burning. I need to run! I have to get out of here.*

My frontal lobes take over, trying to calm everything down: *You can't run. You're not dying, and your family needs you.* My brain is duking it out to see whether a fight-or-flight or a calm response will win, and I get to have a stupid front-row seat to the whole thing, without the popcorn. I stop in the bathroom, deal with the fire in my gut, wash my hands, and splash some cold water on my face.

I head back to the viewing room, where Lisa, her parents, and three of our kids—Josh, Kimber, and Kalyn—are waiting for me before we go in to spend a few final moments with Mitch. Our other daughter, Caity, is on the verge of labor almost a thousand miles away, and she and her husband, Nate, are drowning in the paradoxical emotions of excitement and despair—awaiting the birth of their first child while missing their brother's funeral.

My parents have arrived from Oklahoma, as have my sister Michelle and her husband, Jay, and from San Antonio, Lisa's sister, Jessica, and her husband, Ronnie.

There's a short debate in the hall: Kalyn isn't sure she wants to go in. Ultimately, she decides she has to see Mitch one last time, and she summons the bravery.

Later, on the drive home, I receive a text message from the preacher at the church where Mitch's memorial service will be held the next day:

> Good morning, Doctor. Would you please write a eulogy for the program tomorrow?

At my desk that night, I compose what I hope is something Mitch would have appreciated, something that will make people really know who he was.

Forty-eight hours ago, I wouldn't have believed you if you'd told me that I'd be in a room with my refrigerated, embalmed son and then write what would be the final words spoken over his nineteen-year-long life.

But today I do believe it. Because, just as Thomas found his faith by placing his hand in Jesus's side, I have touched the wounds that killed my son. And because I have the receipt right here on my desk. I look at it again—**ANDERSON FUNERAL HOME WISHES YOU A NICE DAY**.

Apparently, $3,784.36 is the cost of dying.

And then I wonder about the future for all of us now: *What's the cost of living?*

---//---

Lisa and I hold hands in the darkness; she is the tether that keeps me from sliding into the abyss of desperation. In twelve hours, we will gather in a church and say goodbye to Mitchell Keaton Warren.

Every time I almost fall asleep, a thought jerks me awake. The most intrusive thought is of the chocolate-suit-wearing mortician's sloppy suturing of my son's neck wounds.

When our daughter Kimber was in art school at Auburn, she cut her hand with a box cutter one day. Not wanting to personally cause my daughter pain, I let a general surgeon colleague in Auburn suture it. However, Kimber was left with a jagged, very visible scar. I've felt guilty about that ever since because I would have done a more elegant job for her. And this night I'm plagued with the same thought: *I should have done it myself.*

When I finally give in to the stress and fatigue, I have a new nightmare. I see the terrorists and bloody soldiers and burned babies, who have been my almost-nightly companions since Iraq. They climb out of a wrestling ring and are then replaced by a knife-wielding, unknown masked person who jumps across the mat to taunt me in my corner. One of the bloody soldiers looks over his shoulder on his way out and says to me, "Don't worry; we'll be back."

"And there was evening, and there was morning—the third day."[1]

5

A Test Dose

In the world of the very small, where particle and wave
aspects of reality are equally significant, things do not
behave in any way that we can understand from our
experience of the everyday world. . . . *All* pictures are
false, and there is no physical analogy we can make to
understand what goes on.

—John Gribbin, *In Search of Schrödinger's Cat*

Our oldest daughter, Caitlyn—we all call her Caity—is married to
my Iraq War colleague Nate. On August 23, 2013, she is twenty-
four years old and nine months pregnant with Scarlett. Lisa and I
and Lisa's parents have plane tickets to be in San Antonio when
Scarlett is born, but, obviously, your son dying cancels your travel
plans.

So Caity, instead of being able to enjoy us arriving and meeting her
first child (who is Patty and Dennis's first great-grandchild and Lisa's
and my first grandchild) is now grieving her little brother and missing
both his funeral and our support.

Back in Alabama, we attend the memorial service around the time
Caity goes into labor.

Our friend Heather Carson, a brilliant professional photographer,
has created a slideshow using pictures gathered from both sides of
Mitch's family. She set it to a Michael Gungor song called "Beautiful
Things," one of Mitch's favorites.

The opening lines are:

All this pain
I wonder if I'll ever find my way

We watch as Mitch progressed from being a brown-haired newborn to a smiling toddler to a four-year-old, saluting the flag with me at a Fourth of July celebration, to a teenager on prom dates, playing his bass guitar, and graduating high school.

The song keeps playing, the lyrics saying that God can make beautiful things from us, but it doesn't feel beautiful to me, and I haven't been able to get through that song since. Seriously, I just tried while writing this, eight years later, and I'm weeping like it happened yesterday.

The drive home is mostly silent, and the grace of amnesia has covered most of it for me. One clear recollection: a magnificent double rainbow over the highway that some of our family took as a sign that God was watching over us. I wondered if it was another promise: *I'll never flood your world with happiness again.*

By the time we get back to Auburn, Caity's labor is in full force. This baby is coming today.

---//---

In retrospect, it was like being in a dark room and having someone turn the lights on and off every few seconds. Light and dark, light and dark—it reminded me of the strobe lights at skating rinks when I was a kid; the lights made it seem like people were jumping through the spaces between the flickers: *She's there! No, she's over there! No, here she is!*

The flickers take us in and out of the pain, over and over. Every few minutes, a text message from Nate:

The epidural's in!

She's nine centimeters.

She's pushing now.

We have a baby!

These happy messages are interspersed with the doorbell ringing and another vase full of funeral flowers being delivered or a visiting pastor or friend showing up to comfort us. And the silent space in between all those flickers is utterly, desperately dark. *It hurts so much! Oh, the baby's coming! I don't think I can stand it anymore! It's a girl!*

Quantum physics describes a world in which an electron can seem to be in two places at the same time. Lisa and I feel we are in that situation. An impossible-but-true reality in which we simultaneously have the worst and the best feelings we can feel.

—————//—————

Scarlett's arrival brought us, kicking and screaming, into a new world. All the happy things—*How much does she weigh? How's Caity feeling? Send pictures!*—felt like little drops of normal in the vast ocean of grief and shock in which we were adrift. But Lisa and I both saw something very clearly, and it probably saved us.

I said before that losing Mitch pushed us into our own creation story because it was clearly going to change our family forever. But the other metaphor I couldn't see until that Friday was this: Just like Holy Week—in which Jesus dies, is buried, and is risen from the dead—we had a death, a burial, and a sort of resurrection too.

And superimposed on Mitch's death and burial and all that darkness, there was Scarlett's arrival, which Lisa and I both understood to mean that there was still light in the world, even if it was so far away, in San Antonio.

The fourth day of the creation story in Genesis was the day God made "the greater light to govern the day and the lesser light to govern the night."[1] In Auburn, Alabama, on the last day of our most un-holy week, it felt like the darkness might win. But Lisa and I, through the arrival of Scarlett and the miracle of new birth, knew that our family had been given this special moment on this very day for a reason, and that the reason was that we needed hope.

We had a new star in heaven, our son whose life had been so brief, so meteoric, so bright. And we had a little more sunlight here on earth, in the form of a crying, helpless newborn who needed us.

"God set them in the vault of the sky to give light on the earth, to govern the day and the night, and to separate light from darkness. And God saw that it was good."[2]

It did not feel good yet, and we could not yet see the light apart from the darkness. But knowing it was there—that Scarlett was there—somehow made us know it was possible. And that was something, a test dose, a tiny sample of hope.

"And there was evening, and there was morning—the fourth day."[3]

6

Holding the Light, Feeling the Darkness

The LORD said to Moses, "Stretch out your hand toward the sky so that darkness spreads over Egypt—darkness that can be felt."

—Exodus 10:21

I wish I could tell you that Scarlett's arrival was the perfect salve for our broken hearts, that she miraculously replaced the horrific grief with perfect happiness. That as soon as we saw her, everything was right again.

It didn't happen that way.

Amazing, healing things would come from having our first granddaughter on the day we said goodbye to our son, but it did not unfold in real time like a magic trick. It's still unfolding.

Ten days after Mitch's funeral, we flew in almost total silence to San Antonio to see Caity, Nate, and the baby. Lisa and I rented a car and drove to their place in Hondo, about forty miles outside the city. Caity and Nate opened the door and we walked in, and then we all just hugged one another and cried for a while.

There were hardly any words for what seemed like an eternity. What could we say?

We were back to the night Mitch died, experiencing it all again with Caity and Nate since we'd been apart when it happened. And then, when we found our breaths and our voices again, Lisa said, "Where's the baby?"

"Sleeping," Caity said. "Come on. I'll show you."

We walked down the short hallway, and Caity opened the door to the nursery. There was the bassinette Lisa had sent, and we crept over and looked inside.

She was so beautiful, perfect, precious. All the good in the universe, all the potential, all the possibility, radiated from that tiny human. And it hit my heart like an atom bomb. My heart that had been broken into a million pieces, my heart I didn't know could feel again, jumped in my chest and I knew I would give my life for this little girl.

Then something unexpected happened.

Lisa held Scarlett for a long time, and I could see in my sad wife's body language that there was more than bonding happening here. Lisa was absorbing love from Scarlett. She held her close, and it was the most tender, beautiful thing I've ever seen.

Lisa straightened, turned, and held Scarlett out to me. "Want to hold her, Pop?"

Lisa and I had decided that we would be called Missy and Pop by our grandchildren. This was back in the days when we laughed and thought about such silly things. The names were the subject of much debate among our children, since we felt too young to be called Grandmother and Grandfather, and Lisa would never have accepted Grandma in any universe.

I voted for Lady Catherine and Sebastian because those sounded pretty regal—since we were making stuff up anyway and I didn't really want a two-year-old naming me Mr. Buttons or Peepaw. But the kids and Lisa vetoed that before anyone really even thought it through. So Missy and Pop it was, although we all knew there was still a chance Scarlett would have the final say in a year or two, so we knew better than to completely rule out Scooter and Meemaw.

I took Scarlett from Lisa, and the energy transfer began immediately. I held her close to my chest, and for a moment the pain I'd been feeling for a week in my right shoulder blade faded.

Then she looked up at me with those angel eyes and that perfect, tiny face, and I had a terrible realization: She was in danger. I knew I could not protect her. After all, we lost her uncle Mitch before she ever got a chance to know him. Your kids are not supposed to die before you do. If we could lose him, we could lose any of them.

When she breathed, I felt something I'd never felt before when holding a baby. It's always fun, it always warms your heart, but this time I felt like she was giving something to me. Like she was transferring life into my dead soul somehow, and I knew I couldn't survive losing her.

Everything felt so heavy, so dark, so dangerous. But here I was, holding the light.

And it felt awful to be *taking something* from her, this reprieve from the darkness, because I should have been *sending* that energy to her. But I had none to give.

Caity and Nate were awash with emotions—the normal ones that new parents always have, plus the normal ones those who just lost a sibling have. The sum of all that felt impossible for any one person to hold, but they had to hold it anyway.

It felt so unfair to have this time that should have been so happy, so fun, be instead so mixed up. There was a constant struggle between the joy—*Look how pretty she is! Hey, she smiled!*—and the pain. When we talked about Mitch, it felt like we were stealing the moment from Scarlett. When we talked about Scarlett, it felt like we were dishonoring our son, like, *How could a parent who buried their son a week ago be smiling and laughing?*

It was beautiful, horrible, perfect, awful, joyous, and impossible, all at once and one at a time. And there were so many "buts": we have this beautiful baby but a dead son; she's so perfect, but so was he; having a granddaughter is the best, but losing a son is the worst.

Infinitely happy, infinitely miserable. But the math didn't work out to leave us neutral. It was both at the same time. Which just made everything feel wrong.

> Everything felt so heavy, so dark, so dangerous. But here I was, holding the light.

Lisa and I stayed in a hotel that night because Caity and Nate didn't have a spare room. We lay there, holding hands, weeping, talking about how perfect Scarlett was and how much we missed Mitch and how in the world is this ever going to feel different, and we finally just cried ourselves to sleep.

I woke up at some point in a sweat. I'd been having nightmares in which I saw Mitch die and was unable to save him. I had to admit it to myself: I was very, very angry.

Angry at myself because I didn't know what had happened to my son, and therefore there was at least some possibility that I could have stopped it somehow—if only I'd known that one thing I needed to. I was mad that I didn't know it, mad that I didn't know I'd needed to know it, mad that I'd now never be able to know it, and mad that it was too late to matter anyhow.

I was so mad.

So hurt.

So broken.

But the worst part was that every other time in my life when I'd felt this much pain, I could reliably talk to God about it. This time, though, I didn't even feel like trying. Because I was mad at him too.

I'd been to war and seen the worst things people can do to one another. I'd been through divorce, I'd lost patients, and I'd run my hands across what I thought were life's roughest textures. Life had, at times, felt like night, as Elie Wiesel so hauntingly described his experiences with the worst of humanity in the concentration camps of Nazi Germany.[1]

So I'd been around it, had my hands on it, brushed my heart up against it. But I must have been wearing my surgeon's gloves.

Because until now, I'd never felt the darkness.

PART TWO

You Choose How It Changes You

I'm just no longer sure that hope holds the same shape as certitude. Can't I sometimes say, "I don't know," or, "I'm not sure"?

—Jen Pollock Michel, *Surprised by Paradox*

7

The Apogee of Hopelessness

Unfortunately, in this world of ours, each person views
things through a certain medium, which prevents his
seeing them in the same light as others.

—Alexandre Dumas, *The Count of Monte Cristo*

We spent two weeks getting Kalyn settled back into her junior year of
high school. Lisa made sure we had breakfast together every day, to sort
one another out and make sure Kalyn was okay before she left for the
day. I say "okay" not in the normal way, of course, because we now had
a new standard. There was no guitar music coming from her room at
5:00 A.M., which is how we were used to waking up with Kalyn in the
house. This child hears new songs in her heart while she sleeps, and she
writes/plays them as soon as she rises. Kalyn's heart for worship music
was the soundtrack of our lives for years.

Now the mornings were very quiet.

Honestly, I can say that without the responsibility of keeping Kalyn
from falling behind in school, Lisa and I might have just sat down and
faded away in those weeks following Mitch's death.

———— *//* ————

As an aside, I have a shelfful of books that friends and pastors dropped
off in those first few weeks to help us "deal with our grief." It was a very

kind gesture, and I have gained much help and peace from those books over the years. But, as a general observation, it is a terrible idea to give a hurting parent a book in the first thirty or so days after their child dies.

"Oh, you're devastated and can't breathe or eat or think about anything other than the fact that your son is gone? Here's a five-hundred-page Timothy Keller book about pain!"

But those of us who grow and heal through reading *need* those books. Give them to us! Just maybe wait until sufficient time has passed. You can tell when it might be time—for example, when we've resumed shaving, when you ring the doorbell at 1:30 P.M. and we're not still wearing pajamas, or when the contractors have left for the last time after fixing the drywall again.

———— // ————

It had been almost a month since Mitch died, and we were back in San Antonio, taking advantage of one more chance to see the baby before the law of self-employment would make us go back to work. Neither of us could stand the thought, but it was an unavoidable fact: Our business would fail if we didn't open up in the next few weeks. We had ten employees who depended on us economically, and our referring doctors and hurting patients could not wait much longer before they would have to find another surgeon.

In the hotel room that morning, the pain in my right shoulder blade was the worst it had ever been. It had started acutely shortly after Mitch died, and I attributed it to stress and to not sleeping well. But it was getting worse—a dull internal pain that seemed to gnaw right through me. I'd been taking Tylenol and Advil around the clock for two weeks, but it was always there.

I stood at the bedside and took off the T-shirt I'd slept in. I was walking into the bathroom to take a shower when Lisa stopped me.

"Lee," she said, "what are these blisters on your back?"

I reached around and felt my skin, and she was right. There were dozens of painful blisters on my right shoulder blade. One of them popped on my hand, and I saw clear fluid on my fingers. I instantly knew what I'd been feeling and what the diagnosis was: I had shingles.

Shingles. The viral infection from varicella-zoster virus, the same virus that causes chicken pox. Old people get shingles. Sick people get shingles.

I had shingles. "He has made my skin and my flesh grow old."[1]

My heart sank, which surprised me because I thought it was already as low as it could get.

"Honey," I said, "you're going to have to go on without me. Scarlett could catch chicken pox from me. I can't be around her until this clears up."

———— // ————

I called my friend Dr. Michael Roberts again, and he prescribed an antiviral medicine for me, which took care of the rash in about four days. What stayed was the pain.

Many patients tell me they feel their shingles-related pain, the so-called post-herpetic neuralgia, for years after the outbreak. I've seen elderly people tormented by the invisible, punishing nerve-ending inflammation, and it very often wrecks their quality of life.

For me, it's a dull ache inside the right shoulder blade that's never really gone away. The only thing—besides telling Lisa I love her—that I'm positive I've done every single day for the last eight years is notice that pain. I've missed days of work, and I'm sure there have been days when I didn't read my Bible or check email, but I've felt that spot on my scapula every day. It's usually just a nagging, subtle thing, but it's always there.

And once in a while, especially when I'm thinking about Mitch, or, for example, writing a book about how to find happiness again after you've suffered devastating loss, it will stab me like someone took a dull bread knife and twisted it into my back. "Hey, just in case you forgot how much it hurt to lose your son, *pow!*"

———— // ————

Back in Auburn a few days later, I got up one morning, poured a cup of coffee, and sat at my computer to write an email to our kids. Since they weren't all home for me to wrap my arms around them—Josh, Nate, and Caity in San Antonio; Kimber and Kalyn in Auburn—I'd been trying to send them all an email each day to keep us connected and make sure everyone was hanging in there. (These emails to my kids set in motion a newsletter that's now read every Sunday in more than forty countries.[2]) When I checked my email, I saw the name Bob Hudson and I shed the first tears of that day.

Bob was the senior editor at Zondervan, the division of HarperCollins that had purchased the rights to my first book, *No Place to Hide: A Brain Surgeon's Long Journey Home from the Iraq War*. It was due to be released in early 2014, and Bob was in the process of making the final edits to the manuscript. An attached file held several chapters he needed me to make changes to.

His email was so kind: "This is the finest memoir I've ever edited." But also demanding: "I need these pages back in the next day or two, please."

I realized then that I hadn't told my publishing team about Mitch.

In my reply, I told Bob what had happened and asked if I could have a little more time. I didn't think I was up to writing yet and knew I was going to have a problem editing the final chapter of that book. Because in it, I talked about how I'd finally gotten my war demons under control, how my family was together and I was okay, and how we had a happy ending.

But that was now just a fairy tale.

------//------

In medical school the saying goes, "Textbooks are always outdated by the time they're published." This is because medical science is always being updated as researchers discover new information and because it takes years to write, edit, prepare, and publish a book.

Over the course of that day, I had multiple emails and calls from Bob and the editorial team at Zondervan. They were so gracious, and they offered to push back the publication date a few months. At a time when many days I couldn't even leave the house, it would have been impossible for me to attend book signings, speaking engagements, or interviews, and Zondervan was so kind to accommodate my need for time and space.

I struggled to get through the edits in the following days because I was uncomfortable leaving out such a critical part of my story. I wrote an afterword for the book that told the story of losing Mitch and how it felt like going to war again, but it did not make it into the book. The editorial team decided to let the story stand as it had been when they acquired it.

So I realized it's not just medical books that are out of date when they are published: My first book was coming out as a story about putting my family back together, and my lost son was going to be an unpublished afterword.

---------//---------

The next Sunday morning, Lisa and I lay in bed listening to the twelve-million decibel silence of our empty house. Kalyn was in Prattville with her mother, and we were alone with Mitch, who was everywhere and nowhere, all at the same excruciating time.

We were going back to work the next day, and the anticipation of having to interact with all those people asking us how we were doing crushed both of us into the mattress with a seemingly inescapable force.

"We need to go to church," Lisa said.

"I know. But God feels so far away. Honestly, I don't think I've felt him since Mitch died," I replied, although I'm not sure how the words came out through my trembling jaw.

She put her hand on my chest. "I know. I haven't either. But I miss him."

We talked for a while, but I just couldn't convince myself to move.

Finally, we decided to watch the online services of our church, Church of the Highlands.

We'd gone to church as a family the week after Mitch died, and it was too much. Too many people offering their well-intentioned but stunningly painful platitudes like "Don't worry! This will all work out for your good" or "God will use this for good!" Too many friends crying, too many people we hadn't seen since the Phone Call who would make us start the grief clock all over again with them. Too much.

And yet, despite our confusion and anger at losing Mitch, despite both of us feeling like God had abandoned us to the furnace of suffering, we knew the only hope we had of finding our way to life again was to somehow find our way to him again too. So Lisa went to the kitchen and got us coffee, and we logged on to watch church in our pajamas.

The pastor, Chris Hodges, was talking about depression, and he said something that hit both of us right in the chest: "If you want to feel better, step out in faith and start doing something. Faith leads, and feelings follow."

After the service, Lisa said, "Why don't we go for a walk? It's a nice day outside."

We lived on the fifth hole of Moore's Mill Club in Auburn, and in the days before the Phone Call, we often walked the course together. We have many warm memories of walking with Mitch, Kalyn, and Lisa's parents, and carrying our obese pug, Piggy, when he proved unable to make it back up the final hill to our house.

But when Lisa suggested the walk, I realized we had not been outside in our yard or on the street since Mitch died, other than to get in a car.

We got dressed, held hands, and walked out into the sunny fall morning. We took our normal route up Covington Ridge to her parents' cul-de-sac, got onto the cart path by the fourth hole, and walked the entire golf course.

Everywhere we looked we saw Mitch. Here's where he ran his first 5K when he joined the cross-country team in high school, after Lisa convinced him he was a good runner. Here's where the kids had an after-dark game of capture the flag. Here's the field where we had six consecutive Thanksgiving Turkey Bowl football games.

The whole world around us reminded us of him. Except the world was still here.

"I'm just so disappointed," I finally said.

"What do you mean?" Lisa said.

"There's so much *future* that's never going to happen. We'll never get to see him fall in love, pursue a profession, see what his kids look like. It's not right."

She stopped walking and turned to me. Her eyes held a lake of tears, and she pulled me close. "I know. We're not supposed to have to guess at what our kids' lives would be like; we're supposed to get to watch it. That's what makes me saddest, I guess. He had a whole life left."

We hugged for a while since neither of us seemed to have the steam to move. Unlike Piggy, we didn't have anyone to carry us home, so we just held each other's hands and somehow made it back.

When we reached our driveway, Lisa said, "We should get the mail. I don't remember the last time we checked it."

The mailbox was stuffed.

At the kitchen table, we opened dozens of cards and letters, threw away junk mail and catalogs, and made a stack of bills we knew we would have to deal with at some point.

There was one envelope marked **NEW YORK LIFE**. Thinking it was a bill, I opened it and was shocked to see a check. The memo line read **DEATH BENEFIT**.

We both lost it. Seeing a check for $5,000 that purports to be a "benefit" of your son dying was just too much at that moment. Neither of us had even remembered that we had those small policies on each of our kids. My dad is our life insurance agent, and he had encouraged us to have some coverage for our children because he often saw how helpful those funds can be in difficult times.

It didn't feel helpful right then. It was blood money.

The paper felt hot in my hand, and I felt sick to my stomach.

I put the check down on the table, Lisa took my hand, and we went to the bedroom. I'm pretty sure we didn't get up again until the next day. And in retrospect, I'm not sure if we ever deposited that check.

We took action that day to try to make our feelings follow. And it felt awful.

> The whole world around us reminded us of him.
> Except the world was still here.

That night, I kept thinking of my conversation with Lisa about being disappointed at the loss of Mitch's future. I was awash in simply missing him and spent hours a day in his room, smelling him on the clothes in his closet, looking at the things he'd treasured and saved. I could feel his presence in the house and saw him everywhere and in every moment. But superimposed on the normal pain of such a fresh wound was a crushing sense of future loss that I had not expected.

Radio host Dennis Prager suggested that having expectations is the best way to never be happy. He wrote, "Though getting rid of expectations strikes most people as impossible and/or undesirable, minimizing expectations is both realistic and highly desirable. In general, *expectations lead to unhappiness.*"[3]

But although that sounds great philosophically—"Hey, if you want to be happy, just don't let your heart ever expect anything!"—it's practically impossible. No normal mom or dad will tell themselves, "Well, it would be neat for all my kids to survive long enough for me to die first, but I'm not getting my hopes up."

And as I tried to sleep, I admitted it to myself: I *had* expected all my kids to outlive me. I never saw it coming that I could lose one. This realization made me extremely angry, more than I already was, because I work in a field in which I am reminded every day that life is dangerous and kids die.

The German philosophical concept of worldview is called Weltanschauung, the idea that we have a mystical contemplation of how we see the world around us. And I was dealing with the failure of my own ability to have ever contemplated—mystically or otherwise—that such a world could contain dead teenage sons, at least mine. This was, in retrospect, stunningly naïve of me since even my own brother had lost his son Joshua when he was just a little boy. I have had *the Conversation* with many parents: "I'm sorry. We did everything we could, but when he fell off his skateboard and hit his head, there was too much damage."

It was a triple whammy: I was grieving, having to radically alter my Weltanschauung, and I was super angry. I don't mean *super* in the adverbial way of modifying the adjective *angry* in that sentence; I mean it in the scientific sense, in that I had more anger inside my grief-saturated heart than it could absorb, because I don't *do* anger. I've always been the "It's gonna be okay" guy, the guy who gives people the benefit of the doubt, who looks at things from multiple perspectives and tries to keep an even keel. But not now. I was super angry.

Thus, the problem was that the knife didn't just kill my son; it killed everything I thought I knew about the future of our family, all the wishes and dreams we had for him and the ways in which we would relate to the future version of him and *his* family, and it cut loose the "okay" that had always been my baseline. That sense of okay-ness I'd had was rooted in my faith in God and the belief that he was on my side.

And there in the dark of my bedroom, with my shoulder on fire and my brokenhearted wife lying next to me, I felt it: a bitterly angry hopelessness taking root in the fertile soil of the gaping wound where my hope and faith and "okay" had been.

———— // ————

In the Iraq War, I saw and had to do things no one ever should. We don't need to cover that here as I've written extensively about it in my two previous books. But I realize now that my experience of war and the personal trauma I suffered there were buried for years because of what happened when I came home.

The air force, in its great wisdom, had me busy with the work of processing the end of my military career as soon as my boots hit the ground of North America again. I was also going through a divorce, moving to Alabama from Texas, and starting my new practice, all within six weeks of wrapping the bandage around the last soldier's head and pulling the sheet over the last Iraqi civilian I tried to save but couldn't. I didn't have the time to grieve or revisit those months of trouble, so I just closed the lid on them for years.

When they later roared back into my life, the PTSD almost destroyed me. But I never went to the memories on purpose.

Losing my son was different. Perhaps because the trauma Mitch suffered manifested in my life as a sudden absence rather than a trauma I had my hands on, happening in front of me. So much of losing Mitch was in my imagination; so many questions, so many unknowns. There wasn't much to wonder about the sergeant with his mandible shot off who I tried to keep from bleeding to death; I can see clearly in my mind every moment and re-feel every one of the five senses of how it felt to watch the light leave his eyes. But Mitch died alone, and I still don't know how or why.

So I'm left to wonder.

That night, lying in the darkness in my supersaturated angry state, was the first time I remember feeling the pull to go to Mitch in those terrible dying minutes.

It feels so real, and I know it is not a dream because I am wide awake. I'm standing in the darkness at the top of a staircase, and it's just light enough for me to see there is a closed door at the bottom. Somehow, I know Mitch is on the other side. I can smell the distinctive musk of spilled, congealing human blood I know so well from Iraq and a thousand trauma bays elsewhere.

I am drawn to him, but I am so very afraid. Can I help him, comfort him, perhaps save him? Or will seeing him destroy what's left of me?

I am a father desperate to reach his son, a doctor powerless to help, a man paralyzed by terror: I cannot make myself move. There is light at the top of the stairs, but I am pulled to the darkness. There are whispers, "You need to go down there, but God won't go with you. You have to do it alone."

I don't know what to do. I swallow my tears and finally fall asleep.

The sun rose through our bedroom window, but I was already awake. My jaw hurt, and I kept rubbing my tongue against something sharp on the lower left side of my mouth. I finally got out of bed, careful not to wake Lisa, who was miraculously asleep at the moment.

I went into the bathroom and flipped on the light. I washed my face and rinsed my mouth out with some cold water from the sink. When I spit the water out, I saw what looked like a tiny silver rock wash down the drain. I looked into the mirror and saw two very surprising things: (1) in my mouth, the first molar on the lower left side was missing a filling, and (2) on the left side of my sandy blond head was a brand-new patch of perfectly gray hair about the diameter of a baseball.

"He has broken my teeth with gravel."[4]

I started crying—a little earlier than most days back then. I looked into my blue eyes and said to myself, *Lee, your body is falling apart. Something has to change.*

———————//———————

Lisa and I worked with lots of engineers and physicists—people who don't think brain surgeons are all that smart by comparison—along with venture capitalists and entrepreneurs at Auburn University. We helped develop technologies, create intellectual properties, and bring disruptive ideas to the market.

One concept of new technology adoption is called the diffusion of innovations theory.[5] Basically, the idea is that it takes the same amount of time for 10 percent of people to adopt a new innovation—like the internet, cellphones, Bitcoin—as it does for the next 80 percent to adopt it. So if it takes five years for 10 percent of the people in the world to start using cellphones once they're invented, it will take about five more years before 90 percent of the people in the world are using them.

———————//———————

That morning was a low point for me because I realized that my son had been dead about thirty days, and I was rapidly breaking: my hair, teeth, and shoulder blade were crumbling under the new innovation in my life—grief.

It felt like the apogee, the farthest point of hopelessness and despair I thought I could ever reach. But I knew that was just wishful thinking because as my old chief Peter Jannetta used to say, "If your patient's alive, things can still get worse."

What would the next thirty days do to me?

8

The Best-Laid Plans

Devise a plan, but it will fail;
State a proposal, but it will not stand.

—Isaiah 8:10, NASB

Spoiler alert: I didn't die.

Instead, I just went back to work.

Lisa and I made a plan: We would see a few people each day in the office for a couple of weeks, and then I would resume operating and being on call for emergencies in two weeks, which would be mid-September. I could handle that, I thought. It was a good plan.

We saw about fifteen patients that first morning in the office—me with my newly graying hair, broken molar, and shingles shoulder, and Lisa with her less visible but equally broken heart—which was a very light load for me by our standards pre–Mitch's death. Despite the reduced workload, it was terribly difficult because I kept thinking to myself that these patients' low back pain or workers' compensation cases were so trivial in the grand scheme of things. Our pain, our loss, my aching body seemed so much more important, and didn't they know how hurt *we* were?

A few people acknowledged our loss and said kind things like, "We've been praying for you, Doc," or "How you holdin' up?" There were also people who seemed like they *wanted* to say something, but they didn't know what to say, so they just looked a little nauseated and didn't say anything. But most people just seemed not to be aware at all. "I'm Sam Smith, and my neck hurts. What can you do for me?"

I *needed* people to acknowledge my pain, to see me. I'm not proud of this fact, but years of thinking about it have made me realize that acknowledgment is an important and rarely discussed part of grief. And I was aware of it, ashamed of it, even as I coveted it. "Don't you know what I've been through?" I wanted to say when Sam Smith acted frustrated that his disability claim paperwork had been delayed a few days. "Your forms aren't as important as my dead son."

> I *needed* people to acknowledge my pain, to see me.

I found myself struggling to listen to patients as they told me their stories of how they'd been injured or whether they felt ready to go back to work or not. My attention span was nanoseconds. Me, the doctor who was known for empathy and kindness—people in Auburn used to say that Lisa and I ran a "family-practice neurosurgery practice" because we loved our patients so much—couldn't muster ten minutes of active listening without wanting to jump out the window.

The other problem I had was that Mitch was *everywhere* in our office. When we built our new office in 2010, Mitch was my right-hand man in setting up all the technology. Lisa, a professional interior designer before she started running our office when we married, had designed our twenty-first-century office—a technological and interior design marvel that allowed me to see patients in an extremely efficient way, optimizing my workflow while enhancing the patient experience. Lisa's incredible work in designing our office led to her consulting for numerous other medical practices and hospitals over the years.

Mitch had been instrumental in helping me wire the Mac minis we had in every exam room. We used them to display patients' scans when they came into the room, and I had shown thousands of people their MRIs or CT images using specially designed wireless mouse–laser pointer combos that Mitch had put the batteries into, connected, and taught me how to use. Everywhere I turned in the office, I saw a piece of equipment Mitch had helped me install or a printer he'd connected to the network, and I kept flashing back to those days we spent working together to make our office ready to open.

So when Mrs. Jones or Mr. Smith was droning on about how their chiropractor had always been able to pop their disc back into place but now it was way too far out and they needed more oxycodone to tide them over until they could get that shot, I was distracted by the memory of Mitch laughing at me when I couldn't get the mouse to work. We finally figured out it had to be set to left-handed mode or it would always go the wrong way when I tried to use it as a southpaw.

I felt like the guy in the story Jesus told, who was trying to remove a speck from his friend's eye, but he didn't notice the giant log in his own eye.[1] Except in my version, I *wanted* someone to say, "Oh my goodness, there's a huge log in your eye! You poor thing!" But they were too worried about the tiny specks of back pain or a numb finger to care about my giant grief log.

After I saw the last patient, I went back to the office Lisa and I shared. She was sitting at her desk, which faced mine, on the phone with someone. I sat down and wrote the progress notes for the patients I'd seen that morning, and then I turned to look out the window at the beautiful pine forest behind our building. I put my feet on my desk and was thinking about all those people and their various issues that seemed so small to me right then. After all, most of them would go through a few weeks of physical therapy or have a couple of steroid shots and be completely back to normal before they could say *sciatica*. And even for the two or three who might eventually need surgery, I could fix their problems and they would be fine.

But no one could fix *my* problem.

I closed my eyes and rubbed my temples with my hands. The dull headache that started right after the Phone Call a few weeks ago was worse now. I was immersed in the pain, but something was tugging at me. I'd felt so far from God, farther away than I'd ever felt, and for the first time since Mitch died, I thought I felt God there, a presence I can't explain. In a moment when I felt so low and heavy that I didn't think I would ever be able to get up from the chair, I knew I wasn't alone.

It turned out to be Lisa; she came up behind me and started rubbing my shoulders. It seemed like every time I was absolutely desperate in those days, she showed up. I think—I hope—I did the same for her.

In retrospect, I believe this was part of God keeping his promise from Psalm 34:18: "The LORD is close to the brokenhearted." I would get a strong sense that Lisa needed me, and I would go to her and find her crying, holding a picture of the boy who was not her son biologically but who is part of her DNA, and I would just be there. And she did this for me innumerable times and in countless ways—a timely text, a hug, a kind word, a Bible verse she found. Jesus wrapped his arms around us as the third strand. He held us close to each other and kept us alive in those dark days.[2]

"How did clinic go?" she asked.

"Awful. I'm not a very good doctor right now. I can't seem to maintain focus for very long. Nothing seems important."

"That's normal," she said. "You'll get through it. And you are a *great* doctor, honey."

"Doesn't feel like it today. You gotta take me home."

Lisa leaned down and wrapped her arms around my neck. I could feel her warm breath on the side of my aching jaw, the warmth of a heart that had saved mine when I was wrecked and reeling from war. I relaxed in her strong arms, and she held me, just as she had done years ago when we made ourselves a brand-new family. My three kids and I had been lost, and she held us so tightly that we blended right together with her, Josh, and Caity.

Our plan to have only a half-day clinic was wise; I was spent and needed to get away from this place and all these people for a while, to go home, huddle with Lisa against the pain, and rest for another day. But, as the boxer Mike Tyson once said, "Everybody's got a plan until they get punched in the mouth."

9

Extraordinarily Ordinary

I would think of the collective sorrow of the world,
which we all carry in big and small ways—the horrors
that take away our breath, and the common, ordinary
losses of all our lives.

—Tish Harrison Warren, *Prayer in the Night*

My cellphone rang.

Lisa straightened and picked it up off my office desk. "It's the hospital," she said as she handed me the phone.

"Dr. Warren," I said after I swiped to answer.

"Hi, Dr. Warren. This is Claudette in the emergency department. Please hold for Dr. Stinson."

I listened to some horrible Muzak saxophone version of the old George Michael song "Careless Whisper," and then a voice I hadn't heard in a few weeks came on the line.

"Lee, it's Stinson," he said. My friend, the ED physician who looks just like Abraham Lincoln, didn't sound good. His voice was tense, not his usual jovial tone.

"Hey, buddy."

"We've got a problem. I know you're not on call, but do you mind looking at a scan? Eight-year-old boy named Mason Babcock. Fell off the top of the monkey bars at his school's playground about an hour ago. He's been having seizures since he hit the ground, and EMS brought him here. We intubated him and just got him out of the scanner. Doesn't look good."

"Sure," I said. "Hang on a second." I clicked a few keys on my computer—the one Mitch set up on my desk—and logged into the medical center's radiology system. I typed in Babcock, Mason and quickly found the scan. I put Stinson on speakerphone as I scrolled through the images. My heart, which I had thought was as crushed and broken as it could possibly be, managed to instantly feel even worse.

Mason's right temporal bone was fractured, and a piece of it had sliced through his middle meningeal artery, which was now spraying blood into the space between the bone and the brain's covering, the leatherlike dura mater. The brain was very compressed and had shifted from right to left, and there was a lot of pressure on his brain stem. This is the ultimate neurosurgical emergency: If we react quickly enough, we can save the life and usually people will completely recover. But even a short delay can produce permanent neurological damage or death. Literally in this situation, time is brain.

"He's got a huge epidural hematoma," I said to Stinson. I turned my head to look at Lisa, who was now kneeling beside me and looking at the screen. She'd seen enough of these scans over the years to know what had to happen. She turned her eyes to me and nodded slightly.

Everything in me said it wasn't my problem, that no one would blame me for shipping this kid off. But I could see his desperate parents in my mind—wondering if their son would survive, wrecked and crying, probably praying for a miracle, forecasting their own un-holy week in their minds as their little boy lay seizing on the gurney. I couldn't turn my back on them.

"He's not going to survive long enough to fly to Birmingham," I said. "He'll have to have surgery here."

"But you're not supposed to be back yet," Stinson said. "I just wanted some advice for how I could get him stabilized for the Life Flight crew to take him to Children's Hospital. Are you sure you're up to it?"

I looked into Lisa's eyes. We hadn't been apart for more than a few minutes since Mitch died, and the thought of leaving her alone was terrifying. She stared for a beat and then slowly nodded. "You have to go," she said quietly.

"Nothing other than surgery will save him, Stinson. And it has to be now. Tell the OR I'll be there in fifteen minutes."

———//———

During the drive to the hospital, I called my friend Jim, a pediatric neurosurgeon at Children's in Birmingham, Alabama. I told him the situation, and he agreed that me doing the surgery and then flying Mason to Children's for pediatric intensive care was the best plan. We'd have Life Flight medics in the OR ready to rush Mason out as soon as surgery was over.

As we wrapped up talking about Mason, I said, "Thanks, Jim. I'll do my best to get him to you alive."

He said, "Hey, by the way, I heard about your son. I'm so sorry, Lee."

———//———

I met my surgical nurse, Zane, in the pre-op holding area. Zane—who is like a brother to me and who had been in our home for days after Mitch died—looked serious as he approached. He braced my shoulders and looked me straight in the eyes. "Doc, the room's ready and everyone's here. Sure you're good to go?"

"I am," I said. "Where's Mason?"

"Slot four."

We walked across the room to a glass door marked 4, and I slid the door open. An anesthetist named Luanne was putting a dressing on the left side of the little boy's neck. She looked up and said, "I put in a central line. We're ready when you are."

I stepped up to the bedside to see Mason. He had sandy blond hair with a little cut above his right eyebrow, a swollen face, and a breathing tube taped to his cheek. I lifted his right eyelid and looked in the black hole of his blown pupil. The left pupil was still small, which meant he wasn't brain dead yet. There was still a chance to save him. *Time is brain.*

"We have to go now. I'll change clothes. Zane, get him positioned, and I'll be right there."

Zane and Luanne started rolling the stretcher down the hall, and I ran to the locker room to change into scrubs. I opened my locker—the same locker I had been standing next to the last time I had spoken to Mitch on the phone, the day before he died. The last words Mitch said to me were, "I love you, Dad." And the last he heard me say: "I love you, too, buddy."

I looked in my locker. I grabbed the wooden cross necklace that I had worn in every surgery I performed in Iraq and that I've worn in every one since. I slid my wedding ring onto the chain. Lisa's dad gave me that cross right before I deployed, and it's close to my heart every time I operate.

I threw on scrubs and tennis shoes and ran to the OR just as Zane was shaving Mason's head. "Get him prepped and draped while I wash my hands," I said.

I stepped out to the scrub sink and started scrubbing my hands. Suddenly, I felt myself embraced by someone behind me. I turned my head and saw Dr. David Scott, an orthopedic surgeon who is a decorated Vietnam special forces veteran. He held my shoulders for a few seconds. We'd hardly ever spoken to each other, because we usually operated on different days of the week. We'd certainly never hugged before. He said, "I have no idea how you're even standing up right now. And I don't know what to say. I'm praying for you. Go save that boy."

David walked away, and I stepped into the OR. The scrub nurse, Sharon Ray, handed me a towel, I dried my hands, and she gowned and gloved me. Zane had already draped Mason's head, and I stepped up to the table and said, "Knife."

Sharon Ray popped the No. 10 blade scalpel into my left hand, like she had hundreds of times before. But this time, it felt like it weighed a million pounds. It felt hot in my hand, and when I looked at it, I instantly flashed to the knife that killed my son. I felt nauseated and dizzy for a second, and I wanted to throw the scalpel down and run away.

I closed my eyes, swallowed hard, and remembered a time in Iraq when I was trying to save a young soldier in the OR. A mortar round knocked the power out and our tent OR became pitch-black for a few seconds. The alarm red siren wailed, several distant explosions shook the floor, and I was so scared. I whispered, "God, get us through this alive, and let us save this kid." The lights came back on, and we got through the operation. That night I found Psalm 144:1, "Blessed be the LORD, my rock, who trains my hands for war, and my fingers for battle" (NASB).

He had been with me during wartime surgery in Iraq, so I could trust he would be with me now.

I opened my eyes and whispered the same prayer under my breath, "God, get us through this alive, and let us save this kid."

The nausea receded and I went to work.

--------//--------

As far as emergency brain surgeries go, Mason's was straightforward, and the clot came out easily. His young brain did what young brains do: It went from deathly gray to a healthier pink color as soon as the pressure was off, and it shifted back into its normal position by the time I finished putting his bone back together with tiny titanium plates and screws.

I'd like to say I summoned some superhuman strength, rose out of my own problems to save the day for this kid. But the truth is, I just fell back on my training and compartmentalized my pain. As FBI hostage negotiator Chris Voss wrote, "When the pressure is on, you don't rise to the occasion; you fall to your highest level of preparation."[1]

I didn't see it then, but all those battlefield brain surgeries, all the times I'd had to operate under great stress and physical danger, all the horrifying things I'd seen and that God had gotten me through had prepared me for this moment. At a time when some days it was impossible to get out of bed and brush my teeth, I was able to step into the operating room and roll through Mason's surgery—*make a skin incision, saw open the bone, drain the clot, repair the fracture, staple the skin, another day at the office*—because God had trained me to perform under great duress, to turn away from my fear and pain and just get to work.

I wrapped Mason's head in white gauze, took the anesthetist's tape off his eyes, and sighed deeply when I saw his right pupil was now back to normal size.

The Life Flight medics were waiting in the hallway, and they came in and quickly packaged Mason up for the thirty-minute flight to Birmingham. I called Jim to let him know the case went well and that Mason would be there soon.

I went out to the waiting room and saw my old friend Pastor Jon, the hospital chaplain, kneeling in prayer in front of a young couple. There were several other people, probably grandparents and friends, and three small children sitting next to the parents.

As I entered the room, every eye snapped to me.

The parents stood, their faces painted a perfect blend of desperation and hope. My words would determine the arc of the rest of their family's emotional life.

"He's going to be okay," I said.

After hugs and tears and a brief talk about Mason's surgery, I took Mason's parents to the hallway outside the OR just in time to meet the Life Flight crew rolling Mason out on a stretcher. Pastor Jon and the family gathered around the stretcher to pray and say goodbye before Mason's parents would have to get in the car for the two-hour drive to Birmingham.

---//---

I walked back to the locker room and changed into my street clothes. I hung the cross necklace back on the hook in my locker and then put my wedding ring back on my left hand. I walked out of the locker room, and Pastor Jon was waiting in the hall.

"How you holding up?" he said.

"Not so great, if I'm honest," I said.

"Want to talk?"

"I don't know. I should probably get back to Lisa."

"I already texted her and told her I was going to abscond with you for a few. Come on."

We walked together down the hall from the surgery department, past the hospital gift shop and cafeteria, to the small chapel. It was softly lit, and behind the pulpit was a stained glass image of *The Last Supper*. We sat in the back row, and Pastor Jon turned to face me.

Ever since I was a medical student in Oklahoma, I have found myself in hospital chapels when I'm struggling with difficult situations. Something about the quiet, the stained glass, the candles, seems to center me when the world of the hospital is too much to bear. And at East Alabama Medical Center, Pastor Jon had an uncanny ability to show up when I needed someone to talk to. We had covered a lot of ground together here in previous years.

But I hadn't been in this chapel since before Mitch died. I still couldn't make myself go to church yet.

Over the years, whenever I was stressed or hurting, making a hard decision, or preparing my mind for a tough case, I'd come to this chapel. Once, I'd run into a real crisis of faith when I struggled to understand how to doctor someone when I couldn't save them from their brain tumor or head injury. Pastor Jon had helped reframe my thinking, particularly about prayer. He taught me that it wasn't about getting God to do what I wanted but rather learning to shape my heart to want what God wants and to align my will with his. Pastor Jon was my sounding board as I worked through the stitching together of faith and science that led me to begin writing *I've Seen the End of You*, back when I thought I had learned about pain by studying people going through it.

But that was before I lost my boy.

Now, I was in the depths of it myself, and all that study and thought seemed useless from this vantage point. I was a living paraphrase of Romans 1:22: Claiming to be wise, I instead became an utter fool.[2]

It was also in this room that Pastor Jon had told me he'd lost not just one child—a little girl born with congenital heart disease—but his son as well, who had died in a car accident as a young adult.

I'd learned so much from him, had my faith strengthened and so many questions worked out during our talks. But now I felt restless, angry, and I didn't want to be here.

"This is the first operation you've performed since Mitch died, right?" he asked.

I nodded. "Yes. I wasn't planning on coming back for a couple more weeks."

"What a blessing you were here, though, for Mason and his family. You gave them back their son."

I started to cry—it was as automatic as breathing in those days—and he put his hand on my shoulder. I said, "Yes. I'm glad about that. I just . . ."

I felt pressure rising in my chest, climbing its way up my throat, and I wanted with everything inside me to run away.

I stood and walked to the little table in the corner of the chapel where a box of Kleenex sat next to a foot-tall statue of Jesus on the cross. I wiped my eyes and my nose and noticed the ceramic nails in the ceramic Jesus's hands and feet, the ceramic thorns in his crown. My right shoulder was on fire, my jaw ached, and my heart felt as though it was going to shatter into a million ceramic shards.

And I'm back on the dark mental staircase to the furnace of suffering, the depths of life's worst moments.

I've just put another little kid safely back in his parents' arms, and my boy is lying on the ground behind that door, bleeding out. But I'm too scared to move, too alone and powerless here. Yet when the pressure is on, I can always save others, always gut it out and get it done.

So I take a step down, alone, into the darkness. I'm a little closer to Mitch, but the step hurts so much, like all those ceramic shards are slicing my feet to pieces.

Pastor Jon shattered the silence. "You wish someone could give you your son back, too, right?"

I heard him but at the same time didn't. I turned, walked back to the pew, and sat. "I'm sorry. What did you say?"

Pastor Jon put his hand on my shoulder. "You wish someone could give you your son back, too, right? That's why you walked away a while ago," he said.

I shook my head. "'Walked away'? What do you mean?"

He lowered his voice a little. "It's the first time I've ever seen you not stay to pray with a family."

I looked away for a moment. "I didn't even realize I did that. Prayer feels, I don't know, just impossible. I've been involved in saving lives and rescuing people from pain and suffering so many times, but this feels like there's no rescue, no relief, nothing that can ever make it better. Of all the things I've been through—war, divorce, tough cases—this is extraordinary."

Pastor Jon looked at me for a second and his eyes narrowed. "I know. I've been there, remember? And I also know that it doesn't help for someone to say, 'I know exactly what you're feeling.' I *don't* know exactly what you're feeling, just like you could never know exactly what I felt when my kids died. But I know one thing for sure."

I took a deep breath. "What?"

"You're in a lot of danger right now, Lee."

I pinched the bridge of my nose. The headache was back now too. "Danger?"

"Yes. This is the point where it's so easy to make an idol out of your pain."

I straightened. "What are you talking about?"

"Grief can be all-consuming. You've seen it before, right? Remember the lady who dragged her poor husband all over the country trying to save him from that brain tumor long after he'd lost all useful brain function? Because she couldn't let him go? What was her name?"

> "This is the point where it's so easy to make an idol out of your pain."

I nodded. "Mrs. Andrews. Her husband couldn't speak or move the last six months of his life, but she put him through surgeries for feeding and breathing tubes, took him to some quack in Houston who sold her a hundred thousand dollars' worth of snake oil before he finally died."

"That's right," he said. "She made keeping her husband alive the most important thing in her life. She couldn't even see what was best for him or her family, couldn't make room for God to comfort or minister to her because she made her *circumstances* determine how she felt. You told me that, remember? One of the things you discovered in your research was that people who think their circumstances determine their peace of mind, their faith, their happiness—they're the ones who do the worst when hard times come, right?"

I waved a hand. "Yes, but what does that have to do with idolatry?"

"Everything," he said. "Remember the Ten Commandments?"

"Of course," I said.

"What are they?"

"You're really giving me a test right now?"

He smiled sadly. "No, I just need you to remember the first two."

Years of Sunday school training and of not wanting my mom to be disappointed in me came through for me right then.

"You shall have no other gods before me, and you shall not make an idol for yourself."

"Very good! That's it. So you and Lisa have a choice to make here. You're on a mountain of pain and grief, reeling from losing Mitch and wondering how you can ever get over this, right?"

I looked down at my feet and then back at Pastor Jon. "Pretty much."

"Okay, then here's your choice: Are you going to let God help you, or are you going to walk away from him? You can let God be with you on this mountain, like he was with Moses. It's scary. There are thunderclouds and lightning and darkness, and it's terrifying. But he'll be there with you, and he'll give you the playbook, the tools to make it through. And it hurts like he's carving them on the stone tablet of your heart.

"It plays out in finding his promises in Scripture and holding on to them for dear life, in friends coming alongside you, in figuring out your marriage and your other kids in the context of one of you being permanently gone. Books will show up at just the right time, you'll hear a pastor with just the right message, see a sunrise that seems particularly hopeful. Somehow, you will climb off that mountain carrying what you need to find your way again."

His words were exactly true, and I knew it. It was already happening. Every day, someone called or showed up or emailed something that was exactly what we needed that day. The verse of the day on Bible Gateway would speak right to us, or one of the kids would text something that helped so much. And we were doing it for each other and the kids too. God was ministering to us, even when I felt so very far away from him. Every day, there was manna and quail right in front of us, just enough.

Pastor Jon leaned closer and looked directly into my eyes. "But remember what Aaron was doing while Moses was on the mountain?"

I thought for a moment. "He was in the valley, making the golden calf."

He sighed. "Right. While Moses was doing the scary close-to-God stuff and getting the help he needed, Aaron and the rest of the people stayed away from the cloud and the fire and the darkness where God was, and they made themselves a god they could touch and feel.[3]

"A lot of people do that with grief and pain. They fix their eyes and their hearts on a casket or a divorce or a diagnosis, they drink or use drugs or do something else to numb the pain, and they spend their lives holding on to the hurt so tightly that it becomes the only thing they have. That's basically idolatry. It's making a god out of your circumstances instead of letting God help you process them. That's a dangerous place to live, Lee."

I'd never thought of it like that. I'd seen so many patients over the years who had never gotten over something that had happened to them, even if they had survived it. A cancer scare that turned someone's world upside down and left them emotionally wrecked even though they were cured. A loss of a spouse that embittered and enraged someone so much that their whole life was ruined.

"You're right, Pastor," I said. "I've seen that a lot. This just seems so impossible to me. I don't even know what to call myself."

"Call yourself?"

I nodded. "Yeah. When your spouse dies, they call you widow or widower. When your parents die, you're an orphan. But your kids aren't supposed to die before you do. There's no word for a parent who's lost a kid."

"You're right," he said. "I never thought about that before. But you're exactly right. There is no word, and it is impossible. Extraordinary. But there's one more thing you need to know if you want to survive this and find your peace, your happiness, again."

I noticed I was bouncing my foot like Mitch always did when he was nervous, a habit he got from me. I needed to get out of here. As much as I loved Pastor Jon and always learned so much from him, I'd had enough. I was exhausted, adrift, and I needed to see Lisa.

I waved a hand. "What?"

"Losing a child *is* extraordinary. But, my friend, it's also really ordinary."

I started crying again and blew out a long sigh. "How can you say that? I mean, you've lost two kids, which I can't even imagine, so you *know* it's not something you're supposed to feel, and it's certainly not an ordinary part of life."

"Not what I meant," he said. "Take a few deep breaths and close your eyes for a second. Think about what you know from working in this building. I guarantee you that today, probably as we speak, someone is dying or has died. Someone is having a heart attack or holding their wife's hand as she slips away. In the trauma center, one of my chaplain colleagues is comforting a couple who just miscarried a baby or whose kid didn't have a doctor to save them like you just saved Mason. Zoom out to Montgomery or Birmingham or Atlanta and the amount of suffering happening in this very moment is staggering."

"You're not making me feel any better. I hope this isn't your Sunday sermon," I said.

He huffed. "No. I'm making the point that extreme, extraordinary suffering and pain is an ordinary, normal, constant part of life. And that's why you can find a way to make it through."

"That doesn't make any sense," I said quietly.

He put his hand on my knee. "If it really were happening only to you, then it *would* be extraordinary, and it would be reasonable for you to feel hopeless or singled out by God or abandoned. But the extraordinarily ordinary pain of life is mixed in with all the extraordinarily ordinary amazing things too—while we're speaking, people are being born, finding out they are finally pregnant, getting engaged, falling in love, achieving a long-held goal, getting saved, or being baptized. Someone is holding hands or seeing a rainbow for the first time. Yes, life is really, really hard, but it's also really, really good. All at the same time. And when you're submerged in pain, it can be so deep and so dark that you can forget all that light is out there. But it still is."

My phone dinged, a text from Lisa:

Coming home soon?

Pastor Jon stood, and I joined him. "Thanks for the talk," I said. "Lots to think about."

"I understand. You know I do. Go read Lamentations again when you're ready to grapple with this stuff some more. That's where you'll see the perspective you need. And I'm always here for you."

We hugged, and I walked to the parking garage. On the way to my car, my phone rang. It was a local number, but I didn't have the contact saved. I decided to answer it anyway.

"Hello, this is Dr. Warren."

A female voice answered. "Hi. This is Jenny Long. I work in the rehab department."

"Oh, hi, Jenny," I said. I'd worked with her a few times on patients who had suffered strokes and head injuries. She was probably in her early sixties and was a great occupational therapist. "What can I do for you?"

"I wanted to invite you and Lisa to a weekly support group for grief that I'm a part of. It's been really helpful for me over the past several years, and I think it would be good for you too."

Support groups do important work, and I believe they are very valuable to people. But in those early days, the thought of sitting in a group talking about other people's pain seemed abhorrent to me.

"Thank you for thinking of us. I didn't know you had lost a child; I'm so sorry," I said.

"Oh no. I didn't mean to imply that," she said. "My sister's son overdosed fifteen years ago and nearly died. It was the hardest thing I ever went through, but the support group has been so encouraging that I never stopped going."

Fifteen years? Nearly died? I projected myself fifteen years into the future, and I could see a life in between defined by this horrible thing

---

that had happened to me. That redefinition of my life was too much to process right then.

"Thanks, Jenny. I'm not sure we're ready yet, but I'll let you know."

"Okay. Just reach out anytime. It's so hard to do grief alone. We're here for you."

"I really do appreciate it. Thanks."

We got off the phone about the time I pulled up to our house. Lisa was standing in the driveway, checking the mail. I pulled into the garage, and she walked in as I got out of my car.

When I saw Lisa's face, the hope I had of crashing together to recover from the stressful day completely disappeared.

"What's wrong?" I asked.

She extended an envelope toward me, and I took it and looked down. In block letters, it said who had sent it: **STATE OF ALABAMA MEDICAL EXAMINER**.

I thought giving another family their son back while having to acknowledge they could offer no quid pro quo was bad. I thought Pastor Jon lecturing me was awful. I didn't think this day could get any worse.

But I was very wrong.

10

Origami Golden Calf

There's a hole in the world now. In the place where he was, there's now just nothing.

—Nicholas Wolterstorff, *Lament for a Son*

Lisa and I walked into the house and sat down at the kitchen table. I held the envelope for a while, felt it burning my hands as it became heavier.

"We need to open it," Lisa said softly. She put her hand on my forearm, waiting with me for a couple more of Kipling's unforgiving minutes[1] before I finally found the strength to pry open the iron gates of paper and glue and remove the letter.

OFFICIAL DEATH CERTIFICATE was as far as I got before the tears came. Seeing **WARREN, MITCHELL KEATON** with beginning and ending dates was too much. Parents aren't supposed to see that. I'd prevented Mason's parents from seeing it a few hours ago, but there was no preventing this. It was in black and white in my hands, and the permanence of it was crushing.

"It still feels like a bad dream," Lisa said. "I keep thinking I'll just snap out of it at some point, but this . . ."

"This means it's real," I said. "I guess I was hoping we were both just having the same nightmare."

"Yes," Lisa said. She put her head on my shoulder, and we held each other in the space between our breaths. I don't know how long we sat there holding on to the document that signified the end of any hope of this being some kind of mystically shared dark fantasy. The official letterhead and the "Stabbing" under **Cause of Death** snapped us right out of our residual denial phase, even though we were nowhere near ready for acceptance. Kübler-Ross hadn't prepared us for this stage of grief purgatory.

The door sensor beeped, and we turned to see Lisa's parents, Patty and Dennis, come in the door between the house and the garage. Patty was carrying a grocery bag, and as she entered, she said, "Hi, my loves. I brought you some dinner. I know today must have been hard."

We all hugged, and then Dennis noticed the paper in my hand. "What's that?"

I handed it to him, and he and Patty looked at it. Patty started crying. "We have two of those. I hate them. I'm so sorry."

Patty had delivered her first daughter, Rebecca, with all the hopes and expectations of any mother pregnant with her first child. They had the nursery ready, had the name picked out, and were excited to start their family. But Rebecca never left the hospital. She had a fatal birth defect and slipped away from Patty and Dennis, taking their hearts with her.

They were strong and somehow made it through. Eventually, after miscarriages and more heartache, Lisa came into the world in the same army hospital in Georgia where Rebecca had started and ended her short life. Jessica came a few years later, and the McDonalds built a happy family. They added James via adoption, but he was ripped away from them at just twenty-four when he was hit by a distracted driver.

Their experience as bereaved parents gave us a model of how someone could suffer and still find hope and real joy again. And Patty did. She loved Jesus, taught third-grade Bible classes for generations of kids, and loved her family with a holy passion. She and Dennis came alongside me and brought me into their family at a time when I was very wounded by war and divorce, and their love and guidance helped put me back together during a time that had seemed so dark, a time before I learned of the total opacity of losing a son.

We tried to eat, but no one had an appetite. Dennis and Patty led us to the living room, and we all sat on the couch and visited for a while. I was exhausted, emotionally spent, and didn't have a lot to say. But I managed a question.

"How did you both do it? How did you manage to become the loving, caring, happy people that you are, even though you've been through this twice? I asked Pastor Jon the same question, and he basically gave me Lamentations as homework. I'm not ready for that yet."

Dennis leaned back and closed his eyes, taking a mental trip to the deaths of his son and daughter. I could see the memories flood his mind in each furrow of his brow. Finally, he said, "Both times we sat on the bench of 'Ain't it awful?' and spent months telling God how wrong he was for letting it happen. But the problem with that is, you never run out of awful things to tell him about. And I eventually realized that he wants us to tell him, but the process of telling him has to involve entrusting it to him as well."

> "We sat on the bench of 'Ain't it awful?' and spent months telling God how wrong he was for letting it happen."

"What do you mean, Dad?" Lisa asked.

Dennis smiled softly and took her hand. He looked into her eyes and wiped a tear from his cheek with his other hand. "I just had to tell him, 'Have your way. It's your watch, it's your Word, it's your plan, and I don't want to be in charge of it anymore, because I can't understand it and I can't fix it. Have your way.'"

Patty nodded. "We knew we'd go insane or completely lose ourselves if we didn't find a context to put our pain into, some meaning or purpose for it. So Dennis became a chaplain to minister to other hurting people, and I started teaching the little ones about Jesus, and I found out who Jesus was by trying to show him to others. I learned more than I taught. And over time, we figured out that we hadn't died. We came alive again by deciding to live."

We talked for a while, and then they went home. While Lisa showered and got ready for bed, I sat at the desk in our bedroom and opened the file of receipts and papers I'd started when Mitch died. I was placing the death certificate into the file when I noticed the receipt from Anderson Funeral Home on the top. I shed my last tears of the day and sat there as the sun set, thinking about Pastor Jon's warning about turning my pain into an idol.

It would be so easy to just fold up the death certificate and that evil receipt into an origami golden calf. I could pour myself a drink offering and descend into the pain of losing Mitch. Or I could, as Pastor Jon said, go into the smoke and fire and darkness and see if God would really meet me there to equip me for what lay ahead in this journey of bereavement. My mother-in-law said they had decided to live, but that sounded incredibly ambitious to me at the moment.

I didn't know what to do, didn't know what to call this awful situation—this soup sandwich that was gooey and impossible to manage. *They don't have a name for people who lose their kids.*

Staying in the pain didn't seem survivable. The darkness where God might be seemed unapproachably terrifying, and what if he wasn't in there after all?

I lay down in bed and waited for Lisa. I must have fallen asleep at some point, because the next thing I remember was the alarm clock waking me up to another day of not knowing whether to climb the mountain or to brush up on my origami skills.

11

A Little Bit Like Hope

As you do not know the path of the wind,
    or how the body is formed in a mother's womb,
so you cannot understand the work of God,
    the Maker of all things.

           —Ecclesiastes 11:5

The next day, we drove the six miles from our home to our office in almost total silence. Lisa and I have a language we speak, through held hands and the sounds of our breathing, that does not require words; the language we learned in the weeks following Mitch's death. Some days it took so much just to move that we had no energy left for words.

———//———

Our office in Auburn was on the third floor of the Magnetic Resonance Imaging Research Center, a collaboration between the university, several industry partners, medical device manufacturers, and private investors.

A side effect of our office being inside the MRI Research Center was having the opportunity to be involved with research in the evolution of MRI technology, and we had what was then only the third 7T—7 Tesla—MRI machine in the country. Tesla is the unit of measure of magnetic-field strength, and most commercial MRI scanners in those days were between 0.5T and 1.5T. The 7T technology opened the door to incredible things, like being able to image the beating heart. But my interest in the 7T machine had to do with something called functional imaging.

Functional MRI, fMRI for short, uses special blood-oxygen-level-dependent contrast to allow researchers to essentially see what's happening inside a person's brain while they are performing certain tasks or even just thinking about something.

Normal MRI shows you the structure of something, but fMRI shows you the function.

The pictures of the brain we get with 7T are like photographs. The level of detail we can see is stunning, and every time technological developments allow me to look inside the human nervous system on a deeper level, I can see God's design even more clearly. I've never understood the supposed divide between science and faith; for me, when I doubt my faith, science always comes to the rescue.

———————//———————

We had a reduced patient schedule again—our great plan, remember?—but when we walked into the office, our employee Tamara told us that we had a lunchtime meeting on the schedule that someone had forgotten to cancel.

Although neither of us felt like it, we decided to go to the meeting, mostly because otherwise we would have just sat in our office and cried or stared out the window in silence while our staff was gone to lunch. The meeting was in the control room of the 7T magnet and was a demonstration of a new experiment with some of the first human subjects.

The first participant lay in the scanner, wearing a virtual-reality headset, and was shown instructions of tasks to perform and what they were to think about.

First, some tasks: *Move your left thumb, wiggle your right foot, move the small finger on your right hand.*

When the participant performed the task, the screen would show where the blood flow in the brain went, which indirectly showed which parts of the brain were activated during those tasks.

Next, some instructions that only involved thinking: *Think of something sad. The saddest thing you can imagine. Now think of something happy. The best memory you can recall.*

It was fascinating to watch the colors change as various parts of the brain got involved in the process of thought and memory. Negative thoughts increased the blood flow to the amygdala, the emotional parts of the brain where anxiety and depression live. Positive, happier thinking caused improvements in blood flow to the areas that produce helpful neurotransmitters like dopamine and serotonin, the chemicals of happiness.

We were literally seeing the human mind think, watching the neurochemical and blood flow changes in real time in response to changes in thought. "Fearfully and wonderfully made,"[1] indeed.

One of the researchers said something that hit me like a ton of magnets: "She's changing her brain by changing her thoughts."

Lisa held my hand as we walked back up the stairs to our office. "That was really interesting," she said. "But it's funny that they had to spend twenty million dollars to figure out that your thinking can change how your brain works."

> "She's changing her brain by changing her thoughts."

"Why is that funny?" I asked.

"Because it's in the Bible."

"What are you talking about?"

"I can't remember where it is, but didn't the apostle Paul list a bunch of things to think about, to 'set your mind on things above'? And that it will give you peace?"

I nodded. "Yes, something like 'Think on these things,' but I can't remember where it is either." We got back to our office and googled it, and of course, Lisa was right. It's in Philippians chapter 4, and it goes like this: "Keep your thoughts continually fixed on all that is authentic and real, honorable and admirable, beautiful and respectful, pure and holy, merciful and kind. And fasten your thoughts on every glorious work of God, praising him always. . . . The God of peace will be with you in all things."[2]

Lisa half-smiled, about all we could muster most of the time, and said, "See? He's saying that choosing to think about better things makes our lives better."

"How does that help us not be so sad over losing Mitch, though?" I asked.

She shook her head slowly. "I don't know. But it feels important."

That night, mixed into my now-routine nightmares of saving Mason but being unable to save Mitch and the resurfacing horrible dreams of my time in Iraq, there were little flashes of the green-and-red contrast images of the participant's fMRI scan as she thought about different things. Lisa was correct: Paul's words *did* feel important, but I didn't yet understand why.

Nevertheless, there was something there, and it felt a little bit like hope.

12

Seems Easier to Die

I have refined you, but not as silver is refined.
Rather, I have refined you in the furnace of
suffering.

—Isaiah 48:10, NLT

CASPER, WYOMING
DECEMBER 2015

The emergency department at Wyoming Medical Center (WMC) is much larger than its counterpart at my former hospital in Alabama. We'd moved a month prior from Auburn to Casper, and I'd been working at WMC for about three weeks when I met the man who may have saved my life.

The impetus of our move was part practical and part adventure, but it was mostly out of psychological necessity. Since the Affordable Care Act of 2010, solo practice had become increasingly expensive as increased government regulation of healthcare almost tripled our overhead. We hired two additional people to keep up with the ever-changing rules, but with no other doctors to generate revenue, the only way to keep our business afloat was for me to work more. And for the first year after Mitch died, I just didn't have it in me. We saw patients and I took calls and operated, but I simply didn't have the emotional bandwidth to keep adding more and more hours.

Something had to change, especially since the refuge Lisa and I normally had when we came home no longer felt like a safe space. Work was hard, but home was *sad*.

Kimber and Bryce married in August 2014, Kalyn finished high school and left for college in 2015, and we were alone to bake together in the furnace of suffering every night.

The Old Testament prophet Isaiah wrote the words "furnace of suffering" and created the perfect thought-picture for what it feels like to lose a child or to go through any devastating circumstance in your life. But once we went back to work, we quickly gained context for the other part of that verse, the "Behold, I have refined you" part, as the English Standard Version translates it.

Because faced with the choice of blaming God and giving up our belief in him altogether, or clinging to him as the only hope we had of ever finding our way in life *and* seeing Mitch again in the next life, we really had no choice. For both Lisa and me, God was the only way. He was the foundation of our worldview, our upbringings, our marriage, and the reason we believed we had survived all the other hardships we'd both faced in our lives. If we gave him up, we would be anchorless. To paraphrase Oswald Chambers, we came to understand that we had to fear God or fear everything else, since for us, a God who allows a circumstance in which your son can die is still safer than a universe in which there is no loving God nor the future hope of resurrection.[1]

And so, in the furnace of our suffering after we lost Mitch, we went back to work and tried to take good care of people. I started writing again, and I began a weekly newsletter and podcast to try to connect with and serve other people in tough circumstances.[2] Lisa and I both were aware of and had to submit to the fact that we were being refined. I evolved over time into a more compassionate, empathetic physician. I cared more about figuring out how to doctor people even when I couldn't save them with surgery. Lisa became acutely sensitive to anyone who was hurting in any way. And through our interactions with others who were in the furnace with us, we were becoming better people, even though we were in so much pain.

We didn't like it, but we knew it had to be this way, because the choice was clear: Lie down and die, or stand up and live. Be refined or be burned alive.

Earlier in Isaiah, King Hezekiah said, "I will walk humbly all my years because of this anguish of my soul."[3] I no longer had the arrogant belief that living a good life would prevent me from being a victim of the same troubles that literally everyone else faces during their time on this hard planet.

Refined, definitely. But not without an awful immersion in the furnace of suffering.

If you've read my last book, *I've Seen the End of You*, the last six chapters tell the story of how we found our faith and our feet again after Mitch died.

We lived those chapters in Alabama, but I wrote them in Wyoming.

Since we were facing the economic realities of healthcare and living in a house full of emptiness, and I had the luxury of being able to find a job as a neurosurgeon anywhere in the country, we prayed about moving and decided we should. God put the Wyoming opportunity right in our laps the day after we said yes to his leading.

After more than a decade in Alabama, we closed the practice we had built and operated together, left the home in which we'd raised our family, and moved to Casper to start a new life.

But although we had found our faith again—albeit a squishy, infantile version of its former self—something was still missing.

———————//———————

As an aside, right around this time, Lisa did a Bible study by Jennie Allen based on her book *Anything*.[4] In it, you learn to tell God that you're willing to be used by him in order to please him with your life. Lisa convinced me to read the book, too, and we prayed the "anything" prayer and told God we would do anything if he would help us heal and get our fire back. Before *Anything*, we had never thought of moving. A week after we finished the book together, we received a flyer about the Wyoming job, and we both felt 100 percent sure that we were supposed to move. Be careful when you tell God you'll do anything!

————— *//* —————

After Lisa and I had been living in Wyoming a few weeks, several things were already abundantly clear: This place was *so much colder* than Alabama, the hospital was *a lot busier* than any place I'd ever worked, and moving from one place to another isn't a magic fix for all your troubles.

I'm not sure how I'd convinced myself that when we packed all those boxes, our grief wouldn't hide itself inside one of them or why it surprised me so much that it did. That seems foolish when I write it today, but it was genuinely shocking to me then. I thought moving would help, but lo and behold, Mitch went and followed us all the way to Wyoming.

We had decided to sell our house in Auburn furnished. Lisa's aforementioned interior design skills had turned that house into an incredibly warm, beautiful home, and the realtor wisely said, "Don't change a thing. Buyers will be able to see themselves living here, being happy here."

After all, we had been, too, until the Phone Call.

So we left all the furniture and bookcases and artwork as a way to sell someone else the dream of a place where a family could live and grow and be safe from the things that go *bump* in the night, and we moved into a 1,200-square-foot apartment until we could sell the house and buy or build our own place.

It was exciting in a way. Lisa and I started our relationship as a blended family, after we were established, successful adults. We never had the lean years, the apartment years, the pre-kids years together, so it was like a new beginning for us. It was often snowy, and there were tumbleweeds, mountains, all kinds of wildlife—on my first day in the office, they announced overhead that everyone should stay inside because there was a bear on the street—and lots of new people to distract and amuse us during the day. But at night, we sat on the couch and felt just like we'd felt in our old home, only without the comfort of knowing Kalyn was across town in her dorm room or Lisa's parents were just up the street.

All we could do was hold each other, listen to the wind blow across the prairie, and hope it would eventually blow some of the sorrow away. And although our home and office in Alabama had become impossibly sad because Mitch was *everywhere,* our apartment in Casper was equally sad because Mitch was *nowhere.* I missed seeing the places he'd been and constantly found myself wondering whether he'd like where we were now.

I got up every morning at three o'clock, sat at a folding table in the kitchenette, and worked on what I thought would be the final chapters of *I've Seen the End of You.* That book was about the tension between faith, doubt, and the things we think we know. I'd been researching for years how to reconcile the following: my belief in a God who hears our prayers, my doubt that brain tumors like glioblastoma multiforme (GBM) cared whether I prayed at all since everyone with that diagnosis dies, and my knowledge that people who maintain hope when faced with hard things have better outcomes in every measurable way (other than length of life).[5]

But something was missing.

I had started working on the book, the one I thought was going to help people learn to go through hard things and still be happy, as an *observer* and an *expert.* But when Mitch died, I became a fellow sufferer, and much of what I'd thought turned out to be, as my sweet grandmother Floy might have said, horse hockey.

By the time we moved to Wyoming, I had two years under my lab coat as a grieving dad who worked around people trying to process their own grief. I learned so much from them, and I was trying hard to help my wife and my family and my readers see that you could lose everything and still hold on to the hope of faith, and part of me actually believed it. But I'd always had this deep and abiding sense that everything would work out if I just did the right things and prayed and went to church. That if I tried to live a good life, God would come through for me. Losing a son was the first time God had seemed to say, "Here's a situation you can't control or prevent with good behavior, and you can't undo it or fix it."

Losing the notion that it would eventually be okay broke something deep inside me, and Lisa and I talked about it, prayed about it, grieved over it. She was so compassionate and tender to try to glue me back together in those dark days, even as she was a devastated mother who had also lost her boy. So we found ourselves on a foundation of faith in a God who would eventually bring us to heaven to see Mitch again, but for now we were stuck in a world that many times felt an awful lot like hell.

And to be very honest, I spent a good portion of every day on the dark mental staircase, choosing to revisit my pain. Over time, I got farther down the stairs, but it felt so lonely and I never wanted to drag Lisa, let alone Jesus, down there with me. I thought there was something wrong with me, that I needed to open that door and be with my son, even as I knew there was no life behind that door.

I was writing about those things one morning at the card table in our apartment while struggling with a huge case of impostor syndrome: I didn't believe I had the right to talk about how important faith is to deal with hardships like disease or great loss. And yet, I had to, because I needed it.

Then my phone rang, and the sudden noise shattered both the stillness of the room and my train of thought.

"Hello, it's Dr. Warren," I said.

"Hi, Lee, it's Jonna Cubin."

Dr. Jonna Cubin is an emergency department physician and fifth-generation Wyoming rancher. Her husband, Dr. Eric Cubin, is an interventional radiologist. Eric was the first doctor Lisa and I met in Wyoming, and we'd had lunch with him on the day I interviewed for the job at Wyoming Medical Center. Eric and Jonna had invited us to their home for dinner, and we were already becoming friends after only a short time in our new hometown.

"What's up, Jonna?" I asked.

"Well, sorry to call so early, but I have a couple of patients I need you to see in the ED, please."

"No problem," I said. "I'll be there in ten minutes."

"Thanks," Jonna said. "Start with Mr. Hobson in bed six."

"Will do. See you soon."

———//———

In Alabama, the ED front desk was guarded by the never-changing presence of Claudette, who'd been there for centuries and seemed to always be at work. At WMC, it was someone new every day.

Also gone was my friend and stalwart Abraham Lincoln–lookalike, Dr. Elijah Stinson. In his place was Dr. Jonna Cubin, also tall and thin and equally smart, but with fewer bad jokes.

Jonna was sitting in front of a computer with a brain scan up on the monitor, and I could see before I got to her that it wasn't good news.

"Hi there," I said.

She turned in her chair and saw me approach. "Pull up a chair. Here's the MRI." She held a small bag toward me. "Corn Nuts?" she asked.

"No, thanks," I said. "Trying to quit."

I'd noticed Jonna's devotion to always having quality snacks handy, a necessity in the long and hectic shifts she and her colleagues worked in Wyoming's busiest trauma center.

I sat next to her and moved the mouse to scroll through the brain MRI that was labeled **HOBSON, CHARLES.**

"Ooh," I said. "His right frontal lobe is extremely swollen. What happened?"

"He came in as a trauma," Jonna said. "Wrecked an ATV while working his cattle on his ranch up near my folks' place in Kaycee."

"Helmet?" I asked.

She nodded. "Yes, and he didn't lose consciousness. Bruised his shoulder, otherwise unscathed. He only came in because one of his ranch hands saw it happen and called 911. When EMS arrived, he was fine. But he admitted to them that he had a headache, and they convinced him to come in for a scan since he's on Coumadin for atrial fibrillation."

That was smart of the EMTs, I thought. People on blood thinners like Coumadin for heart arrythmias have a high risk of brain hemorrhage even with relatively minor trauma. It made me feel confident to know we had such wise field medics.

"Fortunately," Jonna said, "the CT doesn't show a brain bleed, but it did show the swelling, so I ordered a brain MRI before I called you."

"Outstanding," I said. "You're a good doctor."

She chuckled. "Maybe, but I've dealt with enough neurosurgeons to know that you guys get grumpy when there are 'not enough pictures to look at.'"

I winced. "I may have occasionally been guilty of that. Please tell me if I ever seem rude on the phone."

She waved a finger. "No, I'll tell Lisa! She's coming to our ranch next week for our branding."

Lisa and Jonna were becoming fast friends. Jonna's ranch was in the Red Wall area of Wyoming, famous for outlaws and rodeo cowboys like Chris LeDoux. She wanted Lisa to see where she came from and experience the cowboy culture firsthand, and Lisa was excited about the chance to spend some time with Jonna.

I kept scrolling through the scan, from the top of Hobson's head to about the level of his eyeballs, and then the reason for the brain swelling became obvious. A familiar ache started in my gut and slowly worked its way into my heart.

I knew what I was seeing, and I hated it: I hadn't met Charles Hobson yet, but I'd seen the end of him.

"That's the tumor?" Jonna said as she pointed to the white-and-gray blob nestled deep in the white matter of Mr. Hobson's brain.

"Yes," I said. "How old is he?"

"Sixty-seven," Jonna said.

"That makes it most likely to be—"

"Glioblastoma," Jonna interrupted. "Eric called a minute ago to say he'd read the study. That's his diagnosis."

In the short time I'd worked at WMC, I had already developed a deep respect for Eric's skill as a diagnostic radiologist. In Alabama, I'd been friends with Sandy Jackson, who I had often teased for never committing to a diagnosis. Sandy reminded me of a fortune teller—we jokingly called him "the Oracle"—in that he was so vague in his readings that he was never actually wrong about anything. Sandy never missed a finding, but he rarely came right out and told me what he thought. Eric, I was learning, was more likely to give me only his top diagnosis, and I had already had a few conversations with him in which I had to remind him that there *was* more than one possibility, even though his number one was almost always right. We had a good, easy rapport from the start, and I was excited to have such a skilled and confident colleague to work with.

"Unfortunately, I think he's probably right," I said. "But we won't really know without a biopsy. Would you please order a scan of the rest of his body, just to make sure it's not metastatic from lung cancer or something else?"

"Of course," Jonna said. "Thanks for coming so quickly. I'll tell you about the other lady when you're done."

———————//———————

I knocked on the sliding-glass door of trauma bed six in the ED. I slid the door partway open and said, "Good morning, I'm Dr. Warren. Can I come in?"

"I don't know. Can you?" came the reply.

I chuckled—my third-grade grammar teacher used to say the same thing to me when I confused *can I* with *may I*—then pushed the door open and stepped inside.

Mr. Hobson was sitting on a chair next to the hospital bed, pulling a cowboy boot onto his right foot. He was wearing blue denim overalls and had a cellphone on his lap, a walkie-talkie clipped to his right front pocket, and *two* tobacco pipes sticking out of his left front pocket.

He was a large man, I guessed about six foot four, balding, and built like a refrigerator. He had a kind face, a big smile, and eyes that wondered what I was about to tell him.

"Hello, sir. I'm Lee Warren, and I'm a neurosurgeon."

He laughed. "Neurosurgeon? A brain surgeon?"

"Yes," I said. "What made you come in today—"

He held up a hand to interrupt. "Hey, my wife's cousin's a brain surgeon in Bozeman. I married a city girl," he said. His smile faded, and he looked down for a beat. "Course, we lost her last year. Breast cancer."

"I'm so sorry," I said.

He waved his hand. "It's okay. I know where Wanda is now anyhow. Miss her, though. Hey, I got a joke about brain surgeons I told my wife's cousin at our last family reunion. Want to hear it?"

I shrugged. "Sure."

"What's the difference between God and a brain surgeon?"

I shook my head. "No idea. What?"

He held up both hands and smiled. "God don't think he's a brain surgeon!"

I groaned. This guy was something else.

"Sorry, Doc. Just trying to keep things light. What'd you say your name was again?"

"Lee Warren." I shook his hand.

"Warren? I knew some Warrens from up around Cody. None of 'em was worth killin'."

"No relation," I said.

He smiled. "Good. Charles Hobson, but everybody calls me Lucky Chuck."

About to be Not-So-Lucky Chuck, I thought.

"Do you mind if I sit?"

He shook his head. "It's a free country."

I sat in the chair next to him and turned to face him. "What happened to you today?"

His eyes were a deep blue, and they widened a little as his face lit up. "Crazy cow decided to attack my four-wheeler. It flipped over and I fell out, landed on my shoulder. My ranch hand Nathan called the paramedics because he thought I was hurt. I only agreed to come with them on account of this blood thinner I'm taking. My doctor warned me about bleeding in the brain if I ever fall, so I figured it was smart to come in."

He leaned forward and pulled on his other boot.

"Why are you getting dressed?" I asked.

"'Cause that pretty lady doctor told me I didn't bleed in my head, so I figured I was good to go. Got work to do."

"Well, we need to talk about your brain MRI first," I said.

"Yeah, she said it looked like I might have a brain tumor."

He seemed oddly unaffected about hearing he may have cancer, and I couldn't tell yet if it was Kübler-Ross denial, faith, or the swelling in his brain making him so calm about finding out he was probably dying.

"It does look that way," I said. "We need to run some additional tests to learn more about the tumor and where it may have started."

"You mean to see if it's primary or metastatic," Lucky Chuck said.

I cocked my head. "How do you know so much about—"

"Medical stuff?" he said. "I told you Wanda had breast cancer, Doc. Weren't you listening? We did the whole MD Anderson Cancer Center thing, experimental treatments, surgeries, tried it all. That cancer went all over her body, and it was awful. I learned a lot more than I wanted to about mets and oncogenes and proton beam radiation and triple-negatives, all that. And I may look like an old, fat rancher to you, but I'm not an idiot. I do have a college degree in animal science."

I put my hand on his arm. "Wow. I'm really sorry she and you had to go through all that. But let me show you *your* scan, okay? And then let's talk about what's happening to you now."

He agreed, and I stood, walked to the computer, and pulled up his MRI scan on the monitor. I showed him the tumor and the brain swelling, and I explained that we needed to do a CT scan of his chest, abdomen, and pelvis to rule out primary cancer somewhere outside his head, which would determine the safest place to biopsy and figure out what he was dealing with.

Lucky Chuck stared at the monitor for a few seconds and then looked into my eyes.

"Shoot straight with me, Doc. If there's lung cancer that's already spread to my brain, in an obese, old smoker with a bad heart, the prognosis for me to survive—prognosis *is* the word, right?—ain't good."

"No, not good," I said. "But not impossible either."

"Plus, Wanda and me sat in enough oncology-center waiting rooms next to people with primary brain cancers to know the deal about that. Also not good."

I shook my head. "No, you're right. But we need to know what the diagnosis is before we start predicting the outcome," I said while hating myself for my own hypocrisy—since I already knew that the deadliest cancer on earth was lurking an inch and a half under the skin on the right side of his head.

He smiled sadly. "I've had a pretty good ride, Doc. Married the girl I fell for, went off to school and realized I loved animals more than any people other than Wanda. Got struck by lightning three times—that's why they call me Lucky Chuck. Won some money roping in the rodeo. Had a baby girl, Bea, but she was stillborn." He took in a shuddering breath and closed his eyes for a moment.

I said, "I'm really sorry. We lost our son Mitch two years ago, and it's so hard."

Lucky Chuck shook his head and looked into my eyes. "Sorry, Doc. Nobody gets out of this thing unhurt, do we?"

"No, we don't. Do you have other children?"

He shook his head slowly. "Nope. Me and Wanda just didn't have the heart to try again. So we made a life out on the prairie, and I found God out there in the wind and the sunsets like I never found him in church. But I almost lost him again when Wanda got sick. When I saw her praying while she lost her hair, when she threw up every day from the poison that they kept putting in her veins, when she got so skinny you could see her pulse in her belly. Then she was gone." He looked down at the floor for a second and then back at me, now with a tear on his eyelashes.

"You said you *almost* lost God again. What do you mean?" I asked.

He took a deep breath and slowly exhaled. "Wanda said, when they first told us it was cancer, that we needed to decide right then what we believed about God. That we couldn't wait for the outcome to see if we trusted him or not because everybody dies or has something bad happen to them, so that stuff can't be what determines who God is to us. She told me to decide he was good before she died and not to be getting all mad at him when she was gone, because that would be when I needed him most."

I'd been going to church my whole life, but the best sermon I ever heard about trusting God with my troubles was delivered that day in trauma bed six at Wyoming Medical Center by Lucky Chuck Hobson. And it shook me, because I'd been mad at God for the two years since Mitch died, and I needed him now more than ever.

"Wanda sounds like a wise woman," I said quietly.

"She was. Is. Anyhow, Doc, I don't want to go through any of that stuff. Chemo and radiation and surgery—besides, you probably don't have a drill big enough to saw through my thick head."

I laughed. "Look, Mr. Hobson—"

"Lucky Chuck," he said.

"Okay, Lucky Chuck. I guess you deserve that name after surviving three lightning strikes. Look, no one is saying you have to go through all those treatments. But don't you want to know what the problem is?"

He smiled. "You're a nice guy, Doc. But the only real problem I've had since I lost Wanda was missing her so much every day. I have no mind to spend what time I have left hanging out with you in this place, no offense. I'm gonna go get that crazy cow in the freezer—you don't get to run over Lucky Chuck Hobson and live to tell about it. And then I'm gonna spend the rest of my life seeing God in all the things he made so beautiful on my place. One of these days, if it gets real bad, my horse will come home alone. Nathan or someone will find my body out on the prairie with one bullet missing from my Henry rifle, and I'll be with Wanda."

He stood up, shook my hand, and started to walk out.

"Hold on a second," I said. "There's a couple of forms you need to sign to leave against our advice, or if you agree to come to my office in a couple of weeks after you've had some time to think about it, we can release you now."

"I'd love to come see you, Doc. I enjoy talking to you, and I reckon

I'm gonna have plenty of fresh beef jerky to share. But, just so you know, I'm not ignoring your advice."

"You're not?"

"No, sir. I understand my options, and I'm sure you're a great surgeon. It just seems easier to die."

13

All in Your Head

Just because you have a thought, it doesn't mean you have to think it.

—Max Lucado, on *The Dr. Lee Warren Podcast*

"Mr. Hobson's just going to leave?" Jonna said when I got back to her desk.

"Yep. Says he has no interest in even doing a biopsy. Just wants to ride off into the sunset."

Jonna nodded. "It's pretty common here. That independent spirit that says, 'I'll go out on my own terms,'" she said. "The rodeo cowboys have a saying, 'When you draw a tough horse, let 'er buck.'"

"Wow. I think I would at least want a diagnosis. But he's making a choice of how he wants to die: between knowing—even if he can't do anything about it—or not knowing and still being at peace with whatever comes along. I respect that."

"Let 'er buck," Jonna said again.

"I guess so. Hey, you said there were two patients. What's the deal with the other one?"

She made a *humph* sound. "Tina Tisdale, fifty-seven, in room nine. Thinks she has a brain tumor. She's just back from radiology, so the CT scan should be available in her room."

"She *thinks* she has a tumor?" I asked.

"Yes. She had brain surgery about two years ago for a benign menin-gioma by a surgeon in Cheyenne. The Tisdales moved here about six months back, and she started coming to the ED a few times a month with headaches and other complaints. She said she heard we have a new neurosurgeon, and she wants to see you."

"She couldn't just come to the office?"

Jonna shrugged her shoulders. "She says the pain is getting worse, and she was sure you'd want to go straight to surgery. Last time she was here she brought an MRI she had done at Mountain View, but it was read by their radiologists as normal."

Mountain View was a small surgical hospital across town that had been started by a group of physicians a few years earlier. It sat next to Summit Medical Center, another physician-owned hospital that fo-cused mostly on orthopedics.

"Is the Mountain View MRI available for me to look at?"

"Yes, it should be in our system. Hey, I'm going to meet Eric for cof-fee. Would you like something from Starbucks?"

I shook my head. "No, I had about six cups this morning already. Bad habit, but it's my only vice. Wait, there's a Starbucks in the hospi-tal?"

Jonna laughed. "Yes, on the second floor by the chapel. We might be countryfolk, but we do have coffee shops!"

It dawned on me then that I hadn't seen the chapel in the few days I'd been at WMC. All my time had been spent seeing patients in the ED and the nursing floors, setting up my operating room, and working in the office. Realizing I hadn't even looked for one here stung like another tiny wound in the *lingchi*—the death by a thousand cuts—of grief. The death of my old life, my old faith, another chapter in this new creation story of who Lee Warren turns out to be in the end.

"Thanks for the info," I said. "Enjoy your coffee."

"All right, then. I'll see you in a bit."

Jonna walked off, and I headed for room nine.

———— // ————

Mrs. Tisdale was sitting on the gurney, holding her face in her left hand.

The door was open, so I said, "Hello, I'm Dr. Warren, a neurosurgeon. May I come in?"

Her husband sat to her right on a plastic chair, and he stood to greet me.

"Hi. Rick Tisdale. Nice to meet you."

Tina dropped her hand and looked at me. "I'm Tina. I've heard good things about you. You're going to finally cure me."

"I hope so. What's going on with you, ma'am?" I asked.

"My tumor's back."

"I'm sorry to hear that," I said. "Let me pull up your scan while you tell me about your surgery and everything that's happened since."

I moved to the computer next to her bed and logged in, and Tina told me her story.

"I started having these headaches about four years ago. Really weird, pressure-like sensations just behind my left eye. At first, I thought I had a sinus infection or something, but they just kept getting worse, until eventually it felt like my eye was going to pop out of my head."

She lifted her left hand and traced a faint curved scar just behind her hairline, from in front of her left ear to her forehead. "I had a scan, and they found a tumor. My doctor sent me to the neurosurgeon Dr. Scofield, in Cheyenne. He told me I needed surgery to find out whether or not it was cancer. Turned out to be a meningioma, and Dr. Scofield said it was benign. I was supposedly cured."

"And then what happened?" I asked.

"I started feeling it grow back. About six months ago."

"Right around when we moved," Rick said.

Tina held up a stop-sign hand toward Rick. "It has nothing to do with that. I'm not crazy!"

Rick looked down and stopped talking.

"What do you mean when you say you can feel it growing back?" I asked.

She sat up straighter. "It's the pressure. I can feel it behind my eye again, and it's getting bigger. It's growing every day. And my scar hurts. None of that's ever happened before."

"Okay," I said. "Let me just show you the scan."

I scrolled through the images. **TISDALE, TINA C.** I pointed out the surgical changes and how good her brain looked overall. "It looks like Dr. Scofield did a great job. There's no evidence of recurrent or residual tumor. It's normal."

Rick stood and took her hand. A smile covered his face, and he said, "Honey! That's great—"

"Don't!" Tina said with a look that erased Rick's smile. "Don't you dare tell me this is all in my head."

"No one is saying that," I said. "It's very common for people who have had craniotomies to feel pain or numbness around their incisions and also to have frequent headaches. We can get you set up with a good neurologist who should be able to help you."

"No," she said. "I want an MRI, with contrast, or a PET scan or surgery or something." She stuttered and drew in a halting breath. She began to cry and said, more quietly, "I'm not crazy. Dr. Scofield said it could come back, in the bone, in that covering over my brain, that *something* matter . . . oh—what's it called again—what's the matter?"

"Dura mater," I said.

She nodded. "Right. He told me these things often start to grow again, and I'm telling you, Doctor, I can feel it. My tumor is coming back, and I need you to help me."

I checked on the computer to see what other studies we had on Tina. I found the recent brain MRI from Mountain View that Jonna had mentioned and noticed it was done on an open MRI with a low magnetic field strength, 0.5 Tesla, and without contrast. Plus, she had moved around a fair amount during the study, so the image quality overall was poor. Could I be missing something?

I put my hand on her shoulder. "Look, I don't think you're crazy. Dr. Scofield is right; these tumors can come back, and sometimes we can't see them on CT at all."

"That's why you have to do surgery. You have to find it," Tina said.

I handed her a box of tissues from the counter. She wiped a tear and lowered her head again.

"Tell you what," I said. "I'll get all your old images and records from Dr. Scofield, and we'll get you a new MRI on a more modern scanner, just to make sure we're not missing anything. Can you come to my office next week and we'll go through everything?"

She nodded slowly and finally looked up at me. "Okay. At least you're doing something. Thank you."

"That's what I'm here for," I said.

"Rick, let's go home," Tina said.

———— // ————

Jonna was back at her desk when I left Tina's room.

She sat her coffee down and said, "How'd it go with Tina?"

"She's convinced the tumor's back, like you said. I'm going to get her old records, pathology reports, and see her in the office soon to make sure we're not missing anything. You can let her go home today."

Jonna nodded. "That's what I figured. It's sad; she is actually cured, but she still thinks she's sick."

"Probably. She needs a better MRI, but that CT is really clean. But I've seen it before; it's hard when you face life-threatening issues. Some people get stuck there."

"Well," Jonna said, "we all get stuck sometimes, don't we?"

You have no idea. I can make my shoulder hurt right now if I think about Mitch for two seconds.

"You're right, my friend," I said. "We all do. Thanks for the consults."

She held up a paper sack. "Biscotti for the road?"

I shook my head. "No, thanks, I'm good. I'm going to have breakfast with Lisa before clinic. Have a great day."

———— // ————

I met Lisa at a restaurant in downtown Casper called Eggington's. It was a popular breakfast spot, close enough to the hospital that Lisa and

I would meet sometimes after I made hospital rounds and before I started my clinic day. Another sacrifice of our decision to leave Alabama was that for the first time since we'd married, we didn't get to work together.

Lisa was omnipresent in our practice in Auburn—in the clinic, in meetings in the hospital, often taking video or photos in the operating room for teaching and research projects we did together at the university. She was always there with me, for every hard case or triumph.

She knew the patients and their families as well as I did, and on multiple occasions she had conversations with people at Bible studies—making diagnoses after hearing their symptoms when they asked for prayers—that led to me operating on them. She would say "Amen" when the prayer was over and then say, "You should meet my husband."

She was now alone in our apartment, and I was by myself in a new workplace without my partner. So breakfast and stolen moments in between cases on surgery days were times for us to stay as connected as we could during the long days of me being back in a busy trauma center.

I saw her in a corner booth, the sun highlighting her lovely hair, and I stopped for a beat to float on the thermal currents of my whole spirit lifting at the sight of her. With apologies to Christopher Marlowe, Helen of Troy may have been the face that launched a thousand ships, but it's Lisa Warren I'd fight any battle to get back to.[1] And that's how it felt then; every moment we weren't together felt like I was deployed to some war zone, behind enemy lines, and I had to survive long enough for her to rescue me. Working apart had made me desperate for every second with her—to process things and to see the one person in Wyoming who knew me and what we had been through.

In Alabama, everyone knew us, and many people knew Mitch. People were aware of our version of The Massive Thing, and thus they tried to shoulder some of the load. As much as I hated the Christian platitudes, at least people saw us. In those early Wyoming days, if someone happened to ask the "how many kids" question and we somehow got around to the "our son died" part of the conversation, it was a data point, a sad fact to be noted, guaranteed to elicit an "I'm sorry" but not for them to come alongside us.

We were alone, together.

I slid into the booth next to Lisa and pulled her close. "Hi, darling," she said with her heart-surgery smile that always puts me back together, no matter how badly a particular day has broken me. We hugged for a few seconds and then set about making the most important decision at hand: what to order for breakfast.

Eggington's has a huge menu, and it had changed since the last time we ate there.

"I'm getting option anxiety just reading this thing! There are so many choices," Lisa said.

"Anxiety has been the theme of my morning so far," I said.

She smiled the half smile she'd recovered since Mitch died. "I'm sorry. What do you mean?" Lisa said, just as our server, Mike, came to take our order.

After Mike walked away, I considered Lisa's question. When we ran our practice together, we could talk about everything. But another hard part of our new situation in Wyoming was that, since Lisa didn't work for the hospital, we couldn't talk about patients directly. The Health Insurance Portability and Accountability Act of 1996, commonly known as HIPAA, prohibits healthcare workers from discussing patient information with anyone—including their spouses. In Alabama, Lisa and I could talk about *everything*, and she was an invaluable part of my thinking through things and dealing with tough situations with our patients. She watched over our practice and loved our patients, and we were a great team. Here in Wyoming, we couldn't talk about *anything*, and I hated it.

"I really miss being able to talk about patients with you," I said.

Lisa took my hand. "I know. Me too. Just give me the thirty-thousand-foot view."

I thought for a moment. "Well, I saw one person who probably has cancer but doesn't want to have a biopsy or any type of treatment. And

I saw another person who has most likely been cured of their problem, but they are convinced they're still sick and are basically demanding surgery."

"Wow," Lisa said. "So the first person is so anxious they won't even try to fight the cancer?"

I shook my head. "Actually, I don't think that one's so much about anxiety. That person seems comfortable with their life as they've already lived it, and I think it's more that they think surgery and chemo and radiation would be more trouble than they're worth if the diagnosis is terminal."

"I understand that," Lisa said. "Leah fought so hard and went through so much pain because of her treatments, when we all knew it was hopeless at the start."

Lisa's best friend, Leah, had died of breast cancer back when we were engaged. She had a widely metastatic, advanced disease when the diagnosis was made, and the doctors gave her only a couple of months to live. She proved them wrong; she lived almost a year, but she suffered greatly the entire time.

"Yeah, that was brutal," I said. "The other patient, I suspect, is just so nervous about having *been* sick that they can't move past it."

"It's just like Pain Pump Lady in Alabama, right?" Lisa said just as Mike arrived with our breakfast.

Lisa's egg-white omelet looked delicious, by which I mean to say that it looked like it was so good for me that I wished I could find it delicious. It was a healthy choice, just like my biscuit-and-gravy smoothie with bacon.

———— // ————

Pain Pump Lady was a woman named Martha who had a major spinal deformity. I performed a long corrective surgery and inserted a dozen or so titanium screws and two long rods into her back to straighten her up. The surgery went very well, but the long incision through her muscles was bloody and she had a high output in her surgical drain for the two days she was in the hospital after the procedure. She was doing great other than the drainage, so I decided to let her go home with the drain in place, and she would come back to the office two days later to have my nurse Karen remove the drain.

I saw her at her two-week postoperative visit. She was happy, her wound had healed well, and she was much better than before surgery. I asked her if she needed refills on her pain medicine or muscle relaxers, and her answer shocked me.

"I don't need any medicine, Doctor," she said. "In fact, I never took any in the hospital, and I didn't fill the prescriptions you sent me home with either."

"Wait," I said. "You're telling me you haven't had one dose of medicine since surgery? How did you tolerate the pain?"

She smiled. "I never had any pain. That pain pump you put in controlled everything. I never hurt at all."

"But you didn't have a pain pump," I said.

She waved a hand. "You're pretty forgetful for a brain surgeon. Just like when I had my knee replaced and they had that ball of pain medicine that went into my leg, I never had any pain. I didn't have pain with this surgery either. And once your nurse pulled it out, I figured I was already over the surgery, and it still hasn't ever hurt."

Orthopedic surgeons often use a device called ON-Q* to deliver narcotics directly into the surgical site after hip and knee replacements. This gives good local pain control and reduces the need for potentially addicting oral pain medication. But I had never used one of those in spine surgery.

"Ma'am, what you had was a drain. It wasn't putting medicine into your body; it was draining blood out of your wound."

"Well, however you did it, it worked," she said.

Martha went on to tell everyone she knew about "Dr. Warren's magic pain pump," and we had to dispel those rumors for years. At least monthly, someone with whom I was discussing surgery would ask me about the pain pump they heard about from Martha at the beauty shop or grocery store. We called her Pain Pump Lady, and she probably drove more business to me than most of my referring doctors.

I also verified her story in the hospital chart: She never received even a single dose of pain medication after her surgery. To this day, Pain

Pump Lady is the only person I've ever operated on with no pharma-cological assistance in pain control.

------------//------------

I took a bite of breakfast and asked Lisa, "How does my anxious pa-tient remind you of Pain Pump Lady?"

She reached over and wiped a little gravy off the corner of my mouth with her napkin. "They're both showing you the power of their minds. Pain Pump Lady believed she had medicine on board, and so she never hurt, right?"

"Yes," I said.

"And this person believes they have a problem, and so it's just as real to them. Remember the fMRI in Auburn? How we saw people's brains changing when they thought about different things?"

"Yes, and I remember the conversation we had about Philippians 4 and how God knew a long time ago that thinking about better things can reduce anxiety and give us peace of mind."

Lisa looked down at her plate. She pinched the bridge of her nose and sniffed. She said softly, "I haven't felt that since we lost Mitch."

I took her hand. "Peace of mind? Me either. I keep trying, helping other people, sharing our story, and trying to be a good doctor, trying to be faithful . . . but it's anything but peaceful. I'm still so angry."

> God knew a long time ago that thinking about different things can reduce anxiety and give us peace of mind.

She nodded slowly. "I am too. But it's got to get better eventually, right? How long do we have to 'fake it 'til we make it'? I miss being happy."

Tina Tisdale's and Pain Pump Lady's beliefs changed their realities, and Lucky Chuck chose to fight against his reality. I was trying to "do better" long enough to feel better, and it wasn't working. And I could soldier on forever, taking care of my family and pretending to be okay.

But knowing my precious wife was suffering meant I wasn't okay, and I knew I had to do more.

"I miss being happy too. And you're right," I said. "We're going to have to be like those people in the fMRI scanner in Auburn."

"What do you mean?" Lisa said.

I looked into her sad eyes and said, "If we want to change our lives, we're going to have to change our minds."

PART THREE

Your Choices Will Change Your Life

Those who sow with tears

will reap with songs of joy.

—Psalm 126:5

14

Data Stories

For the revelation awaits an appointed time;
    it speaks of the end
    and will not prove false.
Though it linger, wait for it;
    it will certainly come
    and will not delay.

—Habakkuk 2:3

The data was abundantly clear once I stopped to analyze it.

A few years into my career, I'd started tugging on the Gordian knot of a problem I ran into every time I saw a patient with a brain tumor, which ultimately led to writing *I've Seen the End of You.* Here it is in a nutshell: How can I, as a person of faith, honestly counsel a patient to pray and not give up when I look at their MRI and see a malignant tumor like glioblastoma and I *know* what's going to happen to them?

I'd interviewed several colleagues, people I respected and thought perhaps had already untangled the knot in their own practices. The answers I got ranged from "I haven't really thought about it" to "You're overthinking it. Just do your best."

But it kept bothering me because I wanted to be a good doctor to people even if I couldn't cure them. I'd seen it so many times over the years: Something bad happens, and a person just goes to ground like the rocket-less ejection seat if the handle gets pulled too early. They lose heart, lose faith, and crumble under the weight of all the what-ifs and the loss of the things they thought they had known to be true about their lives.

These people, when they realize that the previously unknown number of future-life days they had left is now much more calculable, are in danger of having the rest of their lives be defined by a single issue. Their story becomes cancer, or trauma, and the rest of their time centers around this, their TMTs. Marriages suffer, and long-standing family matters smolder and get passed to another generation without resolution.

If life is defined by the quality of days rather than the quantity of them, these people die much sooner than their bodies do.

From a neuroscience perspective, I knew that having a positive outlook creates a better chemical environment in your brain, and that produces improvements in your overall physiology. I've seen this empirically in my own practice: a patient's blood pressure and heart rate come down when I redirect their thinking away from fear about their surgery and toward the outcome they're seeking. And there are many reports of people being cured of "incurable" diseases partly through improving their thought lives, as shown by Dr. Bernie Siegel in his bestseller *Love, Medicine and Miracles*.[1] More recently, Dr. Daniel Amen has been the leader in using single-photon emission computed tomography (SPECT) imaging to show the powerful changes in the brain that can be produced by thought hygiene,[2] and I'd seen it firsthand in the even more detailed fMRI images at Auburn.

I'd worked on the problem of how to help people reframe their thoughts about their lives, their diagnoses, and the path forward when they receive terrible news. I wanted to write *I've Seen the End of You* to encourage people to take a breath after they hear the diagnosis or the aneurysm ruptures and decide that whatever the rest of their lives hold, it's still worth fighting for—marriage, family, faith, everything. I knew that some of those people would thread the needle and manage to survive their disease because I had seen some miracles and many improbable recoveries. But the people who recover are the ones who fought hard enough to make it through the awful medical gauntlet of chemotherapy and radiation and surgeries, not the folks who, like I feared for Lucky Chuck, just walked off into the sunset.

And I'd seen many people fight hard, recover their faith, save their family, tell a great story with their lives, and die of their disease anyway. But they managed to have happy endings despite the way it all ended medically.

So all that tugging on the knot of "How do I doctor and encourage people to fight and have faith when I already know the outcome?" turned my own thoughts on the matter upside down. I realized the purpose of *I've Seen the End of You* wasn't for me to solve my spiritual quandary. Rather, I had to learn a new way to look at what it means to be a physician and a man of faith. It was time for me to stop seeing science and faith as two different coats I wore. I needed to become a doctor who was as concerned about people's peace of mind as he was their physical bodies.

And all the way up to August 20, 2013, that was how I saw my role—as both a surgeon and a guide to those people whose lives had fallen apart—and I'd thought I was ready to write that book.

Then I lost my son and realized I had been asking the wrong question entirely.

———————//———————

In the days following the conversation Lisa and I had over breakfast at Eggington's, we both realized something important that we'd been unable to articulate before. By the time we paid the bill that morning, we were full of good food, coffee, and deep conversation. But we were both still starving to death, and now we knew what we were hungry for: We missed the joy, the happiness, the faith, and the life we'd once had. Even though we had carried on and were going through the motions of working, taking care of our family, and trying to encourage other people, we weren't really living.

This dilemma reminded me of when I was a kid. My sister Michelle and a couple of her friends had decided to sing at the McCurtain

County Annual Talent Show. Back then, in small-town Oklahoma, the talent show was the highlight of the year, and getting the trophy could do a lot for a kid's popularity.

I was probably eleven, and I'd just started goofing around with my dad's old acoustic guitar. I knew how to play two or three chords, but I was far from being ready to perform in public. Still, I wanted to be in the talent show, so I asked my mom if I could sign up. I remember her being very skeptical, but my mom knew the value of letting your kids fail sometimes, so she said yes.

I talked Mom into renting a tuxedo with long tails for me, and I borrowed one of her 1970s wigs (didn't everyone's mom wear wigs back then?). When it was my time to go onstage, the announcer said, "And now, please welcome Lee Warren from Broken Bow, who will play classical guitar for us!"

When the applause stopped, I sat on a stool and spoke into the microphone. "Hi. I'm going to play a piece from Beethoven's Fifth." I dramatically strummed one chord and then stopped. "But before I play, did you hear about the chicken that swallowed a yo-yo? It laid the same egg three times."

People laughed, and by the time my five minutes onstage were over, I'd played three chords and told ten jokes. I never had to reveal that I didn't know how to play the guitar, but I won the talent show. Between then and when I graduated high school, I won multiple such events, even a few later on by actually playing guitar by myself and in bands. I gained local fame as an entertainer, and comedy and music became important parts of my life.

I was quick with a joke, always trying to use humor to bring a smile to people, and in my early years in medical school and residency, my bedside manner was informed with the power of lifting the mood.

Then life happened. A difficult marriage, the Iraq War with all its trauma and danger and death, a divorce, PTSD, and then losing Mitch. My ability to feel anything close to real joy seemed as lifeless as my prayers.

And eventually, I'd managed to press on—to control the narrative, to *do better* for my family and others, to win the talent show by presenting a pretty put-together life for the audience to see.

But no one knew I couldn't really play.

Continuing to live in this cognitive dissonance was not a healthy choice, and I knew it was time to make a change.

———————//———————

The next morning at three o'clock I was at the card table in our apartment, and all I could feel was Mitch's absence. I read my Bible and drank coffee and listened to a Tommy Walker song called "These Things Are True of You," which had been instrumental in helping me navigate a crisis of faith I'd been through years before when my legalistic upbringing crashed into the real world of my struggling first marriage.

These lines stood out:

> *Unshakeable, immovable,*
> *faithful and true . . .*
> *these things are true of you*[3]

That morning in Casper, Wyoming, the tears flowed, and I prayed along with Tommy that God would make me unshakable and immovable because I'd been so shaken and moved by the trauma hat trick of divorce, war, and loss. I asked God to make it true of me that I could be, like Jesus, "a man of sorrows,"[4] but also learn as he did to again "[rejoice] in the Holy Spirit."[5]

And then, as suddenly as Habakkuk's revelation that lingered until the appointed time, I began to see it: the question I'd needed to ask all along and the answers that had been there the whole time.

———————//———————

I went to my notes on the patients I'd studied in preparation for what I had intended to be my first draft of *I've Seen the End of You*, when my perspective was that of "concerned doctor with a faith conundrum."

But I had new eyes.

Now I saw it all from the point of view of a person in an equally terminal state of being, a bereaved father who knew his diagnosis would never change or be cured. And what emerged—now that I was looking with a different perspective at these people's journeys through glioblastoma, other major neurological diseases and injuries, harsh treatments, progressive disability, and often death—was basically four stories.

But first, a little context. When scientists look at data regarding people's average survival rates for a particular disease, they usually chart *percentage of people alive* on the y-axis (vertical) and *time* on the x-axis (horizontal). With a malignant brain tumor like glioblastoma, the y-axis approaches zero as time passes, and by the time you get out to five years, there are very few survivors.

NOTE: The following charts are meant to show trends only and do not represent actual scientific data.

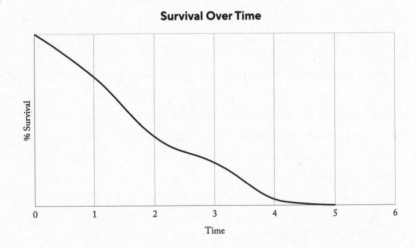

I made charts, too, although they weren't particularly scientific, so I could visually see the trend lines of how several patients seemed to be doing in terms of their *quality of life over time.* I looked at the things they told me about how they were doing emotionally, how their families were, whether they felt more or less connected to God, and how happy and hopeful they felt.

I saw four patterns over and over, which I called Crashers, Dippers, Untouchables, and Climbers. Allow me to explain the difference.

> **Crashers:** People who seemed like they had everything together, self-reported a lot of faith, and were happy—until something bad happened, such as receiving a scary diagnosis or their loved one getting sick. These folks crashed emotionally and never recovered. What shocked me about them was that the curve looked so much like the glioblastoma survival curve; they became progressively less "alive" on the y-axis over time, *even if they or their loved one survived their illness or recovered from their injury.* It was as if the single problem became the defining issue of their lives.

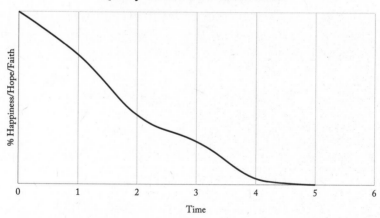

Quality of Life Over Time: Crashers

> **Dippers:** These folks started high on the y-axis with good lives and then dipped lower as they first learned of their problems. They stayed down there for a while and then somehow turned it around and began to climb and ended up high on the quality-of-life axis *regardless of their medical outcomes.*

Quality of Life Over Time: Dippers

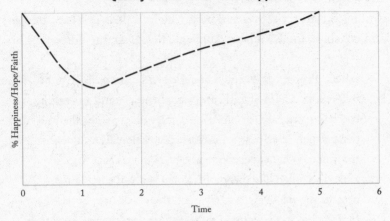

Untouchables: These folks seemed bulletproof. They started high,
   found out about their troubles, but never really wavered in their
   faith, happiness, or their relationships with people or God.
   *These patients did not experience a significant or lasting change in
   their baseline emotional state, even if they ultimately died of their
   illness.*

Quality of Life Over Time: Untouchables

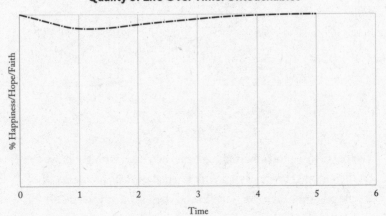

Climbers: This group surprised me the most. They started low, often with a history of trouble, addiction, prior illness, loss, etc. They did not report being happy or faithful or having much quality of life to begin with. When I told them they had cancer, or that the injury would produce paralysis, or that their mom was not going to make it, they often received the news with something akin to having expected it. But then, somehow, *something happened that caused them to discover faith, find joy, and end up being happier at the end than at the beginning.*

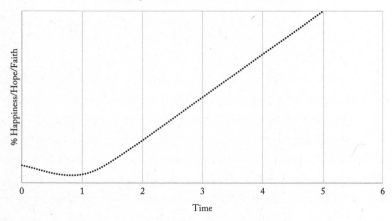

Quality of Life Over Time: Climbers

As I pored over my notes and case studies from the patients who eventually became the "characters" (real people whose names are obscured) in my book, the obvious difference in the graphs was that some people find a way to change directions and climb up the happiness/hope/faith scale, and some people don't. Untouchables didn't seem to need this discovery, since their curves never went down.

The Crashers, people who wound up dead inside even if their bodies lived on, never found this path back up, so their curves turned into a nearly exact copy of the glioblastoma survival graph.

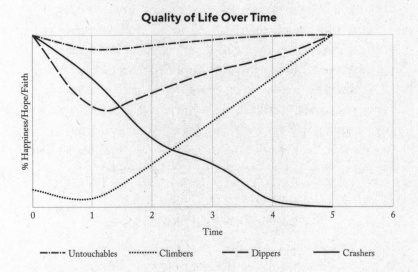

Quality of Life Over Time

Seeing the data displayed graphically made me realize the single thing I'd misunderstood from the start: The deadliest disease known to man is not glioblastoma; it is hopelessness.

This is the explanation for how some people can seem okay and then when life brings them something hard that shatters their Weltanschauung—their worldview, the things they thought they knew—they fall apart. I had a patient named Mr. Andrews, and his wife was the prototypical Crasher. She based her whole world on her husband being well, and when he died, she did, too, even though her body kept on living. She lost hope.

But it also explains how others believe their lives to be destined for misery, feel affirmed in that thinking when they become ill, but then are shocked as people come alongside them, care and pray for them, and love them. Even in the midst of their TMT, Climbers find something that makes them feel better and more hopeful than they ever did when they were well. Joey was a troubled soul, a castaway, and he found love and faith in the cancer center during the last year of his short life, which he told me was his "best year ever" (his whole story is told in *I've Seen the End of You*). He found hope.

And the story clarifies further in people who dip and then recover.

They have their faith challenged, but it turns out that the bottom holds for them, and they climb back up to being happy again, apart from their outcome. Samuel, a young man with a beautiful family, died of glioblastoma, but he finished his story strong. He found his faith to be real, and his quality of life was determined by being grateful for what he had, independent of how long he got to have it.

Untouchables, like my patient Rupert Chang, can absorb life's blows and not seem to flinch. Rupert had a strong faith that was not anchored on the daily circumstances of life, and he had always told his family that no matter what happened, God was enough to get him through. And when something bad *actually* happened, when he learned he had fatal brain cancer, he lived out what he said he believed.

I saw it so clearly that morning: In all cases, a person's ultimate position on the quality-of-life axis depends on *their ability to separate their happiness from their circumstances.* In other words, the people who manage to be okay again when they go through hard things are those who do not define being okay as having a life that is pain-free. They're the people who can accept both of Jesus's statements about life: it's hard, but you can be abundantly happy anyway.

> A person's ultimate position on the quality-of-life axis depends on *their ability to separate their happiness from their circumstances.*

I saw all these patterns in the data, but still I knew there was more to the story of how one person hits something hard and lies down under the weight of it to wither away while another person shrugs it off and carries on. I just didn't know how to tease it out yet.

Even so, in the early hours of that morning, I realized I could not find joy again until I decided that losing my son was not going to be the only inflection point on my quality-of-life curve. Something had to change, and that something was that I had to think about his death differently.

Just as my patients with glioblastoma were not going to survive their cancers, I was not going to wake up one morning and be magically relieved of the pain of losing Mitch *or* wake up and find the whole thing to have been a bad dream and that he was alive and well down the hall.

I was going to have to redefine happiness, rediscover my faith, and find a new "okay" for me. Lisa and our other family members would have to walk that path, too, and Lisa and I would have to lead them.

It was not a matter of waiting for it to heal, because it wasn't going to, at least not by itself. I was going to have to change the way I thought about it.

And I knew where we had to go: The data clearly showed that people do change their lives when they change their minds, and I had ample examples that people could do it.

I just had no idea *how* I could turn it from a fact on paper into a treatment plan for my own life, or if I was even ready to try.

Turns out, Scarlett helped me.

15

You Can't Have That

When we learn to move through suffering, rather than avoid it, then we greet it differently.

—Henri Nouwen, *Turn My Mourning into Dancing*

Tina Tisdale had an appointment to see me in the office on a Tuesday morning. Her new MRI was completed on the Monday afternoon before, so after I finished surgery in the hospital that day, I decided to head down to radiology to look at her scan with the radiologist.

The Cave is a dimly lit room off the main hallway in the radiology department at Wyoming Medical Center, full of high-resolution monitors and state-of-the-art digital imaging workstations. And the Cave is almost always inhabited by a radiologist, reading studies and dictating reports, available to converse with wandering surgeons who need to discuss a patient.

On that Monday, I knocked on the door of the Cave and heard a familiar "Yell-o!" I peeked inside to see Dr. Eric Cubin, Jonna's husband and my new favorite practitioner of the imaging arts. "What's up, Doc?" he said as he sat his Dictaphone down. He grabbed a handful of gummy bears from an open bag on his desk, washed them down with a swig of hazelnut coffee, and then said, "Have a seat."

I shook his hand and sat. "Thanks. I wonder if you have time to look at an MRI with me?"

He agreed, and I gave him Tina's information. He clicked a few keys and moments later we were looking at her brain on the screen.

"What's the story?" Eric asked.

"She had a craniotomy awhile back in Cheyenne to remove a benign meningioma, but she feels something in her head, and she's convinced her tumor is coming back."

Eric scrolled through all the images and pulled up all her prior studies, including the scans from before her surgery. He carefully inspected the pre- and post-contrast pictures and spent a long time scouring her brain from multiple angles in fine detail. I sat back to let him work and watched the great radiologist examine Tina's data intensely for more than twenty minutes, chewing gummies intermittently while he compared new images to old images. The only sounds were the computer fans humming, Eric's mouse clicks, and gummy chewing.

My mind began to wander, and suddenly I'm on the dark mental staircase again, descending into my pain.

I look over and see Eric. There's a picture of his little girls on his desk, smiling, adorable, safe. Eric, the alpha male big-game hunter, has the three most adorable little princess daughters you've ever seen, and he and Jonna are raising them to be the perfect combination of all-lady and all-Wyoming. They know how to fly-fish, shoot a bow, rope a steer, and wear a dress, and it's lovely to watch their family together. But I can't look at his girls right now. I have to find my son.

I look down and take a step into the darkness, feel it enveloping me even as the ceramic cross shards lacerate my feet and send powerful jolts of pain up my spinal cord and into my brain and heart. But I have to go down.

Eric's kids are safe and sound, but my boy is behind that door and he needs me. I need him.

I reach the door and extend my hand to touch the knob. I'm very afraid, swallowing hard against the bitter acid that's rising. Why am I so brave in the operating room but scared to go through this door and see Mitch?

"You okay, Lee?" Eric asked.

I blinked hard. "Yeah, had a long night on call. Must have dozed off for a second; it's so dark and cozy in here."

He laughed. "Yep, that's how we like it." He pointed to his monitor.

YOU CAN'T HAVE THAT

"There's nothing there, pardner. The tumor is completely resected, and I don't see any evidence of recurrence or any residual disease. She's cured."

"Thanks for taking the time. That was my read too. I'll give her the good news tomorrow."

I snagged a few gummy bears and headed out. They weren't too bad, and I strangely found myself wondering how they would taste mixed with hazelnut coffee.

———— // ————

The next morning when I got to the office, there was a note on my desk to call Rick Tisdale. I dialed the number and heard "This is Rick."

"Hi, it's Dr. Warren," I said, "returning your call."

I heard him breathe for a second. "Um, I just wanted to let you know that Tina got her MRI report from the patient portal, and she's really upset."

The government decision that all medical data must be immediately available via the internet for patients to access on their own has created many unexpected issues. People get information without context or without the training and experience to understand everything they're reading, and it often causes them distress. I spend a significant amount of time each week looking at printed radiology reports people bring in, with dozens of words circled or highlighted, and printouts from Google of medical terminology that people have spent hours worrying about. So I spend my time with patients, trying to explain the terms instead of helping them understand how those terms will impact their health. And there have been disasters—people finding out they have cancer from a report on a screen instead of a compassionate physician helping them through it face-to-face.

Yet Tina's report would have encouraged most people. But some of the hardest conversations I ever have with patients are when they think they're sick or need surgery and I tell them something different.

"Why is she upset?" I asked.

"That's the thing, Doc. She read, 'No evidence of residual or recurrent tumor,' and I was excited. But she started crying, saying how no one wants to help her, how you're all a bunch of idiots who can't figure out where her tumor is."

"I know she's frustrated," I said. "I'll try to help her understand when she's in the office today."

"That's the reason I'm calling. She says she's not coming, that we're going to the Mayo Clinic where they have 'real doctors.'"

"I'm sorry she's having a hard time," I said. "I hope she finds what she's looking for in Minnesota."

"I thought finding out she was cured was going to be good news, Doc. But she's more unhappy now than when she actually had a tumor. I'm not . . . I'm . . . um . . . I'm not sure I can do it."

"Do what?"

He was silent for several seconds. "This whole thing. To watch her tell another group of doctors they're wrong. It's like she wants to be sick more than she wants our lives back."

"That's hard. But this is a complex situation, and I don't think it's about her wanting to be sick. Have you talked about going to see a therapist?"

"She won't even let me finish that sentence," he said. "She gets furious and says she's not crazy. I don't know what to do."

"I'm sorry. I'll be praying for you both."

———— // ————

I had a lunchtime meeting at the hospital that day. I finished up the morning clinic just in time to walk over to the hospital conference room for the Wyoming Health Medical Group monthly meeting. This group represented the interests of all the employed providers and staff of the hospital's outpatient clinics. I had been invited to attend because I was the only neurosurgeon, and it was my first meeting.

The hospital administrators were there, including the CEO, who had just announced her retirement. The mood in the room was tense, and as we got started, it became obvious why.

Apparently, a few months before I started working there, administration and one of the bigger physician groups had gone through a huge conflict. The CEO made some major changes, and the physicians felt like their concerns had been ignored. They felt disrespected, and many of them were quite vocal about it in the hospital.

As this would be the last meeting before the CEO retired, the head of that physician group forced a conversation onto the agenda, and it didn't start well. He aired his grievances, raised his voice, slammed his fist on the table, and basically commandeered the entire meeting.

The CEO was patient. She listened intently, waited for him to finish his rant, and then said in a very calm voice, "I hear you. I understand that you're frustrated, and I want to try to make it right. What can we do to make you happy?"

He thought for a moment and then said, "Undo it all. Go back to exactly how everything was before you made that horrible decision and hurt our practice."

Her lips parted slightly, and she shook her head. After a few seconds she said, "Look, Doctor, you know I stand by my actions. But even if I didn't, I couldn't do what you're asking. Buildings have been built. People have been let go or reassigned, new people hired, and we've spent millions of dollars. Overall, the organization has benefited, and many patients have been well-served by the new system. I apologize that you see it as having harmed your interests, and I'm being sincere that we will try to find some way to help you be happy. But to go back in time, and put everything back like it was, is simply impossible."

He scoffed and said, "Well, that's what it's going to take."

She thought for a moment, then leaned forward and looked directly at him and said, "I'm sorry, Doctor, but you can't have that."

—————— // ——————

On Saturday morning, Lisa and I went to Sam's Club to pick up a few things. While we were walking down one of the aisles, Lisa's phone rang. It was Caity on a FaceTime call, and we stopped to answer it. We both smiled and went right into Missy and Pop mode when we saw Scarlett's beautiful two-year-old face on the screen.

"Busy!" Scarlett said. She had started calling us Busy and Bop, but as time passed it became clear that we were heading toward Missy and Pop, and we seemed safely out of the Mimsie and Big Papa danger zone.

We were blowing kisses to Scarlett and her infant brother, Georgie, when a hand clasped my shoulder. I turned around and was face-to-face with Lucky Chuck Hobson.

"Hey, Doc," he said. "Good to see you out here with all the normal people!"

"Hi," I said. I stepped away from Lisa as she tried to wrap up the call.

"Is that a granddaughter?" he said.

I nodded. "Yes, Scarlett. She's two."

"She's a keeper! How've you been?"

"I'm good—"

"You're 'well,'" he said. I'd forgotten he was a member of the grammar police.

"Yes, I'm well. How are you?"

He was wearing his overalls again, with both pipes and his walkie-talkie still in place. He was pushing a large cart, one of the flat ones, and it was loaded with supplies. "Fine as a frog hair. Always have to come into town and restock the ranch on the weekends, you know?"

Lisa clicked off the FaceTime call and turned to face us. I gestured toward her. "This is my wife, Lisa."

He stuck out his right hand to shake Lisa's. "Hello, ma'am. I can see you're into charity work, hanging around with the likes of ol' Doc here. I'm Lucky Chuck Hobson. I'm your husband's patient."

Lisa laughed. "Nice to meet you, Mr. Hobson."

"Lucky Chuck."

"Why do they call you that?" she asked.

"On account of me getting hit by lightning three times and not dying," he said.

"That is very lucky."

"Reckon so. Mighty pretty little granddaughter y'all have there!"

"Thanks. We think so too," Lisa said.

"How many grandkids do you two have?" he asked.

"Two. Scarlett and her little brother, George. We call him Georgie. He's just a few weeks old."

His mouth made a smile his eyes didn't join. "You're pretty blessed. Me and Wanda always thought we'd have grandkids. But then we lost little Bea, so I reckon it wasn't in the cards for us. We had a great life together anyhow."

"I'm so sorry," Lisa said.

He waved a hand. "Don't matter now, I guess. I'll be seeing Wanda and Bea soon enough."

"What do you mean?"

"Oh, Doc probably didn't tell you. I have brain cancer, only I decided not to treat it. Your husband's kind of mad at me, I think."

I shook my head. "I'm not mad at you! And you don't know for sure that you have cancer," I said, even as I wished I could withdraw my words since we both knew they weren't true.

His lips parted a little, and he let out a quiet huff. "Come on, Doc. We're in Sam's Club, not the OR. You don't have to doctor me here. I'm a hopeful soul, but I'm realistic."

"A hopeful soul?" Lisa said. "I like that description. I don't think I've ever heard anyone say that before."

Lucky Chuck smiled and said, "Well, Wanda and Jesus taught me that you can be positive or you can be negative about your situation in life, and they both take the same amount of work. So I just decided I'm gonna be hopeful. Makes things feel easier, even when they're hard."

Lisa nodded and said, "That's beautiful. But I'm really sorry you're having to go through this."

He smiled. "It's okay. I'm good to go. I know where I'm heading, and I don't want to spend any part of the rest of my life in the hospital with your man there—no offense, Doc."

"None taken," I said.

Suddenly, Lucky Chuck's face lit up. "Hey, Mrs. Warren, do you know why they bury neurosurgeons ten feet under instead of six feet?"

Lisa shook her head. "No. Why?"

He said, "Because deep down, they're nice people."

———— # ————

We received a text message from Caity that evening while we were having dinner. Lisa, in addition to her skills as a neurosurgery office administrator, entrepreneur, and interior designer, also went to culinary school and worked as both a caterer and a personal chef before I met her. I often tell people that our house is always the best restaurant in town. This evening was no exception: oven-baked wild Alaskan salmon with lemon butter sauce and broccolini. It was perfect. She lit a candle, and I marveled at her talent that was second only to her beauty, wit, and charm.

When the phone dinged, Lisa said, "Caity sent us another bedtime video."

I moved my chair around the table to sit next to Lisa. Caity had been recording the conversations Nate had with Scarlett at bedtime. He'd turn out the lights, snuggle with his little girl, and talk to her while she fell asleep. Those messages were lifegiving, and we looked forward to them every day.

The videos were all too dark to see, so we just listened. Scarlett, since she was born at a time when all the adults in her life were sad about her uncle Mitch dying, had naturally dealt with some anxiety and trouble sleeping. Nate would pray with her, comfort her, and sing to her, and it was precious to listen to.

Caity and Nate had told Scarlett about her uncle, making sure she knew of his life even though she was too young to understand that he was gone. In this video, Nate was going through a routine that had comforted Scarlett against the terrors of going to sleep. She wanted to hear him say all the people who loved her, so he said, "Jesus loves you, Mommy loves you, Daddy loves you, Missy and Pop love you, Uncle Josh loves you . . ." and so on. Then, in an angelic, quiet voice, Scarlett clearly said, "And Mitch loves you."

Somehow, she knew Uncle Mitch loves her.

Lisa and I looked at each other and the tears came as they still did every day. This time, though, they weren't purely tears of pain. There was some joy mixed in, too, because Scarlett reminded us that Mitch still *is*.

She didn't say, "And Mitch loved you."

She said "loves."

That night, I lay in bed, staring into the darkness, my right shoulder blade incinerated with the post-herpetic neuralgia of my ongoing grief. The week's events tumbled around in my head like SuperLotto balls, but they wouldn't land in any combination that made sense to me.

I could see the angry doctor in the meeting: white turtleneck sweater, round glasses, perfectly bald head. He looked a little like Dr. Evil, the villain in the *Austin Powers* movies. He'd said, "Undo it all. Go back to exactly how everything was before . . ."

And Lucky Chuck said he and Wanda might have had grandchildren, "But then we lost little Bea."

It hit me then that I'd been wallowing in "buts":

We used to have a beautiful son, *but* he died.

We love our granddaughter, *but* we miss Mitch so much.

We used to have faith that God would protect us, that he loved us,
   but TMT happened and now we doubt everything.

The buts seemed insurmountable; whatever flickers of light tried to spark our hearts back to life felt extinguished under the weight of them.

Then Scarlett said "and."

"And Mitch loves you."

I had nineteen years with Mitch, *and* he loves me.

I had a wonderful, smart, funny son, *and* I have a perfect
   granddaughter.

I'm immersed in the darkness, *and* I can see light.

It all started to coalesce for me in the painful darkness of our little apartment where Mitch had never been. I'd been so angry, like the table-pounding doctor, because I wanted it all to be like it had been. And that crashed me into Tina Tisdale's choice: Rick Tisdale had said of Tina, "It's like she wants to be sick more than she wants our lives back."

I didn't think that Tina *wanted* to be sick. I thought that her having faced her mortality with the terrifying tumor and brain surgery ordeal made her psychologically unable to believe she could ever be well again. She was a classic Crasher-type from my earlier data analysis.

I *wanted* to find a way back to our old lives—happy, faithful, feeling close to God—and I *needed* to help my beloved wife and family find it again too. I realized that I was going to have to decide to accept the "and."

But I was so tempted to just wrap myself in the covers, focus on my pain, and let the smoke of my smoldering anger rise like incense on the altar of grief.

It was so clear in that moment: Once TMT happens, you want so badly to go back to before, to the way things were. But as life unfolds, other beautiful things come along, other blessings appear, your story continues. It can never go back to the way it all was if you also want the good parts of life now.

You want it all, but you can't have that.

16

Reanimation

We are hard pressed on every side, but not crushed;
perplexed, but not in despair; persecuted, but not
abandoned; struck down, but not destroyed.

—2 Corinthians 4:8–9

"Sorry to wake you, Lee," Jonna said when I answered the phone.

I checked the time, 4:30 A.M. I'd had a busy stretch of surgery and being on trauma call and hadn't slept past three in a couple of weeks.

"No problem," I said. "Whatcha got?"

"I have a young man here who is going to need surgery. He's drunk and hammered, and he can't move the right side of his face."

"On my way," I said. While I walked to my truck, I realized she hadn't said "hammered drunk" but rather "drunk and hammered." I figured I was just sleepy and misheard her.

———— // ————

"Thanks for coming so quickly," Jonna said as I walked into the emergency department. "He's in Trauma One."

"What happened?"

"He's twenty-seven, assaulted on the reservation near Riverton. Multiple lacerations and bruises on his head and neck. Here's his head CT."

I sat next to Jonna at her desk and clicked through the scan of **WALKER, ANTHONY**. "The brain looks normal," I said. "But holy cow . . . I count six depressed skull fractures that will need to be re-paired; all these small, round areas of his head where the bone is pushed in, like he's been hit with a . . ."

"Hammer," Jonna said, "like I told you on the phone. He got drunk, and someone hammered his head."

I thought I'd seen everything, but I had never seen that before. Drunk *and* hammered.

"Still," I said, "those fractures shouldn't paralyze his face. Brain looks really clean. Did you do a CT angiogram?"

In head injury cases where the patient has a neurologic deficit like weakness or numbness but no obvious trauma to the brain such as bleeding or swelling, we do an angiogram to look more closely at the blood vessels. A damaged or dissected brain artery can cause a stroke, which will not show up for several hours on a plain CT scan.

She tilted her head and her lips parted slightly, like she was about to say, "Do I look like I just finished medical school?" But thankfully, Jonna's gracious spirit prevailed, and she instead said, "It's early; you probably need some coffee. Of course, I did. They're having some trou-ble pushing the images to us, but they said it should be only a few more minutes. You want to see him while we're waiting?"

We walked into Trauma One, and I saw a thin young man who looked like he'd had a very rough night. His face was swollen on the right side, and there were multiple bandaged lacerations on his head. Blood seeped through the white gauze in several places. He was resting in the quiet of a concussion, a blood-alcohol level that would have killed most people, and the IV sedation Jonna had given him so he would hold still for his scans.

As Jonna and I approached Anthony's bed, I noticed that his right eye was partly open, and his face drooped on that side like he'd had a stroke.

I touched his chest lightly. "Good morning, sir. I'm Dr. Warren."

He opened his left eye and turned to the sound of my voice. "Hi," he said with a slur to his voice, partly because half of his face was para-lyzed.

"What happened?" I asked.

He shook his head. "I don't know. I was just minding my own business, walking to my grandma's house, when these two dudes jumped me."

It is a universal law of trauma centers that, at least once a month, someone will report that they were randomly attacked by "the Two Dudes." In my twenty-plus years of practice, I have taken care of patients in multiple hospitals and cities around the world and have discussed this public health crisis with many other trauma surgeons. The Two Dudes have a consistent MO: They only attack inebriated, unaccompanied males between the ages of seventeen and thirty who are bothering no one, and who usually are en route to perform an altruistic task such as helping an elderly relative walk to church.

The Two Dudes were actively menacing young men in Oklahoma City when I was a medical student, terrorizing the Pittsburgh streets while I was a resident, and wreaking havoc in San Antonio and Auburn. And now, shockingly, they were running amok in Wyoming. They must be on the FBI's Most Wanted list by now.

I performed a detailed neurological examination on Anthony, and everything was normal other than his face. When I asked him to smile, his left side worked, but his right forehead and eyebrow did not lift, his right eye would not close, and his right lower face did not move at all. The unopposed left side "smile" pulled the right side over, which turned his smile into more of a grimace—picture a pirate saying, "Aaargh."

I noticed a perfectly round bruise just in front of his right ear, and my heart sank as I realized the diagnosis.

"This isn't a stroke," I said. "It's a—"

"Crush injury to his facial nerve," Jonna said.

The seventh cranial nerve is also called the facial nerve. It exits the brain stem and travels through the temporal bone to enter the face just in front of the ear. All the muscles of facial expression are innervated by it. It is vulnerable to injury from tumors growing in the parotid gland, surgeons making incisions, and, apparently, hammer-wielding dudes.

"My what?" a groggy Anthony asked.

"Your facial nerve," I said. "One of those hammer blows hit you right here"—I pointed to the bruise in front of his right ear—"and it damaged the nerve that moves your face."

The left side of his face fell hard enough to make up for both.

"Am I gonna be okay?"

I nodded. "Hopefully it's just bruised. We're going to give you some steroid medicine and put ice on your cheek to get the swelling down. There's a good chance it will get better."

"And if it doesn't?"

"Well, there's a really good facial plastic surgeon in Denver we can send you to. They can do a surgery called facial reanimation, and many times that can help the nerves reconnect and get you smiling again."

Jonna's pager went off, and I turned to see her look down at it.

She said, "I have to go. Someone needs me on the other side of the department. See you in a few."

When I looked back at Anthony, he had passed out again. I didn't want to wake him, so I went to write some orders and my note on his case, and then I called the specialist in Denver.

He said my plan was solid, but that since Anthony was going to need several of those skull fractures fixed, he suggested that we go ahead and transfer Anthony to Denver now so he didn't have to be cared for in two different hospitals. That way, he said, he could see Anthony earlier and make sure there was nothing else he could do to improve his chances of restoring facial function.

That sounded smart to me, so I called a neurosurgeon at the University of Colorado who agreed to accept him in transfer. The trauma team took care of the details, and within a few hours he was in the air.

I never saw Anthony Walker in person again.

But I couldn't stop thinking about him that day as I went about my business in the office and as I tried to sleep that night. Crush injuries are devastating to nerves, which rarely recover without surgical intervention. Anthony's flaccid, paralyzed facial muscles would not allow him to show his emotions, express his feelings, or even close his eye all the way.

Over time, if the nerve did not recover, his eye would be dry and in danger of corneal abrasions or scarring, and he would be at serious risk of blindness from the damage the constant exposure would cause.

You must be able to close your eyes if you want to protect them. If you want to keep seeing, you have to stop looking all the time.

When Mitch died, I had suffered a crushing blow to my faith and my heart. After two years, parts of my life were still working, but they pulled the dead parts along like the pirate's grimace on Anthony's face—it didn't look right. I still had a general belief in God, but it felt like all the things I believed no longer applied to me; I could tell patients to have faith and press on, and I believed it mattered. I could pray for a patient and believe God cared about them, but I believed he didn't care about me anymore.

And it felt worse than if I could somehow just not believe at all. But that would mean I'd have to give up on believing I'd get to see Mitch again someday, which is what the apostle Paul was getting at when he said that if our only hope is in this life, we're more pitiful than anyone.[1]

I was staring 24-7 into the void, trying to see how I could find my feet again, feel something other than the pain in my shoulder blade again, find the happy, vibrant "it's gonna be okay" Lee Warren of the pre-TMT days.

My heart was flaccid and paralyzed, and the crush injury, I finally realized, was unlikely to heal on its own. Lisa and I had seen little flickers of hope here and there—from Scarlett's "and" and the flashing colors of the fMRI scanner in Auburn, to spectacular sunsets and double rainbows, to being there for each other in the hardest moments.

But my eyes were getting scarred from the constant looking and longing for how it used to be, and I was terrified that I would eventually be blinded to even the slightest light perception of faith that it could ever be okay again.

Anthony was unlikely to recover without surgery, but it would take some time for his doctors to know that for sure. It was still possible he could get better on his own.

But it was not possible for me. I'd watched this wound for two years, and it was failing to heal. Lisa's precious broken heart was just as damaged as mine, and it was time to do something about it.

We needed reanimation, to come to life again, but it was going to require surgery.

I'd been writing *I've Seen the End of You,* about how other people could handle the hardest things in their lives and find hope and happiness again, and I knew the answer was in the stories I'd collected. I'd made the charts, mined the data, and learned a lot. But the one question I had left was, How could I ever move from my general, desperate hope back to a living, animated life again?

I knew I had to take another look at the data, but I also knew that at some point it would be time to stop studying and start operating.

17

Data Stories, Part 2: Gap Theory

> We'll watch for the dawn while acknowledging the
> dark.
>
> —K. J. Ramsey, *This Too Shall Last*

As a neurosurgeon, I have a pet peeve about the word *visualize*. Surgeons often use it incorrectly in operative reports or when they're describing an operation, as in, "After inserting the laparoscope, I was able to visualize the gallbladder."

But the fact is, friend, I can visualize your gallbladder while I'm typing this sentence, even if you had it removed in 2004. Visualize has two meanings, and neither one of them is "to see with the eyes."

Visualize means to "see or form a mental image of" or "make visible" to someone else's eyes.[1] I can close my eyes and visualize your brain, or I can use a saw to open your skull and visualize your brain by making it *visible* to someone else. But when we both look at something with our eyes, we are not *visualizing* it, we are *seeing* it.

Similarly, as a writer of nonfiction books, I have a pet peeve about the word *denouement*. This is a fancy-sounding French word (pronounced *day-new-maw*) that refers to when a writer ties up all the loose ends of a story right at the end. It's what you want if you're watching a police drama or a romance movie—your crime explained, the bad guy in jail, the couple to finally kiss. That's denouement; everything working out in an orderly, understandable way.

But romances and police procedurals are fiction; real life is messy. We don't get the story wrapped up in a bow, and the more we want it, the more disappointed we become.

———— // ————

I was thinking about these things after Jonna called to tell me that Tina Tisdale had killed herself.

"Lee, this is Jonna. I thought you'd want to know that Tina Tisdale is dead," she said.

I don't know how long I paused before I finally said, "What? What happened?"

"She took a whole bottle of hydrocodone and a handful of muscle relaxers. Rick woke up this morning and found her dead in the bed next to him with the pill bottles on the bedside table."

"But why? I thought they were going to the Mayo Clinic."

"Rick said that she became despondent over the last few days because Mayo reviewed her records and agreed with you; they didn't see any reason for her to have an appointment. He said she just couldn't live with that. She gave up."

Tina had post-craniotomy syndrome, a sensation that many people have after brain surgery in which their scalps never feel normal, they have frequent headaches, and they feel a sensation of pressure inside their heads. It's literally all in their heads, but to them it feels like something's wrong in their heads.

It's just as real as the post-herpetic neuralgia in my shoulder blade, the phantom pain my granddad felt in his amputated leg for the rest of his life, or the vague pains that people who have had joints replaced feel in their artificial knees or hips when the weather changes. It's real, but it's a diagnosis of exclusion: Once you rule out everything else that could be wrong, then you decide it's just a pain syndrome, and you adjust your mind to the fact that you're going to have some abnormal sensations there.

Leftover pain is the price of not having a brain tumor anymore, of not having the crippling arthritis in your trick knee, or of having had shingles or leg-destroying peripheral vascular disease.

Tina looked into the void of the rest of her life and could not visualize herself being okay again unless someone could cut something out of her and make the pain stop. She needed the story wrapped up: "Here's why you're hurting and here's how we can fix it." She needed denouement, and when she read the letter from the Mayo Clinic, she knew she wasn't going to get it.

When she needed to find the "and," she got stuck on the "but."

She could have said to herself: "I had a brain tumor, and I had surgery that cured it. I had a potentially fatal disease, and now I only have some pain to deal with."

Instead, she died with this on her lips: "I know there's something wrong with me, but no one can help."

I felt so bad for her, for Rick, but I hadn't thought she was crazy. The problem was, I completely understood her.

---//---

I finally saw it: I'd been on the *Thomas* side of the Doubting Thomas story the whole time. I didn't actually believe my son was dead until I touched his cold, beautiful face and saw the poor suturing and the funeral home receipt, and then I didn't believe I could ever have a happy life again unless I could somehow get over his death.

But after Tina died, I realized I'd been waiting for a tidy *progression through* and *ending to* my grief story just like Tina had needed denouement: loss → pain → healing → happiness.

I wanted the pain to go away, my faith to be restored to its previous state, and to be happy again. But unless my son walks in the door while I'm typing this sentence, his loss is always going to hurt.

I can't have that.

So with two years of data to show me that it wasn't an orderly, simple path to wholeness, I came to see what the Bible means when it says it was necessary for Jesus to be just like us, his brothers and sisters, *in every way.*[2] And that was the moment I finally was able to reconcile how Jesus could say life was going to be hard, but also that he wanted us to live abundantly.[3]

To line those up, I had to remember that Jesus rose from the dead, but he brought his wounds back with him.

You get to live, but it leaves a mark.

He was just like us, the walking wounded. He was like Jacob after wrestling God all night; he got the blessing, but it came with a limp.[4] He was like me: alive but still bearing the evidence of evisceration. He was like you: alive but with whatever scars you're carrying around from TMT's visit to your life.

I still couldn't visualize how I could ever really be happy again in a world without my son's giant smile, but the truth was plain to see: The huge hole in my side was never going to heal. I wasn't Thomas in the story; I was more like Jesus.

Lisa and I would have to embrace the "and": to live with the trauma of TMT *and* somehow find real hope and peace of mind again. To bear the injuries but be neither destroyed nor defined by them. To clear our throats and say, as Jesus said to Thomas, "If you want to know me, touch my wounds."[5]

—————— // ——————

When I had graphed out the data of how people respond to hard things, it became obvious that the first inflection point happens when people encounter a problem that challenges or destroys something they thought they knew—and the inflection can happen in either direction. But although these challenges to our worldviews can alter the curve, the degree to which they change and how long those changes last depend almost entirely on our ability to separate happiness from circumstances.

In other words, the more tightly happiness and circumstance are coupled in your heart, the more vulnerable you are to negative inflection points when TMT happens, and the more resistant you are to positive inflection points later in your life.

This is what creates Crashers.

When you thought your spouse was healthy but now they have cancer, you will likely have a downward change in the direction of your happiness/faith/hope curve. And, unless you somehow learn to uncouple happiness and circumstance, no future event will restore you to your original state.

"But wait," you might say. "If I'm cured, if she is cancer-free, then I'll be happy again."

But my analysis would suggest that this is incorrect. And Tina Tisdale would disagree also: If you determine that a particular circumstance is required for you to be okay, to have your faith restored, to feel happy, then the reality is that you're just one more negative circumstance away from crashing again. You'll bounce from up to down with the rhythms of this hard life, like the yo-yo-eating chicken who laid the same egg three times.

Why? Because tumors come back, and even if the person you've tied your hope to is cured of the cancer, they're still human and someday they will die. Because markets crash, pandemics happen, people cheat and lie and steal and fail to like your Facebook posts.

TMT is coming for you. Or phantom limb syndrome or post-herpetic neuralgia or something else that's all in your head that will make you live as if TMT is on your doorstep even though it's actually hanging out in Omaha with the Two Dudes this weekend bothering someone else.

Climbers like my patient Joey figure out along the way that there are realities around them that are more important than their problems. Joey was down and out, but somehow his eyes opened to the light and hope around him, to love and possibility and peace, even as his body was wrecked by TMT of brain cancer.

Most of us, hopefully, will be Dippers. We're rocked by TMT for a while, and we negatively inflect toward hopelessness until we remember that we've been through hard things before, that there's more to life than length, that we're loved and we have a life beyond this one, that God is with us.

And then we climb back up, rung by rung on the ladder out of the furnace of suffering. We escape the fire, but we still smell like smoke.

I looked at my graph again and pondered the differences between where Untouchables and Crashers end up over time:

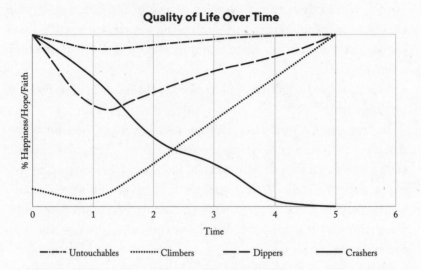

Quality of Life Over Time

Looking at the data, Untouchables seem to have a perfect uncoupling of emotion and circumstance from the start, and it has a lot to do with faith.

It dawned on me that Lucky Chuck had this figured out because of what Wanda had told him when she first got sick. He'd said, "Wanda said, when they first told us it was cancer, we needed to decide right then what we believed about God. That we couldn't wait for the outcome to see if we trusted him or not because everybody dies or has something bad happen to them, so that stuff can't be what determines who God is to us. She told me to decide he was good before she died and not to be getting all mad at him when she was gone, because that would be when I needed him most."

And that reminded me of a scripture, Romans 4:18, in which the apostle Paul said of Abraham, "Against all hope, Abraham in hope believed."

And that is when Warren's Gap Theory came together for me:

Faith lives in the gap between against *and* hope.

Take another look at the graph, but notice the gap:

Quality of Life Over Time: The Faith/Hope Gap

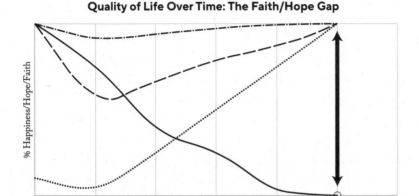

It's important to point out again that these graphs are not meant to show actual data, only trends I could see of whether people were more—or less—happy, hopeful, etc. over time. I don't mean to suggest that everyone with faith winds up perfectly happy and that those without it end up hopeless and miserable.

Obviously, most of us live in between the two extremes, and the graphs of our lives would more likely zigzag toward and away from both of them.

The truth is that any inflection toward hope produces huge improvements in how people feel. In a dark room, a tiny candle is enough light to get you through.

Warren's Gap Theory simply points out that the distance between hopelessness and happiness changes most profoundly (in either direction) in response to the weight we place on the circumstances of our lives.

> Warren's Gap Theory: Faith lives in the gap
> between *against* and *hope.*

Abraham, *against all hope,* still believed *in* hope. This is the quarterback in the huddle with two seconds left in the game and down by six points on fourth-and-twenty, telling his team, "We've got this." It's hopeless . . . unless it's not. They still have two seconds, so they decide to try anyway.

But it's also the prayer on the lips of the dying man, thanking God for the life he had and the one he believes he's about to step into. It's the "but even if he doesn't" faith of Shadrach, Meshach, and Abednego.[6]

And the more I investigated my own experiences and what the Bible has to say about hope, faith, and happiness despite life's hardships, the clearer it became. I didn't have to visualize it anymore, because I could see it in real life: Hope doesn't just happen.

Hope is a verb.

18

Hope Is a Verb

I say to myself, "The LORD is my inheritance;
therefore, I will hope in him!"

—Lamentations 3:24, NLT

Scarlett said, "And." Tina died with a handful of pills labeled "But."

Then I remembered Pastor Jon's assignment. In the chapel in Alabama on the day I saved a little boy's life shortly after being unable to save my son's, he told me that I needed to go to the book of Lamentations to find perspective.

So I did.

It's a five-chapter poem that tells a terrible story: Jerusalem has been sacked by the Babylonians, and the first two chapters give a blow-by-blow account of the destruction of God's temple, the pillaging of the city, and the despair of the people. There's murder, rape, theft, and all manner of horrifying events happening to a people who were called "God's chosen" but who had forgotten who they were.

The first two chapters are full of super-encouraging verses like:

- Her fall was astounding; there was none to comfort her.[1]
- This is why I weep and my eyes overflow with tears. No one is near to comfort me, no one to restore my spirit.[2]
- Without pity the Lord has swallowed up all the dwellings of

Jacob; in his wrath he has torn down the strongholds of
Daughter Judah. He has brought her kingdom and its princes
down to the ground in dishonor.[3]

And my personal favorite, which is even more poignant when presented as is, in poetry form:

My eyes fail from weeping,
   I am in torment within;
my heart is poured out on the ground
   because my people are destroyed,
because children and infants faint
   in the streets of the city.

They say to their mothers,
   "Where is bread and wine?"
as they faint like the wounded
   in the streets of the city,
as their lives ebb away
   in their mothers' arms.[4]

This is not the upbeat daily-devotional stuff that evangelicals tattoo
on their wrists or ankles, like Jeremiah 29:11 or Micah 6:8.[5]

So as I read the gruesome tale from the unidentified author, I wondered why Pastor Jon thought that making a bereaved father who was
crushed by the loss of his son read about kids starving to death in their
mothers' arms would bring any comfort.[6]

But Pastor Jon had earned the right, through dozens of conversations in the chapel over the years, to have me listen to his advice. So I
pressed on. Then two things broke my brain as I reached chapter 3.

The first verse of Lamentations 3 is a self-contained lesson in how
suffering can make us extremely self-focused: "*I am the man* who has
seen affliction by the rod of the LORD's wrath."[7]

Are you kidding me? I thought. The entire city had been pillaged, the king murdered, the women raped, their kids starved, and this guy thinks he is *the man* who has seen affliction?

How could he be so obtuse?

I was giving old what's-his-name the business when I felt a gentle tug in my heart and a voice in my head saying, *"Really? You think he's the only one who's ever made it all about himself when he's hurting?"*

In an instant, I remembered approximately 647,000 times since Mitch died that I took note of someone else going through a hard situation and I silently judged my pain to have been worse, more intense, or less deserved than theirs.

I'm not proud of these thoughts, but they happened:

My dentist shared that his son had been diagnosed with a rare form of liver disease and had about three months to live. I thought, *At least you get to see it coming; make sure you spend lots of time with him. That's better than suddenly finding out like we did.*

A friend's wife died in a car accident, and I said to myself, *At least she got to live more than nineteen years.*

I saw the mortuary workers loading a sheet-draped stretcher into a hearse behind the hospital, and I thought, *Probably an old person who outlived their kids.*

Someone's loved one, spouse, child, parent, all notched up in my mind as a less painful, less tragic, discounted version of TMT.

The best book I've ever read about the prayers we learn from Lamentations, *Dark Clouds, Deep Mercy,* is by a pastor named Mark Vroegop. If he had written the book in 2015, it would have saved me a lot of mental gymnastics to understand this point, but he didn't write it until 2019. However, Vroegop perfectly summarized the point I scratched out of my misery that day when he wrote, "Our natural bias is to individualize suffering."[8]

The "I am the man" lamenter was no different from me. I remembered something from physics class in college about the properties of gases—they will expand to fill any size container you put them in. This is how the aroma of a freshly baked loaf of bread fills the entire room, but so does a rotten egg's sulfuric stench.

Pastor Jon didn't reveal it to me, but I figured it out: *The devastation of TMT will expand to completely fill the person who experiences it.*

So comparing your grief against someone else's won't make either of you feel less—or more—full of pain.

I discovered Warren's Law of Suffering that day:

> Grief isn't a competition; it's a condition of being human.

I appreciated Pastor Jon pointing out that my suffering had made me myopic, but I wasn't prepared for what happened next. It seemed like the point was to help me see outside myself, to broaden my vision to the pain of those around me, and in so doing, remember the extraordinary ordinariness of my TMT in the larger context of humanity's universal "in this world you will have trouble" plight.

But in the verses that followed Lamentations 3:1 I found the real reason he sent me there, and it changed my perspective forever. The connection between profound loss, physical pain, and the fear, isolation, and darkness of hopelessness was all right there. Here are some of the highlights (or lowlights) found in the New Living Translation:

- He has made my skin and my flesh grow old, He has broken my bones (verse 4).
- He has buried me in a dark place, like those long dead (verse 6).
- Though I cry and shout, he has shut out my prayers (verse 8).
- He has hidden like a bear or a lion, waiting to attack me (verse 10).
- He has made me chew on gravel (verse 16).

In the writer's words, I saw all the bodily ailments that grief had brought me: the bitter taste of acid reflux in my mouth, my broken molar and lost filling, the pain in my shoulder from the fiery shingles and its persistent neuralgic pain. I'd felt so isolated (*No one else could ever understand how much this hurts!*), afraid of everything (*I can't protect my kids or grandkids!*), and the world had seemed so dark all the time.

It was all right there for me in black and white: I wasn't alone.

Now, please understand that I was never *alone*, as I had Lisa and the rest of our family and many friends come alongside me during those years, and I alongside them as well. And although I jokingly named the things I learned Warren's Gap Theory and Warren's Law of Suffering, I did that to make a point: Your experience of TMT will teach you your own laws and principles of how pain and loss affect you and what to do next. Hopefully, my words here will change the slope of the learning curve for you, offer you some assistance along the way. But you will put your own name on the things you discover in the aftermath of your hardship.

Because a corollary to the law of suffering, one that I had not articulated until I empathized with who I will refer to going forward as "the Lamenter" of Lamentations, is that *we may suffer together, but we grieve alone.*

> Warren's Law of Suffering: Grief isn't a competition;
> it's a condition of being human.

From my perspective (thousands of years later), the writer's situation is typical of the people around him in the story and in human history in general, but from *his* perspective it is all-consuming and total.

But he was also teaching me—teaching all of us—what to do when you face overwhelming suffering: He brought his pain to the only one big enough to handle it. He was mad at God for allowing the problem but also falling on God as the only possible problem solver.

It gave me permission to acknowledge that maybe it *was* okay, after two years, that I was still complaining about it too. And I wasn't just complaining, either, because anytime it was quiet or dark or I'd had a moment in which something reminded me of Mitch, I found myself back on the dark staircase of my mind, revisiting the whole trauma all over again.

Fighting through Lamentations allowed me to see that maybe I wasn't stuck after all; perhaps I just needed to keep reading. *Thanks, Pastor Jon.*

Then the writer came to a low point—I know you're thinking, *Wait, that wasn't the low point?*—that I knew Lisa and I had felt, and I'm sure every bereaved parent, widower, orphaned child, cheated-on spouse, bankrupted businessperson, or newly diagnosed cancer patient feels:

> Peace has been stripped away,
>   and I have forgotten what prosperity is.
> I cry out, "My splendor is gone!
>   Everything I had hoped for from the LORD is lost!"
>
> The thought of my suffering and homelessness
>   is bitter beyond words.
> I will never forget this awful time,
>   as I grieve over my loss.[9]

Those words perfectly summed up my situation—everyone's situation after TMT. No peace, no prosperity to be had in earthly accomplishments or wealth, the lost splendor of the beautiful family now broken, all the things we'd hoped for Mitch's life now impossible, unspeakable bitterness, unforgettable awfulness.

Lisa and I were sitting on Dennis and Patty's bench of "Ain't it awful?" and Lamentations made me see that our family wasn't alone in our suffering.

It's a long bench.

But then something utterly unexpected happened, and I never saw it coming:

> But this I call to mind,
>   and therefore I have hope.[10]

Faced with the bitterness, physical affliction, and utter despair of his situation, the writer was left on the bench, crying out all his problems, but *he doesn't give up*.

He uses a verb, an action word, and he *calls* hope to mind.

Other translations use other verbs, but they are all active verbs: *recall* (NASB), *think of* (NCV), *turn to* (YLT).

He *does* something to his mind, and that's how he finds hope. Look at it again (emphasis added):

But this I *call* to mind,
    and therefore I *have* hope.

There it was: the first time I'd noticed self–brain surgery in the Bible.

What was it that he called to his mind? That God is good despite the terrible circumstances the Lamenter and all of Jerusalem were facing. He's setting his mind on the goodness of God, apart from the situation he's in.

He's channeling Lucky Chuck's wife, Wanda.

Look at it in context:

Yet I *still dare* to hope
    when I remember this:

The faithful love of the LORD never ends!
    His mercies never cease.
Great is his faithfulness;
    his mercies begin afresh each morning.
I say to myself, "The LORD is my inheritance;
    therefore, I will hope in him!"

The LORD is good to those who depend on him,
    to those who search for him.
So it is good to wait quietly
    for salvation from the LORD.[11]

He *dares* to hope. He learned Warren's Gap Theory all by himself, that faith lives in the gap between *against* and *hope*. There was no reason to be hopeful here. Things were objectively terrible. But he chose to hope anyway. He realized that if there's a problem big enough that God must have allowed it, then the only rational hope is that God can help him through it.

And most important, this *daring to hope* business isn't placed neatly at the end of Lamentations. It's squarely in the middle, and there are two more lovely chapters full of misery and pain to follow. The kids are still starving, and the people are still utterly sad.[12] He's not even sure that God is going to deliver them by the very end of the book, but he knows he's talking about it with the only possible Deliverer.

In chapter 5, he says both, "Restore us, O Lord, and bring us back to you again! Give us back the joys we once had!" *and* "Or have you utterly rejected us? Are you angry with us still?"[13]

He's not crazy, and he's not indecisive; he's choosing "and."

This is horrible, *and* God is my only hope.

Vroegop wrote that lament is "a prayer in pain that leads to trust."[14] That's what's happening here in Lamentations, and it happened to me in Wyoming while I was in Pastor Jon's school of suffering.

The Lamenter took action to make himself see God even in the darkest hours of his pain. He worked the second definition of *visualize:* an action taken to make something visible. He *visualized* God being good when things didn't feel good, so he could see the hope of God being who he's been all along and will always be. "The faithful love of the Lord never ends!"[15]

And that's when I realized what I had to do to feel joy again, find my okay again, be a new version of myself, and lead my wife and family to this happier place too:

The prophet found it through *visualization,* but I chose a different word.

I needed some *happification.*

19

Memory, Movement, and the
Science of Happification

Anxiety in a man's heart weighs him down,
but a good word makes him glad.

—Proverbs 12:25, ESV

Happification is a made-up word. But it's a good word, a word that refers to the act of moving anxiety and hopelessness aside to see that happiness is in there somewhere, no matter how deep and dark the hole seems. That's what the Lamenter was doing, moving his eyes off the present situation long enough to see the possibility of God coming through for him, which then gave him the peace of mind to endure what he was experiencing.

And after my Lamentations deep dive, I realized something extraordinary, at least for me: I could start flexing the muscles of hope instead of sitting around waiting to feel better.

I was mourning the loss of my son, but I was also mourning the loss of my happiness, because it had always been such a core element of who I am and it had gotten me through some awful times before.

> I could start flexing the muscles of hope instead of
> sitting around waiting to feel better.

Someone is going to post a review of this book or send me an email to tell me that I shouldn't worry about happiness, and that the Bible never says that God wants us to be happy. They will say that happiness is a feeling, an emotion, and that what Christians have is better: *joy*, some sangfroid, spiritual state we achieve by knowing that we are going to a better place after death and that our responses to life's hardships are earning us millions of points in the afterlife.

I'm not going to debate that here, but let me say this: Before Mitch died, I didn't *feel* happy, I *was* happy.[1] No matter how many times I was mortared in Iraq, I was always able to say, "It's gonna be okay." As my first marriage crumbled and I had to fight hard for my relationship with my kids, I always found a way to hold on to hope.

After the war, I stuffed all those memories inside a trunk and left it in my garage. I didn't talk about it, didn't share the pain with Lisa or anyone else. I just worked. When it all came roaring out of me in the form of nightmares and daymares, I learned about post-traumatic stress disorder. PTSD surprised me because I thought I could just leave the war behind and that I was strong enough to move on by choosing not to think about it. And then I was in the middle of its storm, and I learned to manage it by talking about the things I was feeling and by Lisa encouraging me to write about it. It got better by opening the trunk and walking those memories out into the light.

But even in the worst of it, when I thought I was going crazy, I never felt hopeless. I talked to Lisa, prayed, sought help, and knew there was a path forward. Back then, I knew it was going to be okay.

I've always tied words like *faith*, *hope*, and *happiness* together, because in my Weltanschauung, they are mixed like the flour, sugar, and salt in my everything bagel—I can't separate one ingredient from the other in the recipe of how Lee Warren finds his way in the world.

But since Mitch's death, the recipe had been off. I could intellectually admit that I still believed in God. I could objectively see that I had many other blessings and an amazing wife and wonderful kids and grandkids. Still, nothing tasted right.

When big things happened that should have filled with me with great joy—weddings, the release of my first book (*No Place to Hide*), births—I went through the motions of outwardly acknowledging them, but inside I had just one unemotional thought: *Noted.*

However, after Lamentations taught me that hope requires action, I was immersed in a baptistery filled with scriptural Baader-Meinhof phenomena. That's what psychologists call the selective attention bias that happens in your brain when you notice something unusual or new—like a yellow Ferrari driving down Main Street of a small town in Nebraska—then you begin to notice yellow Ferraris everywhere. It seems like something has changed in the number of yellow Ferraris nearby, but the truth is that you just never noticed them. Now that your brain is attuned to their presence, you notice all of them.

I began noticing hope-grabbing action all over the Bible. Then I applied my scientist's eye to try to understand what they had in common, and I discovered the science behind how happification happens.

In every case of a biblical writer moving through pain and into peace of mind, there are two elements that combine to allow the hope muscles to flex into action: *memory* and *movement.*

Here are two examples: Asaph in Psalm 77 and David in Psalm 143.

Asaph was in trouble at the start of his Psalm:

I cried out to God for help;
    I cried out to God to hear me.
When I was in distress, I sought the Lord;
    at night I stretched out untiring hands,
    and I would not be comforted.[2]

He's hurting so much that he can't sleep. This was my life, Lisa's life, for so many nights after our horrible Black Tuesday, un-holy week, and in the years since. It's so scary; you can't stop hurting enough to sleep, and you're also afraid of the dreams that will come when you do.

And now look at David, who was equally upset:

The enemy pursues me,
    he crushes me to the ground;

he makes me dwell in the darkness
    like those long dead.
So my spirit grows faint within me;
    my heart within me is dismayed.[3]

Asaph and David both faced terrible peril and pain, and they handled it in the same way.

Here's Asaph:

I remembered you, God, and I groaned;
    I meditated, and my spirit grew faint.
You kept my eyes from closing;
    I was too troubled to speak.
I thought about the former days,
    the years of long ago;
I remembered my songs in the night.
    My heart meditated and my spirit asked:

"Will the Lord reject forever?
    Will he never show his favor again?
Has his unfailing love vanished forever?
    Has his promise failed for all time?
Has God forgotten to be merciful?
    Has he in anger withheld his compassion?"

Then I thought, "To this I will appeal:
    the years when the Most High stretched out his right hand.
I will remember the deeds of the LORD;
    yes, I will remember your miracles of long ago.
I will consider all your works
    and meditate on all your mighty deeds."[4]

Notice the two elements: I *remembered* (memory) and *appeal/con-
sider* (movement). Asaph used songs, prayer, meditation, and memory
to *call* (there's that word from Lamentations again) the true things

about God back to his mind and into his heart. Asaph *made a decision* to get off the crazy train of catastrophizing ("Has his unfailing love vanished forever? Has his promise failed for all time?"), and he used memory and movement to do it.

I love this. He's in the middle of this pity party. He's reminding himself how hosed he is. "Everything is over; I'm done for. God's forgotten me, all is lost, things are as bad as they can get. I'm resigned to this being the end of me."

But then he *decided:* He said to himself, "Hey, time out. Stop. Get off this worst-case scenario ride that you're on, and remember that you've been here before. You've been through hard things, and God's always come through." And *then* he arrived at this, in verse 13: "Your ways, God, are holy. What god is as great as our God?"

This is a crucial point: Asaph decided to change his mind before the situation was resolved.

Just like the Lamenter got to the *taking hope* part with two horrible chapters left in his story.

Now let's go back to David:

> LORD, hear my prayer,
> 　　listen to my cry for mercy;
> in your faithfulness and righteousness
> 　　come to my relief.
> Do not bring your servant into judgment,
> 　　for no one living is righteous before you.
> The enemy pursues me,
> 　　he crushes me to the ground;
> he makes me dwell in the darkness
> 　　like those long dead.
> So my spirit grows faint within me;
> 　　my heart within me is dismayed.[5]

This is present tense; his trouble was happening *now*, in real time. It's not something that happened in the past and he's still upset about. He was in the middle of it.

But look what happens next.

> I remember the days of long ago;
>   I meditate on all your works
>   and consider what your hands have done.
> I spread out my hands to you;
>   I thirst for you like a parched land.
> Answer me quickly, LORD;
>   my spirit fails.
> Do not hide your face from me
>   or I will be like those who go down to the pit.
> Let the morning bring me word of your unfailing love,
>   for I have put my trust in you.[6]

When I read this, I was overwhelmed with all the verbs, all the action in David's words.

He was amid all this despair; he was despondent. He even came to the point where he said out loud, "I'm losing hope. I'm done for, guys. I'm out. I'm crushed to the ground with fear."

But then, just like Asaph, he checked himself before he wrecked himself. "I remember." "I meditate." "I spread out my hands to you."

You see all that action? There's movement in there. There's a memory. *I'm going back. I'm thinking about other times when I felt the same way, when I've given up hope, when everything seemed to be lost, but somehow you helped me get through it. I remember.*

He acknowledged the darkness while he waited for the dawn.

There's a huge amount of power in memory: not in going back and looking at all the mistakes, all the fear and shame, but in remembering the fact that whatever you felt in times past, somehow God got you through it. He made it possible for you to survive it.

It's memory, pondering, deciding, and then action, *movement*. It's saying to God: "I lift my hands to you. Let me hear you. I'm trying to hear you, God. I'm trusting you. I give myself to you. I'm going to sleep, and I know tomorrow will be better."

Memory and *movement* are the component parts of hope.

There's all that action in there. We see Asaph and David using memory and, like the Lamenter, using movement to call hope to life. Verbs—action words. It is not passive. It's how we see "and" and not "but."

It's the science of happification.

Here's an analogy I saw in these scriptures, although I knew then and acknowledge now that it is imperfect:

If you followed a treasure map into a field, and the map led you to a rock that was supposed to mark the treasure buried beneath, you could move the rock to visualize the treasure and make it yours. Asaph and the gang were moving aside the anxiety, the current problems they were facing, and they were happifying themselves in the knowledge that God was still God and that he was big enough to help them, even though their problems didn't just magically end when they believed it.

But here's why it's not a perfect analogy:

If you move the rock and find the treasure, you can grab the loot and walk away, leaving the rock behind forever. What once hid your treasure is now in the past and you don't even have to think about it again.

Not so with grief.

The Lamenter spent the rest of his days wounded by the pillaging of his city and people, no matter how God resolved the situation. Asaph and David lived with the memories of their troubles even after God got them through. And I knew I would go to my grave mourning my son Mitchell, even as I started to understand how to smile again. I can grab the treasure of learning to survive and perhaps even become happified, but I have to carry the rock with me.

Memory and movement produce happification. They are the component parts of hope. And hope gives us the understanding that we can walk toward the light despite our scars and unhealed wounds. Seeing these writers make headway in their hardships by practicing self–brain surgery gave me confidence that perhaps I could too.

But even as the lights started to flicker on in my heart, a dark figure lurked in the corner, and I knew a fight was coming.

20

The Happification of Hopeful Souls

The cave you fear to enter holds the treasure you seek.

—popularly attributed to Joseph Campbell

I have a picture of Mitchell on my computer screen. It's Thanksgiving, probably 2010, and we're on the field in our neighborhood in Auburn where we played the annual Turkey Bowl football game with our family, neighbors, and friends. That year, a fire truck full of sweaty firemen pulled over and played with us, which our teenage daughters enjoyed immensely.

Someone, most likely Lisa, snapped this picture of Mitch, who was standing in the sunlight, looking up into the sky. The light hits his sandy brown hair and his face just right, and it looks like he's glowing, almost like those old paintings of saints with the golden gleam painted around them.

Every time I see that picture now, it makes me cry. But the tears are a mixture of sadness over how much I miss him and of a desperate hope that this is exactly how he looked and felt in his spirit when he took his last breath. The hope that he looked up and saw Jesus, like Stephen from the Bible, who while being stoned to death saw Jesus reaching out to comfort him in his dying moment.[1]

But that picture has also become a portal, and it's a dangerous place for me.

Earlier, I told you that I cannot listen to Michael Gungor's song "Beautiful Things" since it was the soundtrack to Mitchell's funeral slideshow. The main reason I can't listen to the song, however, is that it is one of the triggers I absolutely know will serve as a portal to the open pit of grief I can fall into even now, eight years after Mitch died. Similarly, when I look at that picture of Mitch looking into the sunlight, I'm aware that I can step into the picture in my mind, and the darkness of losing him will envelop me.

---//---

I need to pause for a moment and make sure you are with me, that you're clear as to what I'm trying to describe here so that we can move into the next section together. I'm going to get to the treatment plan shortly, but before I do that, I need to spend a little bit more time explaining how this very sad father experiences the trauma of losing his little boy every day even after all these years, and here's why:

Your TMT, whatever it is, has been, or will be, is a serious trauma that you will have to endure. I've been studying the effects of various forms of trauma on myself, my family, and my patients for many years now:

- the aftermath of the war
- my divorce
- meeting and marrying Lisa and the difficult and beautiful process of blending two families
- losing Mitch (and more losses we will get to later in this book)
- working with hundreds of patients and families, and hundreds of thousands of people online in their darkest hours of disease, injury, death, and pain

Those are my bona fides to talk about trauma and TMT. So in the rest of this chapter, I'm trying to tease out how to best describe what

I've observed and am living through. (I say "I" here not to leave out Lisa and the rest of our family but to again make the point that our experiences with TMT and trauma are all individual even as we live them, thankfully, together. It is among God's greatest graces to me that I am not living this out alone.)

And thus, the next pages are not me wagging my finger and telling you how to "do" your trauma. Rather, see me extending my trembling hand and offering to hold yours as we navigate this dark staircase together. Not as your doctor or some wise writer with all the answers but as another TMT alumnus trying so hard to make it back to hope. And if TMT is our alma mater, maybe "Beautiful Things" should be our fight song: "You make beautiful things out of us."

To that end, I've been stuck for three weeks on writing this chapter and what comes next because each time I try to illustrate what trauma feels like and how it drove me to realize that I had to have a treatment plan, my writing voice kept sounding like I'd slipped from patient to physician. Friend, I want to walk this hallowed ground with you as a fellow patient. Because the treatment plan is for you, for Lisa and our kids, and for me—all of us together.

So since I can't possibly know what your TMT feels like for you—when you get sucked into its black hole and when it pushes you up and out into finding a way to heal—I'm going to tell you what it feels like for me to live in between those two realities. Maybe it will help you recognize where your own choices end and begin.

Here are four simultaneously true things I feel and experience every day in different degrees of severity since Mitch died. I have discerned that they are familiar to other trauma sufferers as well.

Please know that I'm not saying these make sense, but that they *are true:*

1. I feel guilty about still being so sad after so much time has passed, but I also feel guilty that I still need to feel it. To be honest, sometimes I want to feel it because it makes me feel close to Mitch again. Sometimes I go to the dark mental staircase on purpose and will myself to go down to my son.

Then Satan (or my limbic system) whispers in my ear that I don't have enough faith—otherwise I'd be "over it" already—and that I'm pitiful. The voice I hear sounds a lot like Tom Waits singing, "Come down off the cross, Lee, we can use the wood."[2]

2. I feel an equal amount of guilt when I find that some time has slipped by without me thinking about Mitch, and I worry that maybe psychologically I'm trying to move on. In those times, it feels as if I'm dishonoring him by not having him front and center in my heart. This happens annually to Lisa, one of the kids, or me on his birthday or the anniversary of his death, when it's not the first thing we think of that day and then another one of us sends a text or mentions it. We cry and feel bad for not being the first one to say it, like somehow that means we didn't love Mitch as much as whoever remembered first.

3. I feel completely out of control when the uninvited darkness of PTSD wraps me up. Recently I found myself standing in a Hallmark store in front of a Willow Tree figurine of a man and his boy, and I realized I'd been standing there for ten minutes, I was crying, and I couldn't remember why I'd come into the store.

4. In the same breath, I feel as though revisiting the scene of Mitch's death in my mind is *the only thing I can control.* Since I can't bring him back to life, at least I can choose to walk down those mental stairs and sit with him.

I present this quadruple-edged reality of trauma to you as the Rubik's Cube it is: complex, hard to understand or describe, and awful to experience. But those are the best four bullet points I can elucidate from my own deep immersion over the last three weeks of trying to write this chapter, and the last eight years of trying to live it.

Thales said the easiest thing in life is to dispense advice, and I don't want this chapter to sound easy, because then when you hit TMT you'll say, "Whoa! Dr. Warren is full of it. He made this sound so much simpler." Fortunately, Thales also said that the hardest thing in life is to know yourself.[3]

So grab my hand and let's walk through what I feel when I see Mitch's picture on my computer desktop or when I'm standing at the portal. Because sometimes I choose to walk into it, sometimes I get sucked into it, and sometimes I just wake up and find myself in it. Here's what that's like for me.

————— // —————

When I find myself thinking of the night of August 20, 2013, its gravitational field begins to draw me in. I can feel the darkness enveloping me, and it has a surprisingly dual quality of pain and pleasure, daunting and irresistible, like Sour Patch Kids but with mental anguish and reunion with Mitch instead of sour and sweet candy.

Each time I dwell in this darkness, it's as if I need to join my son in his dying moments. I need to be there to comfort him or try to protect him or—if I could only get there soon enough—to push him aside and allow the knife to plunge into my own neck and allow him to escape. Of the thousands of times I've walked down those mental stairs, this is the outcome that seems most just to me. And even though I know that no amount of wishing can give me the opportunity to take Mitch's place or to save him, it feels like I need to take this journey, to sit in the darkness with him, so at least he doesn't have to die alone.

I've never related to the type of psychological release that cutters get by injuring themselves, but in the times I've spoken to them, their impulse to slice themselves open and bleed seems to relate to the need to feel something tangible and focused instead of the vague inner pain they can't process. In the moments when I'm at the top of the stairs that lead my mind to the dark room in which my son died, I understand. I'm trying to fix something, like a good surgeon, and going down those stairs seems to be my only way of fighting against the reality that Mitch is really gone, because that is a reality I can't possibly live with and survive.

I can soak in it, wallow in the what-ifs and the what-happeneds. And I do, more often than I wish to admit, pick up those scalpels and carve my heart with them, to feel the pain again. Then Lisa will say, "Honey, what are you thinking about?"

I usually, to my shame, lie. "Nothing."

But she knows. She'll reach over and take my hand and say, "I miss him too."

———— // ————

I was in this hole one morning shortly after my Lamenter-David-Asaph epiphany, tears flowing, when I noticed a verse that I'd somehow missed in the dozens of times I've read the Psalms in my life.

David wrote, "Please, don't turn Your ear from me. If You respond to my pleas with silence, I will lose all hope like those silenced by death's grave."[4]

This was the moment—a moment of exceptional clarity—when I realized that trauma puts us down in the pit, lying to us that God is silent. Trauma tells us we will not survive, that darkness is our only friend, that we are doomed. God has turned his ear, isn't speaking to us, isn't listening to us, won't even look at us.[5]

> I realized that trauma puts us down in the pit,
> lying to us that God is silent.

In that exceptional moment, the Great Physician gave me the first real dose of hope I'd had in years by reminding me of another verse that was written by the same suffering man, David, in Psalm 139:

Can I go anywhere apart from Your Spirit?
   Is there anywhere I can go to escape Your watchful presence?

If I go up into heaven, You are there.
   If I make my bed in the realm of the dead, You are there.[6]

Some translations use the word *pit* to describe the dead place to which David is referring. The Hebrew word is *Sheol*, the realm of all dead things.

The pit is where you land after TMT.

For me, the trauma of losing my son tries to convince me that there is only one picture of Mitch that is true, and it is what happened to him when he died. I can't make sense of it, and I can't hear God's voice when I am caught in the lie. I can pray Psalm 28:1, "Do not turn a deaf ear to me," but trauma tells me that he is.

Our choice is not whether we will become like those who go down to the pit; trauma sends us there against our will. Our choice is whether we believe that God is silent, absent. If we stay in that darkness, it will swallow us. It's where Crashers get stuck when they allow the loss or the event to become more real than the voice of God. Like the tormented soul in Edvard Munch's classic painting *The Scream,* their hands are clasped over their ears, shutting out the voice of God.

Trauma pitched me into the pit. My choice is whether to stay there.

I remembered that the same David who covered his ears in Psalm 28 had his own epiphany when he realized that not even the pit can keep our God from coming alongside us in our pain.

Now I fully understood Pastor Jon's warning about the danger of turning grief into an idol. It's where Crashers get stuck worshipping in the church of TMT, where the loss or the event becomes bigger and more real and more desirable to sit at the feet of than God's. I understood it because I was continually drawn to its darkness, and it was very real. What *wasn't* real was the pit. It is a lie that God is silent. But it feels real—so how do we break its hold?

David had also been stuck on the staircase, and he knew exactly how it felt to be in the pit of grief and pain. He also knew that the pit was a lie, and what broke its hold on him was his conviction that God is not silent. He remembered all the times before when he'd felt alone, but God had sung a louder and more beautiful song than the death metal silence of the pit.

Fear is what tells us that God is silent. If we choose to live in this fear, we will become like those who go down into the pit and stay there.

> Not even the pit can keep our God from
> coming alongside us in our pain.

What turned David around was the memory of God's voice and his movement to take his hands off his ears. He engaged the verb of hope.

Suddenly, I remembered all the times I'd been teetering between despair and hope, when I didn't know whether to cut the wound open again or to let God bandage it, when doubt filled my heart so full it felt like I was made of questions. I realized that each time there had been an invitation: *"Lee, don't look at that picture and see your boy bleeding out all alone. See the sunlight on Mitch's face—notice that he's looking up!—and know that I was there with him more fully than you ever could have been. If you really believe I'm God and that I have a home for you someday, then believe me: Mitch is already where I created him to be."*

My heart broke open right then because I had to admit something to myself: I had been afraid to let light into the place I let myself go to feel the pain, because I was afraid it would show that I had lost my son forever.

I realized that in every vision I have of that night, I see myself looking at the scene, hurting and crying and covered in my son's blood, but Mitch is gone. They've removed the bodies. The vision is not actually set at the scene of the tragedy. The vision is set in my own heart. I am reliving the trauma, giving it power because it is familiar, and when it beckons to me, I follow it.

David said, "If you be silent to me, *I become like* those who go down to the pit."[7]

David didn't say that if God was silent, he (David) could go down to the pit to spend time with those he had lost. He said that he would become like them. Become one of them.

And that's the choice I saw so clearly in that moment: The inflection point that matters most in a hurting person's life is when they choose either to hear God calling them to become hopeful souls like Lucky Chuck or to stay in the pit of believing that trauma has triumphed and clasp their ears to tune out God.

It was my breakthrough, when I finally made the diagnosis and named the disease that was killing my heart: hopelessness that I had lost my son forever. That I was the victim of the worst cruelty the universe could inflict.

But I wasn't the victim here.

Mitch was.

I was hurting, missing him, crushed by his loss, but he was the one who had died. And God had been there with him, ministering to him like Stephen, and was with him now.

I had been living, for more than two years, like those who go down to the pit. I had been swallowed up in the darkness of experiencing my own personal version of God's silence. It wasn't because God was silent. It was because I believed the lie that my trauma around Mitch's death was the only reality that mattered.

---//---

The first and most important step my patients must take before I can make them better in the operating room is to admit to themselves that they need surgery. Recognizing that they have a problem they cannot fix and giving me permission to help them is critical. I cannot repair something unless the patient signs an informed consent, performs the proper pre-operative clearances and testing, shows up at the hospital, and gets onto the surgical table to allow me to operate.

In medical training, we have a mantra: *See one, do one, teach one.*

I'd *seen* the Lamenter, Asaph, and David perform self–brain surgery under God's direction to change their minds in the middle of their horrible hardships.

Now it was time for me to *do* one, because I had Lisa, four living children, two sons-in-law, Scarlett, Georgie, and thousands of newsletter readers and podcast listeners all over the world who were waiting for me to *teach one.*

The dark figure that had lurked in the corner of my mind when I first became drawn to the idea of happification for my hurting heart turned out to be the liar of trauma, convincing me that my world had shrunk to sitting in the shadows with my pain. Now I knew that my very attempt to be with Mitch, by visualizing his death over and over again, was keeping me stuck with the Crashers in the pit of TMT, hands clasped over my ears in fear of losing Mitch forever, but Mitch wasn't going to be there with me. And the liar of trauma was convincing me that God wasn't going to be there with me either.

It was a fight, all right. Listen to the liar and stay in the pit or listen for the voice of God and discover the truth.

It was time for me to consent to self–brain surgery, to change my mind and change my life.

But I had to learn how to perform it first.

I had to go back to school, and my first professor was Lucky Chuck Hobson.

PART FOUR

Welcome to Self-Brain Surgery School

There is almost nothing outside you that will help in any kind of lasting way, unless you are waiting for a donor organ.

—Anne Lamott, *Almost Everything: Notes on Hope*

21

Lucky Chuck's Last Ride

Amid cancer's agony and wrongness, I have found
graces that tear praises from my pressed lips.

—Eric Tonjes, *Either Way, We'll Be All Right*

I owe my career in neurosurgery to my son Mitchell.

In my third year of medical school, Mitch decided to be born. I had
a busy schedule around his due date, and I asked my academic advisor
if I could rearrange my clinical rotations to have a few days off when he
came into the world (this was long before the days of paternity leave).

My new schedule required that I choose an elective rotation in either orthopedic surgery or neurosurgery, as they were the only rotations that had availability that month. I had never thought about either
of them as career choices, but they sounded interesting. A little further
investigation into my choices made it easy to pick neurosurgery: The
orthopedic rotation required students to be on call at the hospital every
other night for a month, and the neurosurgery rotation did not require
any overnight call.

So I thought it would be fun to observe brain surgery for a few
weeks, and I chose the easier rotation. Mitch was born on February 9,
1994, and I started my neurosurgery rotation at what's now called OU
Health University of Oklahoma Medical Center on March 1.

On my first day, I was assigned to help the chief resident operate on a baby with a skull deformity called sagittal synostosis, in which the skull bones grow together prematurely, preventing the brain from growing normally, and if left untreated, it causes a very abnormal head shape.

The resident made several saw cuts and removed large pieces of the baby's frontal and parietal bones, rearranging and spacing them out, then carefully suturing them together to make sure her head shape would be normal as she grew. At one point, he handed me the drill and said, "Do you want to drill a hole in her skull?"

He guided my hands as I used the drill to make a tiny hole through which he placed a suture to anchor the bone pieces together.

By the end of the surgery, I was hooked: I was going to become a neurosurgeon.

The problem was, I was late to the game. Neurosurgery is extremely competitive, and hundreds of students apply for the few training spots available in the country each year. Most of those students seem to have been born wanting to become brain surgeons, and they have done research, been published, worked in operating rooms, had tattoos of famous neurosurgeons, and sold body parts to gain favor with selection committees. Or so it felt.

I was late in my third year and had done none of those things; my chances were slim.

I signed up for an extra month with the neurosurgeons, and on the first day of the second rotation, I walked into the department office to learn that a visiting professor was in town to spend time with the residents. I was told to join them in the conference room, and there I found all six residents, from the chief down to the first-year, sitting around the table, waiting to hear a lecture from Dr. Laligam Sekhar, a famous brain tumor surgeon from Georgetown University. They said he was currently being given a tour of the hospital by the department chairman, Dr. Phil Carter.

They pointed me to a chair in the corner, and as I sat, I saw a small book on the chair. It was called *Handbook of Neurosurgery* by Dr. Mark Greenberg. I'd noticed that all the residents carried this little book in their lab-coat pockets, and it served as a sort of Bible for them as they learned to be neurosurgeons.

I'd never looked at it until that day.

As we sat and waited for Dr. Sekhar to arrive, the exalted residents chatted and ignored me, a lowly student. So I flipped through Greenberg's handbook and amused myself dreaming of someday knowing all those neurosurgery facts and having my own place at their table.

I came upon a picture of a brain tumor at the base of someone's skull, which was called an olfactory groove meningioma, in a section on something called Foster Kennedy syndrome, which I had never heard of. This fascinating syndrome, Greenberg wrote, causes anosmia (inability to smell), optic nerve atrophy and inability to see on one side, along with papilledema (swelling of the optic nerve) on the other side.

About that time, the door opened and Drs. Carter and Sekhar walked in. Dr. Carter introduced all the residents to Dr. Sekhar, and they shook hands while I remained invisible.

Dr. Sekhar then presented a case to the residents. He told the story of a young woman who presented to his clinic with the strange complaints of having trouble smelling things, headaches, and vision loss in one eye. He then showed them several brain scans, which revealed a large brain tumor of the cranial base.

In a crisp, English-educated Indian accent, Dr. Sekhar asked the chief if he could name the syndrome. The chief thought for a few seconds and shook his head, which produced a huff from Dr. Carter. One by one, each of the six residents made guesses as to the diagnosis, and none of them were correct. Dr. Carter was turning red at having his residents fail to impress Dr. Sekhar, and it was excruciating.

Then, unexpectedly, my invisibility cloak must have worn off, because Dr. Sekhar called on *me*! "You, the student in the back with the blond hair. What do you think?"

All eyes were on me, the student who'd been on the service for one month and one day and who knew nothing.

But *Handbook of Neurosurgery* burned hot in my hands, and I couldn't really believe what was happening. In a quiet voice, I regurgitated what

I had literally just read for the first time in my life a few moments earlier.

I said, "Is it Foster Kennedy syndrome caused by an olfactory groove meningioma?"

Dr. Sekhar nodded, Dr. Carter smiled, and all the residents hated my guts.

Later, Dr. Carter would write a letter of recommendation to support my application for neurosurgery training in Pittsburgh, in which he mentioned that "Lee Warren knew more as a third-year student than any of my residents." With my solid academic performance in medical school, a strong interview, and Dr. Carter's support, I was selected for the spot among several hundred applicants that year.

I never told Dr. Carter or any of the residents that Greenberg's handbook had given me the answer. God put me in the right chair and provided the manna—the one fact in that one-thousand-plus-page book—I needed that day.

I became a neurosurgeon after completing the longest and most arduous training program of all medical specialties and passing the most difficult written and oral board examinations possible. I finished my training at age thirty-two, after fourteen years of continuous schooling after high school.

And all of it happened because of Mitchell.

———— // ————

I was wrapping up clinic one afternoon when my phone dinged. It was a text message from Jonna Cubin. I clicked to open it:

> Charles Hobson is back in the hospital. Nothing for you to do, but I thought you might want to know.

Lucky Chuck was back.

I called Lisa on my way out of the office and let her know I was going to swing by the hospital to see him on my way home.

I walked into the emergency department to find Jonna at her desk. She looked up as I approached and said, "Hi, Lee, good to see you."

"Hey, Jonna. How are you?"

She raised her eyebrows and sighed. "Busy day. Flu season. We've been slammed the whole shift."

"Sorry," I said. "Hope it slows down for you. What's going on with Lucky Chuck?"

She looked down for a beat. "Pneumonia probably. Collapsed at Walmart and EMS brought him in. He won't let us put him on a ventilator or even do a chest X-ray. He wants to go home. I thought maybe he'd listen to you."

"I don't know. He's been resolute in not wanting anything done. I'll go talk to him, though."

She smiled. "Thanks. Bed nine."

----//----

I knocked on the door of Lucky Chuck's room and said, "It's Dr. Warren. Can I come in?"

I heard a cough and then Lucky Chuck said, "I don't know. Can you?"

I rolled my eyes. *Shoot! I did it again!*

Lucky Chuck was lying in the bed, skeleton thin and pale. He'd lost a lot of weight since I'd last seen him at Sam's Club. He was wearing an oxygen mask and breathing like air was his food. I glanced at the bedside monitor and saw that his pulse oximetry reading was in the mideighties, far too low given that he was on supplemental oxygen. His heart and respiratory rates were very high, and he had a fever.

I sat on a stool next to his bed and took his huge hand. "It's good to see you. You look good," I said and immediately regretted it.

He shook his head. "You're a terrible liar," he wheezed, sputtering the words.

"Looks like you have pneumonia, according to Dr. Cubin," I said.

He nodded but did not try to speak.

I noticed he had bruises all over his left arm, and he saw me looking at them.

"I've been falling a lot lately. Headaches somethin' awful too."

"Your tumor is probably growing," I said.

He sniffed. "The guy mopping the floors over there could have told me that."

I shook my head. "I know. I'm sorry, my friend."

He coughed again and then said, "Sorry, Doc. It's really hard to breathe."

I called for the nurse, Helen, who came in and set up a handheld suction for Lucky Chuck, which he used to clear the secretions from his mouth.

"That's better," he said. "Thank you, ma'am."

Helen said, "You're welcome. Let me know if you need anything else."

She started to leave, and Lucky Chuck grabbed her hand. "Hey, young lady, may I ask you a question?"

She nodded and said, "Sure."

He looked right at me and said, "How many neurosurgeons does it take to screw in a lightbulb?"

Helen shook her head. "You got me. No idea."

"One. He just holds it in the socket, and the world revolves around him."

Helen laughed, I groaned, and Lucky Chuck coughed and spit up more phlegm.

His oxygen level dropped lower, now in the low eighties. Helen said, "I better go get Dr. Cubin."

Helen left the room, and I said, "Lucky Chuck, we should get you a chest X-ray, see if there's some fluid that could be drained to help you breathe. And if you let me do a head scan, maybe there's something I could do to help your headaches and balance."

He clinched his jaw muscles and stifled another cough, and his eyes watered. "No, Doc. I'm done. I'm so tired."

"You're ready to give up?"

He shook his head slightly. "I'm not giving up; I've just run my race. No more IVs or X-rays. I want to see Wanda, Bea. Maybe even your boy. What'd you say his name was?"

"Mitch," I said softly.

"Mitch. That's a nice name. I'll say hi to him for you."

"You have a lot of faith," I said.

He nodded. "Took a long time to find it. Like I told your wife, I'm a hopeful soul, though, and somehow, God kept me looking up all those years. And if Jesus isn't alive, if God's not real, then it's all for nothing. But he is, and so are Wanda, Bea, Mitch, all those folks in the 'great cloud of witnesses.' And I'm ready to be there."

"I think we could make you a lot more comfortable, though," I said.

"No sense dragging things out. We both know where I'm headed, and soon." He coughed again. "And I'd rather take the escalator, 'stead of the stairs."

"I understand. I wish I was as strong as you."

"Were," he said.

"What?"

"It's 'I wish I were.' Now get on out of here and go see that pretty wife of yours. I need to rest."

I stood, clasped his hand, and said, "I'm praying for you, my friend. I'll come see you tomorrow."

He nodded, coughed a few times, and waved me out.

I walked out of his room just as Jonna was coming in.

"He's not looking good," I whispered.

She looked at the monitors. "I'm going to turn up his oxygen. See you tomorrow?"

I nodded and said goodbye.

As I pulled into my driveway a few minutes later, Jonna texted me again:

He's gone.

---//---

Lisa and I spent that evening talking and thinking about Lucky Chuck Hobson. I realized that I never would have been there to meet Lucky Chuck if it hadn't been for Mitch coming along and wrecking my third-year schedule in medical school.

And as sad as I was that Lucky Chuck had died, I was inspired at how he, like all the Untouchables I'd previously met, had faced his ill-ness with such courage, hope, and faith.

I smiled as I imagined Lucky Chuck telling Mitch all those neuro-surgeon jokes, since Mitch and Josh had often teased me about being a nerd. Once, Mitch asked Josh what neurosurgeons say instead of "It's not brain surgery." Josh thought for a moment and said, "They probably say, 'It's not like trying to talk to girls.'"

And then I realized, in the twentysomething years since Greenberg saved the day for me, that the two patients I'd learned the most from—about how important mindset is to wellness—I'd never operated on. Tina Tisdale descended the staircase alone because she let her mind convince her that something was wrong and that no one, not even God, could help her. Lucky Chuck developed a fatal disease in the setting of a life full of hard things, like *TMT: The Third Act,* but he re-membered (memory) that he'd survived the loss of his baby girl, Bea, and his wife, Wanda, and that God had been there the whole time. And he chose the action (movement) of maintaining hope even while he decided not to pursue painful treatments. Lucky Chuck was a flesh-and-blood exclamation point on my lessons from Lamentations and Psalms on the idea of self–brain surgery to cut through the darkness of trauma and pain and find God waiting to sit with or walk through it beside me.

Sometimes we need to fight—Tina could have fought hard to over-come her pain syndrome or learn ways to live with it, like the rock of grief I'm carrying along with my hope while I type these words—and sometimes we need to sit and let God be enough for us.

I'd taken what I thought was the easy path when I chose neurosur-gery over orthopedics in medical school to be there when Mitch was born. That "easy" choice, ironically, led me into the hardest medical training there is and a career of walking among people in the worst pain, with the most malignant cancers, and taught me to perform some of the most delicate procedures ever devised.

The contrast between Tina and Lucky Chuck was stunning: Self-brain surgery saves lives, and hopeful souls are those who decide to learn it. I was convinced that I was now ready to become an expert practitioner *and* patient. I knew it was going to take a lot of work to align my faith and my heart like Lucky Chuck had, but I also knew the alternative was a lifetime of walking down the stairs, afraid to open the door, holding my hands tightly over my ears while convincing myself God wasn't talking or even there.

> Self-brain surgery saves lives, and hopeful souls are those who decide to learn it.

Thomas Aquinas defined hope as "a certain stretching out of the appetite towards good."[1] I had a deep hunger for the happier and better version of my life I'd known before TMT thrust me into that awful un-holy week and the subsequent darker world. I knew it was not an *either-or* but a *both-and* I had to accept, a quantum reality in which pain coexists with abundant life.

And, likely because I am a surgeon, the whole manner of explaining to myself (and you) the treatment plan for creating this life-changing mental shift presented itself to me wrapped in surgical metaphors. If I were, say, a plumber, this book might have been called *Plumbing the Pain: How to Flush Fear and Unclog Your Life*. We write what we know, right?

Lucky Chuck had been smart enough to decide what he believed about God before he ever faced his TMT and was thus an Untouchable.

I was a Dipper—most likely you are, too, or you wouldn't be reading this book about how to find your way up again—but I had a voracious appetite for happification, and I would not be denied.

Yes, life is so hard. Let 'er buck.

I was ready.

As I fell asleep in Lisa's arms that night, I smiled as I imagined Mitch laughing when Lucky Chuck said, "An insurance agent, a priest, and a neurosurgeon walk into a bar . . ."

22

The Punch Line

They offer superficial treatments
    for my people's mortal wound.
They give assurances of peace
    when there is no peace.

—Jeremiah 6:14, NLT

My father is a natural and accomplished public speaker. When I was a boy, my dad would try out his jokes for an upcoming speech on Mom and, during breakfast with us, he'd practice something he was going to present later that day. He would often provide us with the principles for how to make your content resonate with your audience.

I can visualize him now, wiping the biscuit and gravy from the corner of his mouth (my mom frequently prepared such healthy choices in those days, before my uncle Dick had a heart attack and started our entire family's War on Salt and Flavor that lasted the rest of my childhood) and saying, "If you want folks to remember your message, here's what you do: Tell 'em what you're gonna tell 'em, then tell 'em, and then tell 'em what you told 'em."[1]

Lucky Chuck died around the time I completed the manuscript for my book *I've Seen the End of You*. That book was about my experience with people facing terminal brain cancer and other big problems in their lives, and how I'd learned through losing Mitch that hopelessness was more fatal than anything that can happen to our physical bodies. In the last chapter, I wrote this:

Life is a series of beautiful moments interspersed by great trials. The trick to being happy is to learn to have beautiful moments *during* the trials. Faith isn't a belief that God will spare you from problems; it is a belief that he's still God and will carry you through those problems.[2]

I can see now that I was just beginning to understand the ways hope and faith play into our ability to "learn to have beautiful moments during the trials." In the epilogue I indicated that I was starting to see through the lens of faith all the things that are still true, even when we're hurting. I wrote, "Faith doesn't keep us from having problems. It just gives a clearer view of how God is responding to them."[3]

In that book, I told you that Lisa and I survived losing Mitch, and I tried to explain the rudimentary steps we were taking to find our faith again and rekindle our hearts. Now I'm going to break down the process and talk about how we did that and how I'm now teaching other people to do so—in the style I learned from my father.

Here's what I'm going to tell you:

TMT can either be *a* thing that happens in your life, or it can be *the* thing that happens in your life. The difference in how you see and respond to it will determine the shape of your life's curve and where you end up on the happiness/faith/hope axis.

People do not wander through life, encounter hard things, and then randomly wind up either crashed in despair or somehow at peace again. Self–brain surgery school is where Climbers and Dippers are made. Untouchables are prodigies who don't really need school, and Crashers are dropouts who don't want it or never knew it was available.

> TMT can either be *a* thing that happens in your life or *the* thing that happens in your life. The difference lies in how you see and respond to it.

Self–brain surgery is painful and scary, and it's so much easier to crack open a beer (or scroll through Amazon or eat Cheetos or name-a-surrogate) and numb it all away or clamp our hands over our ears and believe the lies of trauma. Another alluring alternative is to follow the self-help gurus who offer an easy path to making it all better—but unless we actually change our minds, we can't make any real and lasting changes to our lives, and we will find ourselves victims of the "superficial treatments" for our mortal wounds that Jeremiah warned us of in this chapter's epigraph.

If we want to find hope and happiness again after TMT, we need surgery.

That's the punch line of what I'm going to tell you, the preface to the course syllabus called the Treatment Plan: TMT can either be *a* thing, or it can be *the* thing.

Now, let me tell you.

23

Choosing Your Treatment Plan

> Feeling out of control, survivors of trauma often begin
> to fear that they are damaged to the core and beyond
> redemption.
>
> —Bessel van der Kolk, *The Body Keeps the Score*

One Tuesday morning in my office, not long after Lucky Chuck died, I sat face-to-face with Clyde Weatherby, the cowboy-est cowboy I'd ever seen. Clyde was twenty-seven, and his wife, Mavis, sat next to him. She was tall and pretty, and they had held hands since I began showing them Clyde's brain scan on the wall-mounted computer screen.

I was used to ranchers wearing their hats indoors, but Clyde's was more than a ten-gallon hat—it must have been twelve gallons—lined with black felt and a long feather on the side. His Wrangler jeans were starched so stiff I wondered how he sat without cracking them.

"The area here, the white circle around the dark center in your left temporal lobe," I said. "There's a lot of swelling around it, which is why you've been having the headaches."

A familiar pain rose through my body with the knowledge of what I saw on the screen and what I projected mentally over Clyde's future. I was seeing the end of him, like so many Clydes and Samuels and Joeys before, a slideshow in my brain of all the previous conversations like this one, and everything that would inevitably happen in the months to follow.

I looked directly into Clyde's eyes and said, "This is most likely a brain tumor called glioblastoma, or GBM."

"Tumor?" Mavis said. "You mean like, like cancer?"

I nodded. "Yes. I'm sorry, but I have to tell you the truth."

Clyde said, "That's what we want. That doctor at the hospital said . . . shoot—what's her name? Venezuela or something?"

"Cubin," I said, "with an *i*."

"Right. My memory's not great lately. Anyway, she said there was a spot on my brain and that I needed to see you to figure out what's wrong with me for sure."

"Yes, we'll need to remove it to know what it is, since the other tests Dr. Cubin ordered—your labs, the CT of the rest of your body, everything—are all normal. That means it probably didn't spread from your lungs . . ."

He waved a hand. "I don't smoke."

I shook my head. "You don't have to. Several types of lung cancer happen in nonsmokers. But like I said, we didn't find anything outside your head, so we will need to do a procedure called a craniotomy to remove the mass and determine what other treatments you need."

Clyde looked at Mavis, and they shared an intimate couple's almost imperceptible nod.

He turned back to me and said, "Let's do this."

I said, "Hang on. We need to talk about the risks and alternatives to surgery. Before that, though, can I ask why you left the emergency department and went home the other day? When Dr. Cubin called, she told me that she was going to put you in the hospital. We could have done this last week."

"Well, it was marking time," Mavis said.

"What does that mean?"

"We're sheep ranchers," Clyde said. "We had to earmark, vaccinate, tail-dock, and castrate several hundred more lambs before I could spend any time away from the ranch."

I'd met sheep ranchers before, but they usually sported overalls and work boots rather than the cowboy-hats-and-jeans uniform of the younger cattlemen in Wyoming. "Oh, I thought you were a cattle rancher."

He made a soft smile. "You mean 'cause of how I'm dressed?"

I nodded. "Well, yes."

"These are my church clothes," he said. "Anyway, we don't have big community brandings like the cowboys do, and since my dad died last year, I'm having to do all the work. Sheep ranching is mostly a one-man operation."

Mavis made a soft sound with her throat, and Clyde said, "I mean, one family."

When Lisa had attended Jonna Cubin's family's branding, she was impressed at how ranchers from all over the area gathered to help one another sort and vaccinate the calves, as well as "cut" the steers, to prepare them for sale. It was a big job, and the community spirit made it doable.

The sheep ranching ecosystem, apparently, was more solitary.

"That's hard work," I said. "I understand now why you needed to go home."

"Yup," Clyde said. "But we're situated now. And I need to get this taken care of because we just found out Mavis is expecting."

"Congratulations," I said, even as my mind saw Mavis raising the baby alone.

Mavis's eyes flickered between the computer monitor and Clyde, then back to me. She rested her hand on her stomach and said, "Yes, it's our first. Can you finish telling us about the surgery, please? I'm not feeling very well."

I began telling him all the things that could go wrong with the surgery. Infections, seizures, strokes, and brain hemorrhages. Before I had gotten all the way through the list, Clyde held up his hand like a stop sign.

"Whoa," he said. "I trust you. We don't need to talk about all that scary stuff. You make it sound so dangerous."

"I know; it's a lot. And it *is* dangerous. But I have to tell you everything that could happen, no matter how unlikely, because you need to make an informed decision about whether to have surgery, to get another opinion, or to do nothing."

———— // ————

The following day, I prayed with Clyde and Mavis in the pre-op area, Clyde signed a consent form, and we rolled him on a stretcher into the operating room at Wyoming Medical Center for brain surgery.

Mary, the anesthesiologist, administered a few medications, and I had my hand on Clyde's shoulder as he drifted off to sleep. I shaved some of Clyde's hair, positioned him on the surgical table, and attached the Mayfield head holder to his skull to keep him from moving during the surgery.

I went to scrub my hands while the nurse prepped Clyde's skin. As I was scrubbing in, I let my mind wander down the path of Clyde's future—a sad conversation we would soon have about his cancer, then weeks of radiation and chemotherapy, followed by months of declining health as glioblastoma carried out its inevitable death march through his brain. The average survival for GBM is about fifteen months, and his first child would be born in seven.

In times past, before I'd lost a son and had my worldview shattered with the reality that I was not just on planet Earth to help other people in their worst moments but to also go through them myself, I prayed *for people* in times like this—*God, save him from this disease!* But I'd been through a mental shift since then, and now I often found myself praying something more like the prophet Habakkuk in the Old Testament—"How long, LORD, must I call for help, but you do not listen?"[1]

I walked into the operating room, picked up the scalpel, and set out to prove what I already knew.

———— // ————

Peter Jannetta was a world-famous neurosurgeon best known for perfecting a procedure called microvascular decompression, in which painful or disabling cranial nerve problems—like trigeminal neuralgia, a facial pain syndrome—can be cured. He was my chairman for a while in Pittsburgh during my training, and, along with teaching me delicate surgical procedures, had arguably more influence on my daily practice than any of my other professors. The main reason for that influence was not that he was technically better than anyone else—I was trained by master surgeons like Dr. Jannetta, Joe Maroon, and Takanori Fukushima, men who would be in the Neurosurgery Hall of Fame if there was such a thing—but rather that he had a different philosophical approach.

PJ, as we called him, insisted on keeping things as simple as possible. I would be about to perform a difficult and elegant microsurgical procedure, and he would look at me and say, "Don't make an operation out of it, Lee."

No matter how hard or dangerous the case, PJ always reminded me to be efficient, keep calm, and have a plan to carry out the procedure— the literal *operation* we were about to perform—in the smoothest, safest way possible. He said, "Slow is smooth, and smooth is fast," which he'd heard was a motto of special forces soldiers, and he was right. When we had a good plan and kept moving forward in surgery, being thoughtful about the next step before we got to it and not wasting time in between, surgery wound up being safer *and* faster most of the time.

For years, every time I scrubbed in to a case, I asked my team, "Do y'all want me to make an operation out of this?"

And they always shouted out, "No!"

But since Mitch died, I had been an empty suit. All those little things, the sayings and music and humor I'd always brought to work with me, had seemed so unimportant. I showed up, worked hard, did a good job, but it wasn't the same; *I* wasn't the same.

And I missed it. Missed myself. I knew that even though I was starting to learn how to walk back up that staircase, the one that kept leading me down to revisit the trauma of losing my son, I had left so much of myself down there too. Unfinished business resided there, and I didn't know if I could reclaim it all.

Was I damaged to the core? Was that happier part of my life over? Why was it taking so long to find my way?

I held the scalpel over Clyde's skin and repeated my silent prayer, *How long, Lord? I'm so tired of all these brain tumors and people hurting, and I'm tired of hurting too, just so tired. And this poor man, just getting started in life. He's going to be another sad story I'll have to tell. How long?*

I felt a nudge in my spirit and a thought: *"Nothing changes until you change something, Lee."*

And for the first time in more than two years, I decided it was time to do something to apply all the things I'd been pondering in my studies of the Lamenter, David, Asaph, and in my conversations with Lisa, Pastor Jon, Dennis, and Patty. I'd come to intellectually understand the importance of memory and movement as the component parts of hope, and I remembered PJ encouraging me to simplify things.

> Nothing changes until you change something.

Sure, I was here in the OR with another patient, about to confirm their terminal diagnosis. But I had a job to do—accomplish this surgery in the best way possible, establish the diagnosis, and then be a good doctor for Clyde and Mavis, even if I couldn't save him from his disease. Because I'd learned so much about hopelessness and how it was far deadlier than any cancer.

Clyde was going to need my help to set his mind on the rest of his life, no matter its length, to help Mavis prepare to raise their child alone, and to tell a brave and good story with his response to the fight he was in against his will. I was in this place at this time to be there for him, walk through it with him, and I needed to step into it.

I looked at my team and said, "Do y'all want me to make an operation out of this?"

The team had no idea what I meant because I hadn't brought those stories and that part of my personality with me to Wyoming. But I was determined to be present from now on, and I believed that since God had me here, I needed to *be here.*

As I made the skin incision and used a saw to make a small opening in Clyde's temporal bone, I told my team the story of PJ and how he taught us not to *make an operation* out of every operation.

And I felt a little better.

Using a computer-guided neuronavigational system that's called StealthStation, I easily found the capsule around the tumor in Clyde's left temporal lobe. The brain was very swollen, and I decided to put a needle into the tumor so I could drain some of the cyst fluid. This would make the tumor smaller and thus safer and easier to remove.

I inserted a hollow brain needle into the tumor, and a large amount of fluid gushed out. But it was not the yellow-gold cyst fluid I'd expected.

Instead, it was foul-smelling thick white pus.

Clyde did not have brain cancer; he had an abscess.

He was not going to suffer through months of radiation and chemotherapy; he was going to take antibiotics for a few weeks.

He wasn't going to die from his version of TMT; he was going to be a father.

——————//——————

In the recovery room, I shared the good news with Mavis and the still-groggy Clyde. They were overjoyed, and I was reminded (again) that, although there are many sad cases and a seemingly endless stream of hard things in this world, not *everything* is sad. Sometimes it's not cancer, even though I thought I knew that it was.

The next morning, I met with the infectious disease doctor in Clyde's room. We had a long conversation I'll never forget about *exactly how* some sheep ranchers manage to vaccinate, earmark, tail-crop, and castrate a lamb all by themselves. I'd never thought about it before until Clyde said in a matter-of-fact way: "Well, when you don't have help, you grab the lamb and hold on for dear life. If you try to let go and use a knife, you get kicked or the lamb just runs off. And sometimes you don't have enough hands, so you have to do certain things with your teeth."

My jaw probably hit the floor, and he noticed my face, which was probably white (or maybe green). He smiled and said, "I forgot, you're pretty new to Wyoming."

He went on to explain how, every year, they have one or two sheep ranchers in the state who develop infections from the practice of using their mouths to help them castrate the lambs. It is an old (and thankfully dying) practice born of the ranchers' lack of help and need for efficiency.

Apparently, Clyde had been trying not to make an operation out of it.

24

A Controlled Form of Trauma

Heaven have mercy on us all—Presbyterians and Pagans alike—for we are all somehow dreadfully cracked about the head, and sadly need mending.

—Herman Melville, *Moby-Dick*

Sleep brings the dream-that-is-not-a-dream: I'm on the staircase again.

I can see all my enlightened thoughts about uncovering my ears and can hear David's words about lifting my hands and letting God help me up out of the miry clay. I know it's all true and that it will help me, but it is distinct from the tractor beam that's pulling me down these bloody steps, sucking me back into the void where I can sit with my son. I'm an M. C. Escher lithograph, an impossible construction, and I don't know if I'm going up or down.

Before, it has been presented to my slumbering brain as a Hobson's choice:[1] I can either have the light up the stairs or the darkness down them. Either-or, take it or leave it. But now it feels possible to carry the light down with me, as if I can have "and."

My strength falters, and I stumble down a few steps. My hand reaches for the doorknob I've previously been too paralyzed by grief, pain, and fear to grasp. I can smell the trauma, but I need to see it. There are parts of me in there on that soaked floor that I need to find in order to be whole again. It has been the locked door of despair for more than two years, the door I can neither ignore nor pass through. It has been my barricade and my wailing wall.

Is it time to open it?

———— // ————

Jonna called me to the emergency department again on a Thursday afternoon to see an elderly man who had fallen. She sounded tense on the phone: "Marcus Green, eighty-three. I think he has a spinal cord injury. Not moving much at all."

"On my way," I said. "Do you have imaging yet?"

"He's in CT now. Eric's on today."

When I reached the hospital, I headed straight to the Cave to go over the scans.

Eric turned as I entered the room. "Hey, Lee. The CT doesn't show a fracture, just severe degenerative changes and spinal stenosis. I went ahead and got him an MRI, which is just coming across now."

I sat next to Eric, and we went over the scan. Marcus had a contusion—a bruise—on his spinal cord at C3–4.

Over the eighty-three years of his life, Marcus had developed degenerative arthritis in his neck, which narrowed the pathway for his spinal cord and created osteophytes—bone spurs—that displaced the soft spinal fluid environment with bone. When he fell, he banged the delicate cord into the hard spurs, bruising the cord and producing swelling of its white matter.

The swelling caused his cord's dysfunction, leaving him partially paralyzed.

"Doesn't look good for him," Eric said.

I nodded. "It's significant, especially for his age. But sometimes these folks recover pretty well. I better go see him. Thanks for your help."

Minutes later, I stepped up to the stretcher in trauma bed six, the same room where I'd first met Lucky Chuck. Jonna introduced me to Marcus, his wife, Doris, and their daughter Susie. Jonna stayed in the room while I examined him. As always, Jonna's diagnosis proved correct. Marcus could shrug his shoulders and flex his hips a little but otherwise could not move or feel anything.

"It's called a central spinal-cord injury. Your spinal cord is very swollen, which is why you can't move most of your body. The muscles to your diaphragm are also innervated by your cord, and there's a chance the cord swelling could cause you to have trouble breathing. If that happens, we will have to put you on a breathing machine."

"I don't want that. No life support," Marcus said quietly.

"I understand," I said. "But these injuries often improve and sometimes completely heal with time. We're going to give you some steroid medication, and you may start to get better in a few days or weeks. You will need surgery at some point, and you'll definitely need aggressive rehab, but there's a good chance you can recover if you're willing to fight for it."

"Why can't you just fix it now?" Doris said. She reached down to take Marcus's hand, but he did not react.

"I can fix the stenosis, remove the bone spurs to give the spinal cord more room, but we need to wait a few days to let the swelling go down first. Surgery causes heat and vibration that can actually make the cord more swollen and worsen the injury if we operate too early. It's not the narrowing that's causing the problem; it's the bruising of the cord. Surgery won't fix it, but steroids and time might."

Susie looked at her dad and then blinked hard and said, "So if surgery won't fix his injury, why would you do it at all?"

"Good question. It will make the environment for the spinal cord healthier, protect him from future injury if he falls again, and improve his pain and numbness that I'm sure he's had for a while. Haven't you, Marcus?"

He nodded slightly and said, "Yes, my neck's been killing me for years, and my hands tingle all the time."

Doris snapped her head toward him. "You never told me that! Why haven't you seen a doctor about it?"

He shook his head. "I just figured I was getting old. Didn't really think about it much."

Susie asked, "So his spinal cord *could* get better? Right, Doctor? If he needs the breathing machine, it might not be forever?"

I nodded. "Yes. The reason you're not moving well right now, Marcus, is because of two things. One is called primary neurological injury, and that's caused by the actual damage your fall did to cells in your spinal cord. Those cells are dead or permanently damaged, and we can't fix that problem. But there's also a lot of swelling in other cells from the contusion. Those cells could go either way, and the steroids and eventual surgery will give you a chance to save them. When we lose other cells from the late effects of the trauma or from swelling, it's called secondary injury, and that's what we're trying to prevent. You're likely going to improve some after all the swelling goes down, so we want you to fight, even if you need to use a ventilator for a few days. Because we don't really know how bad this injury is until some time has passed and the primary injury declares itself. Sometimes it's not as bad as we think."

Susie said, "So we have to wait for surgery because you don't want to add any more stress to those injured cells, to prevent the secondary injury. Is that right?"

I nodded. "Yes. Surgery is a controlled form of trauma. There's always risk." I went through the informed consent process and told them all the things that could happen in or after surgery. I finished with, "And you could die, get an infection, form a blood clot, have trouble with your hardware, or fail to improve. And in the wrong time or setting, surgery can make things worse instead of better."

Marcus looked at his wife and daughter and then back at me. His eyes narrowed and he said, "Okay, I understand the risks. But I've never backed down from a fight before. Whatever it takes, let's do it."

The nerves that supply function to the diaphragm muscle leave the spinal cord between cervical vertebrae three, four, and five, which we refer to as C3–5. In medical school they teach this fact with the saying "C3, 4, and 5 keep the diaphragm alive."

These nerves are vulnerable to damage in patients who fall or experience other trauma, especially if they have underlying degenerative disease such as Marcus Green's bone spurs and stenosis. The impact kills many cells, interrupts neural connections, and causes a physical alteration of the spinal cord's ability to transmit and receive information from and to the brain and muscles. This is the primary injury, one that we have no ability to protect ourselves from, and it comes on suddenly, without our consent.

In the first seventy-two or so hours following such neurotrauma, the degradation of these cells and the swelling surrounding them release harmful chemicals into the adjacent tissues and trigger a complex cascade of abnormal physiologic events. This progressively worsening environment begins to affect and threaten the function and even survival of cells that were spared from the primary (initial) mechanical trauma. In Marcus's case, the swelling and ongoing cellular degradation would threaten his ability to breathe on his own in the coming days, or perhaps forever.

The only treatment for primary injury is prevention.

Our opportunity to improve after brain or spinal cord trauma is defined by the extent of the primary injury and the prevention or limitation of secondary injury.

---//---

The pain in my shoulder returned while I finished charting and writing admission orders for Marcus. I said goodbye to Jonna and walked out of the emergency department with my right shoulder blade on fire. I stopped in the OR locker room and took some ibuprofen from my locker. I grabbed a bottle of water from the doctors' lounge and headed for my truck.

My path took me past the chapel, and I noticed as I approached that it was empty as usual.

I knew Lisa was at a meeting to discuss fundraising for the hospital's annual gala, which she'd been asked to direct. Lisa is a tremendous event planner and has a gift for pitching vision, so she's perfect at building an event around a story and inspiring people to donate money for a good cause. She wouldn't be back for a while, and I didn't feel up to driving home to be alone.

I stepped into the chapel, which is smaller and quite different from the one in Alabama where I'd spent so much time with Pastor Jon. In Wyoming, I rarely saw a chaplain in the chapel, although I commonly worked with them on the floors and at the bedside of many patients. My favorite chaplain was Zach, a gentle and kind man whose wife, Beatrice, was one of our excellent hospitalist physicians.

But Zach was not in the chapel when I walked in that afternoon. There was no stained glass *Last Supper*, only a simple cross and some battery-powered candles on the altar.

I sat in the front row and said a prayer for Marcus while I rubbed my right shoulder blade with my left hand. I prayed about his spinal cord, for complete healing, and for the delicate surgery I would perform in a few days.

Many perils lay ahead for Marcus, besides the dangers of the surgery. Older patients with spinal cord injuries have a high risk of blood clots, bedsores, pneumonia, infections, and a general failure to thrive. The thirty-day mortality rate approaches 20 percent in published studies, mainly because of these complications and the host of preexisting conditions and comorbidities elderly patients bring to their injuries.[2]

As I prayed for Marcus to be spared from these dangers and to be healed from his injury, I became slowly aware that *I was just like him.*

———#———

Marcus and I had talked about primary and secondary injuries, about the timing of surgery, and about how his underlying spinal stenosis had predisposed him to spinal cord injury. While I was thinking about this, I finally figured out why it had taken me so long to begin to heal after losing Mitch.

Since post-traumatic stress disorder was first widely studied in the aftermath of the Vietnam War, therapists and healthcare providers have come to understand the importance of *trauma-informed* care. This paradigm of treatment seeks to shift the conversation with patients from *What's the matter with you?* to *What happened to you?*

Everything in your life prior to TMT is relevant to how you will react and respond to it when it happens. Every trauma, hardship, illness, surgery, fear, and abuse, even if you haven't consciously thought of them in years, can color how you face this one.

I'd been asking myself, *What's the matter with you?*

I'd been beating myself up about why I couldn't just, like I had a million times before, decide to feel better.

And I started to see that I hadn't been a very good doctor to myself, because the real question was, *What happened to you?* I had failed to practice good trauma-informed care, which is why I'd been so mystified about my own progress.

TMT had crashed into my life—our lives—and laid waste to my heart like the fall that crushed Marcus's spinal cord. Losing Mitch was the primary injury, but it came in the context of my prior exposure to war and divorce, and they had been the hard surfaces Mitch's death had thrown me against.

In the years since TMT, the secondary injuries had piled up. Not so much that I'd had more loss (yet) but that the grief, pain, and emotional swelling endangered the parts of me that still lived.

People's attempts to help—the Christian platitudes, the offering of scriptures like Romans 8:28 ("In all things God works for the good of those who love him"), and their uncomfortable attempts to avoid it altogether—had served as secondary wounds, layered on top of my TMT.

During the un-holy week and the months following it, those Christian-y words had sounded distorted to my trauma-deafened ears. The cards and books that well-meaning folks sent to assure me that "he's in a better place," or to teach me to "walk with God through pain and suffering," had seemed blurry to my tear-filled, swollen eyes.

> Trauma-informed care shifts the conversation from "What's the matter with you?" to "What happened to you?"

Now it all made sense. The injury was too fresh, and so my brain had resisted what I'd learned from biblical professors and the studies I'd done on how to help people who were hurting. While spinal-cord injury patients sometimes need seventy-two hours or more of steroids to make surgery safer, grief apparently takes longer than that. Years, in my case.

But now it felt safe to proceed, after years of witnessing the stakes involved in doing nothing like Tina, accepting the situation peacefully like Lucky Chuck, or like Marcus Green, accepting the risks in exchange for the potential benefit of walking again.

I wanted to walk again, too, back into my happier, more hopeful life. I wanted TMT to be *a* thing that had occurred in my life, not *the* thing.

Surgery is a controlled form of trauma, but I was ready to accept the risks. Like Marcus, I would do whatever it took to stop being pulled down those stairs against my will whenever TMT decided to resurface in my heart. I knew there was unfinished work down the staircase, knew that if I wanted to walk into the light again, I was going to have to walk into the darkness first and have surgery to put myself back together. Or, more correctly, I'd have to consent to the process and let God do it.

I left the chapel to head home. I was excited to share with Lisa all that I'd figured out—and for us to start making things right together.

My drive time, as usual, consisted of listening to an audiobook. Since Mitch died, I'd been working through all those books about grief and loss, faith and doubt, and how to survive and thrive despite life's hardships. I'd just started *The Body Keeps the Score*, Bessel van der Kolk's book about the mind-body connections that are crucial to understanding the impact trauma has on our lives. As I drove, I recounted the various ways in which losing my son had affected me: TMT had grayed my hair, broken my teeth, incinerated my shoulder, and hamstrung my heart.

My body had, indeed, kept the score.

25

There's No Failure in Prehab

I said, "This far and no farther will you come.
Here your proud waves must stop!"

—Job 38:11, NLT

I told you in the beginning of this book that I needed to take you down the dark staircase and into the furnace with me before the treatment plan would make sense. At this point, you may be saying, "Quit telling stories, and give me the plan already!"

But imagine you've been sitting in a dark room for hours. Someone quickly opens the door and flips the switch, flooding your eyes with blinding white light. It almost hurts, doesn't it? You can't see, and you reflexively throw your hands over your eyes, protecting them from too much light.

There's a story in 2 Samuel in the Old Testament, after David murdered Uriah to cover up the adultery David committed with Uriah's wife, Bathsheba, that illustrates what can happen when this switch gets flipped. The prophet Nathan told David that God was going to punish him for his sin by taking the life of the newborn son who was conceived during David's sinful act.

David spent seven days in seclusion, praying, mourning, and fasting, hoping that God would spare his infant son. But once David learned that the child had died, he did something I cannot fathom.

David got up from the floor, washed his face and combed his hair, put on a fresh change of clothes, then went into the sanctuary and worshiped. Then he came home and asked for something to eat. They set it before him and he ate.[1]

The Bible doesn't give us any direct evidence of King David's mental health, but the account of the rest of his life shows that his family was a disaster. Applying a trauma-informed reading to how he handled the grief over losing his son—which was a direct result of his own actions—it's easy to imagine that some of the problems he faced later were the result of secondary injuries caused by his failure to properly heal from the primary wound of his boy's death.

I know what my office staff would have thought if I'd shown up at work on Wednesday, August 21, 2013, the morning after Mitch's death. If I had said, "Well, he's gone and there's nothing I can do about it. But I've got an office full of people to take care of," they would rightly have thought I was overcome by grief and making irrational decisions.

But that's exactly what David did:

His attendants asked him, "Why are you acting this way? While the child was alive, you fasted and wept, but now that the child is dead, you get up and eat!"

He answered, "While the child was still alive, I fasted and wept. I thought, 'Who knows? The LORD may be gracious to me and let the child live.' But now that he is dead, why should I go on fasting? Can I bring him back again? I will go to him, but he will not return to me."[2]

Over the next several chapters, David lived as if nothing had happened: He made love to his wife and he fathered another son (Solomon), started a war to expand his kingdom, and then took no action when one of his sons (Amnon) raped his daughter (Tamar) and another of his sons (Absalom) murdered Amnon (his brother) in revenge for Tamar (his sister). The Bible mentions that David was "furious,"[3] and that he spent three years wanting to go to Absalom, but he never did.[4]

Sure, the prophet told David that one consequence of his sin would be that "the sword will never depart from your house."[5] But through my lens as a fellow grieving father, I can see that part of the fulfillment of the prophesy was that David used surrogates like sex and war to numb and distract himself from the pain of his loss. Then he failed to parent and lead his living sons in a healthy way, which led to generational disasters in his lineage that are well-documented in the Bible.

Today, people turn to alcohol, drugs, pornography, shopping, or other substitutes to take their minds off what's really hurting them. But, as we see from David's life, surrogates are for suckers.

If you don't find the treatment plan and let God carefully stitch you back together after TMT wrecks you, you'll do crazy things that don't really help (or even create other problems), and years later you'll wonder why it seems like the sword never departed from your house.

David, after days in the darkness, just flipped on the light switch and stepped back into his life. But his eyes weren't working well. He couldn't see the nightmare his family life was becoming because he didn't give himself time to adjust after TMT.

> Trying to intervene too early after TMT can
> make the primary injury worse.

As I wrote earlier, part of the treatment plan is to be trauma-informed toward yourself. You must understand the difference between primary and secondary injuries and that the early post-traumatic period produces so much swelling and alteration of normal function that it is simultaneously impossible to predict the ultimate outcome *and* unsafe and ineffective to attempt anything other than supportive care.

Just as I send almost all my patients to physical therapy or to pain management to try nonsurgical treatments for their pain before considering more invasive options, I've tried to show you the long path I took to letting the primary injury settle down before I acquiesced to needing surgery.

In many cases, time and a little rehab will take care of my patients' problems. And in this context, if your TMT was losing your pet gerbil Commander McFluff to a horrifying Roomba accident, you'll probably pull through eventually without too much trouble.

But when the event is too devastating to process alone, too out of your Weltanschauung to understand, then you will find yourself needing a treatment plan to get better. The nice thing about sending my patients to conservative treatment first is that it often turns out to prepare them to have a more successful recovery after surgery. Studies show that the concept of *prehab* is valid; the time invested in getting stronger physically and more ready mentally for surgery helps you have a better outcome and prepares you for the work required in rehab after surgery to maximize your recovery.[6]

I've used these pages to take the bandage off my wounds, not only to show you their severity but also to show you that healing takes time. I wanted to reveal the path I took to finally come to grips with the fact that the unhappy, existing-but-not-living life I'd settled into was no longer acceptable, and I had no capacity to "fix it" on my own.

Some people, perhaps, heal faster and with less needed intervention than I did. For me, all those talks with Pastor Jon, Dennis, and Lisa, all my studies of Lamentations and Psalms and Habakkuk, had served as prehab. It helped me become strong enough to admit I was unable to heal alone, and now that the emotional swelling had gone down enough for me to think a little more clearly, it helped me articulate the treatment plan I would need to find my hope again.

But it took years.

You cannot just wake up the day after TMT happens and put on a smiling face, like the face Eleanor Rigby kept in a jar by the door, and carry on with your life.[7]

Well, you *can* do that, if you want. David did. Millions of people do.

But I would like to remind you once more of the graph from a previous chapter.

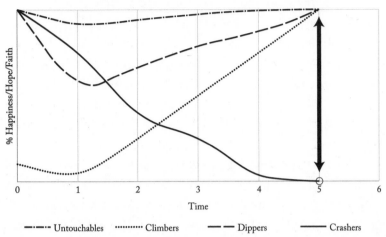

Quality of Life Over Time: The Faith/Hope Gap

% Happiness/Hope/Faith

Time

0   1   2   3   4   5   6

—·—·· Untouchables   ·········· Climbers   — — Dippers   —— Crashers

In my decades-long walk among the sick and broken, and my now eight-year-long experience as a fellow intra- and post-TMT person, I have come to notice that there are two types of Crashers.

Note that the graph does not mention *affect*, our outward expression of happiness/hope/faith. There are clearly Crashers who are outwardly dead, depressed, chronically drunk, or otherwise numbed to the pain, sometimes suicidal, and not trying to pretend otherwise. But there are plenty of people who put on a good show of looking like they're okay, even though they are dead inside.

Perhaps this was David. It was me for a long time. Maybe it's you too.

But I suspect that you've read this far because you do not want to just carry on anymore. Your TMT left you, like me, in the darkness, on the staircase, disoriented, deaf to God's voice, and blind to the direction your life needed to go to find healing. You don't want to settle for carrying on, limping through life while your family falls apart and the wars you started in your grief rage around you. And neither do you want to try to numb your pain with booze but then find yourself unable to feel anything good.

You want more.

And I do too.

But we can't change our lives until we change our minds.

And we accomplish that via the treatment plan: prehab, self–brain surgery, and rehab.

If you're my patient, and we've already tried physical therapy, shots, medications, and time, and all those things have failed, you'll come back to my office for another visit. I will sit on a stool and look into your eyes, and you will say, "Doc, I can't deal with this anymore. I'm ready for surgery."

At this point, we both know there are no other options. You've acquiesced to the fact that the problem is not going away on its own and that you need more help. You're no longer willing to let this issue be *the* thing in your life. You're ready to say, like God said when he defined the edges of the oceans, "This far, and no farther."[8]

And you won't be discouraged that all that time and effort hasn't solved your problem, because you'll see that prehab has prepared you for what's next. You will understand that failed conservative treatment *is not failure;* it's the vital prehab part of the treatment plan.

Now I'm convinced that we have exhausted all reasonable conservative measures, and that the risk of the ongoing issue outweighs the risk of the procedure. I'm confident that your eyes are open enough to the realities of the situation and that you're tired of being in the darkness of your pain.

You're ready to let the light back in.

That's when I put my hand on your shoulder and say, "Okay. Let's get after it."

26

Understanding Your Brain on TMT

A good doctor should not avoid performing surgery or prescribing a bitter pill if it is in the interest of the patient. Similarly, a wise person must not avoid taking unpleasant and difficult decisions.

—Awdhesh Singh, *31 Ways to Happiness*

Neurosurgical training is long and difficult. After college, medical school is four years, followed by a yearlong general surgery internship during which we learn surgical principles and techniques from general, vascular, and trauma surgeons to develop basic skills and prepare us emotionally and practically to specialize in the delicate and dangerous work of brain and spine surgery.

After internship, we train for an additional five to eight years, depending on subspecialty interests and fellowship training.

As I mentioned previously, I was thirty-two when I finished my program and began practice in the air force at what was then called the Wilford Hall Medical Center in San Antonio, Texas—fourteen years of continuous education after I graduated high school in Broken Bow, Oklahoma.

During all that time, I was being formed into a careful and competent diagnostician and surgeon by the slow exposure to hundreds of physiological and anatomical problems, diseases, and injuries. We saw developmental, congenital, and acquired pathologies, as well as the various infections, degenerative diseases, cancers, and vascular aberrations human bodies can develop. I was taught all the things that can go wrong due to the person's diagnosis *and* their treatments.

Eventually, I was allowed to participate in surgery and given small roles with increasing responsibility over time. All those lessons served as building blocks in my development, which would be refined later in practice over the years of my career.

I learned dozens of operations, approaches, techniques, technologies, and options for hundreds of different kinds of disorders. But it wasn't just technical training; all those years in medical school and residency were strategically designed by my wise professors to make sure that I would be able to make the right diagnosis, choose the correct approach to treatment, and be competent and skilled enough to safely perform the necessary surgery at the right time.

But now, here I was in Wyoming three years after Mitch died, and I felt like I was back in school. I'd finished writing my book *I've Seen the End of You,* in which I recounted that "hope is faith waiting for tomorrow," a phrase I ~~stole~~ borrowed from John Ortberg.[1]

At the end of the book, I wrote, "I have seen people face the worst diseases known to humanity, who stood up to the test and became the best version of themselves they could possibly be despite their bodies losing to their illness. And I have witnessed people miraculously survive incurable cancers, people who were nevertheless rotted and malignant humans by the time they were 'cured.'"[2]

My book was honest and vulnerable, which is why it's been helpful to people who are going through hard times, even if they don't have glioblastoma or haven't lost a child. But if you read it, you won't find me telling you that Lisa and I had been completely cured of our grief and were back to our old selves again. I had found my way back to some form of my former faith, and I could see or at least visualize the hope it offered. But I was struggling with a huge incongruity in that I had just written a book to tell you *that* I believed in hope again, but I hadn't figured out *how to achieve* it, for myself or anyone else.

I wasn't sure where I was going to land among those people I'd observed as a doctor and presented to my readers. Would I be a Crasher, a Dipper? I was certainly not an Untouchable. And the reason I wasn't sure was that I didn't yet have the treatment plan. I just knew I wanted it, I needed it, and that you did too.

I told you before that I named Warren's Gap Theory and Warren's Law of Suffering after myself to make the point that learning to overcome TMT is an individual journey, and that you'll have to come up with your own treatment plan. I also told you that my version of the treatment plan is wrapped in surgical metaphors since I'm a brain surgeon and not a watchmaker or a plumber. That's why this book isn't called *Time to Get You Ticking Again.*

But even though writing that made me laugh, there is something real about me presenting the treatment plan to you as self–brain surgery. We've seen it in the fMRI patients, in graphic form from my patients' responses to their TMTs, and in our journey through Scripture with the Lamenter and his friends.

So however you want to envision *your* treatment plan, understand that you must literally learn how to change your mind about TMT in your life if you want it to move from being *the* thing to being *a* thing. And that, my friend, takes self–brain surgery. (Look at me telling you what I'm about to tell you again!)

Prehab is the first part of the treatment plan. Self–brain surgery is the next.

When I was a kid, there was a commercial from a group called Partnership for a Drug-Free America. It showed a man holding an egg and saying, "This is your brain." Then the camera panned to a skillet on a stove. "This is drugs," the man said. He cracked the egg into the skillet, and as it began to fry, he held the skillet up to the camera and said, "This is your brain on drugs. Any questions?"[3] With the image of the frying egg in my head, I could easily visualize what would happen to me if I took drugs. It was a very effective warning for me, and apparently it worked because I never fried my brain on drugs.

Now imagine me holding up an egg and showing it to you. "This is your brain," I say.

Then I show you a skillet on a hot burner: "This is TMT."

Finally, I crack the egg into the sizzling skillet and say, "This is your brain on The Massive Thing."

You can take an egg out of the skillet after a few seconds or minutes, and although it will be forever changed, it's still edible, even good. All the king's horses and all the king's men can't put the egg back together again, but the hot skillet can still be just a thing that happened to the egg.

Or you can leave the egg frying until it's a burned-up, completely destroyed, unrecognizable, useless wreck.

The skillet can be *the* thing that happened to the egg in its short life, or it can be *a* thing that happened on the egg's journey to whatever purpose it was supposed to serve. (I know—I can feel you rolling your eyes as I stretch the metaphor, but it's a great visual, right?)

If we let the egg burn to a crisp in the pan, then TMT is *the* thing that happened to it.

It would be silly to ask the egg, "What's the matter with you?" The egg needed a treatment plan, but all it got instead was TMT.

Remove the egg before it's completely destroyed, and we can ask it, "What happened to you?" Then the egg can answer, "I was in the skillet for a while."

TMT puts you in the skillet. The treatment plan pulls you out before it's too late.

———— # ————

I went to school for all those years to become a doctor who could help people when they were going through their worst troubles, and then I had already started writing a book about it when I was thrown into my own worst troubles. Losing Mitch put me in the position of being one of the sufferers instead of someone simply studying how to help them.

And in all that time of evaluating people's responses to TMT and then observing my family and me walk through ours, I've come to an important conclusion:

The response of our brains to the emotional assault of TMT parallels how our brains respond to the physical diseases I've spent my career treating.

Our brains on TMT go through a process of progressive disease and dysfunction that keeps us down with the Crashers until we learn to handle our traumas and tragedies in a healthier way.

- We have intrusive thoughts about our TMTs that lead to mutated, unhealthy emotional responses.
- Left unchecked, this emotional cancer then spreads into a network of bad thinking that interacts with trauma's lying voice (wrong conclusions, false stories, etc.). These repetitive thoughts and behaviors can become programmed over time, just like the sick synapses that cause seizures to spread in epilepsy patients.
- Our diseased synapses then allow this negative atmosphere to create lousy attitudes, which now have some agency in our choices. Then we're reacting to our own attitudes instead of the real situations we're in.
- The lousy attitudes feed on partial truths, and reasonable regrets devolve into toxic shame and blame as the power of focusing on the past grows.
- This deranged neurochemical nightmare then mutates into paralyzing doubt and metastasizes throughout our entire systems. As a result, we are so full of TMT's malignancy that we crash into despair, disconnected from faith and crushed by hopelessness.

The egg is hopelessly fried to a crisp unless the chef rescues it in time with a spatula. The pilot will crash to the ground if the yellow handle is pulled too soon, unless the parachute opens. And our heart-and-hope charts will flatline, too, unless we implement the treatment plan before it's too late.

> The response of our brains to the emotional assault
> of TMT parallels how our brains respond to the physical
> diseases I've spent my career treating.

We need to learn to interrupt or reverse this process before the final crash shatters our fibrillating ceramic hearts. To do that, we must come to believe the two most important realities in learning to survive and really live again after TMT: (1) Not every thought is true, and (2) feelings are not facts.

Building on the crucial prehab process, we can now learn the life-saving self-brain surgery operation I call the *bad-thought biopsy*. The biopsy teaches us to think about our thinking,[4] which gives us a chance to turn around the malignant crash I just described, like this:

- We pause when an intrusive thought barges in—*You're never going to be okay again!*—and wait a beat long enough to investigate the thought before we allow ourselves to emotionally react to it.
- This short pause between thought and reaction allows us to close the gap between *what we think* and *what is true* before we allow emotion to enter our choice of reaction. It gives time for light to flood the darkness of our feelings with facts.
- We can then critically examine whether it's the actual situation we're in that is keeping us down or whether our own attitudes are contributing.
- Seeing things more clearly can reanimate us when we've been paralyzed by doubt. It can help us find our hope again as we climb out of the hole of regret and shame and back onto the solid ground of healthier perspectives on our post-TMT lives.

Prehab gets us ready for surgery by strengthening our resolve to get better and giving ourselves informed consent for the hard and painful procedure of changing our minds.

But self-brain surgery is not the end of the story. It's not a one-and-done cure for all the ailments TMT brings. In my practice, I insist on my patients going through physical and occupational postoperative rehab so they can maximize their recovery. And we must do the same for ourselves as we recover from TMT's trauma on our lives.

Rehab is where we engage the hope muscles of memory and movement. It's when we choose to *do something* to get stronger, move forward, and begin to heal. But it's not helpful unless we understand what's happening with our brains on TMT and until we learn to biopsy our thoughts before we act on them. And that, my friend, is the treatment plan: prehab, surgery, rehab. It's that simple, but it's not easy. You have to go to school to learn it.

Are you ready?

PART FIVE

Comfort Care for Terminal Lives

As he said this, his countenance became expressive of a calm, settled grief that touched me to the heart.

—Mary Shelley, *Frankenstein*

27

The Biopsy Will Change Your Mind

We are taking prisoners of every thought, *every emotion,* and subduing them into obedience to the Anointed One.

—2 Corinthians 10:5, Voice

What is your first thought when you remember your version of TMT?

Or, if you haven't really had TMT yet but your life feels like a "death by a thousand cuts" from a series of disappointments or troubles, what pops into your head when you think of why things aren't as you'd want them to be?

Most of us, if we're honest, hear an almost constant inner voice that is negative. This inner voice blames us for TMT happening, shames us for other people letting us down, and tells us it's really our fault. It screams that we're a failure, or that all is lost, that it can never be okay again.

But that is a lie.

I took Clyde Weatherby to the operating room, certain that the spot showing up on his MRI was a cancerous tumor, but then I was surprised when the fluid within it was white and not yellow. At that point, I no longer thought he had GBM but rather an infection. I submitted the removed tissue to the pathologist so she could analyze it. Because even though it looked like pus and not tumor fluid, I still had to be sure.

The pathologists have a saying about how to know what something really is: "When tumor is the rumor, tissue is the issue." And the tissue showed an infection.

Can you imagine what would have happened to Clyde if I had treated him for GBM because I was sure of my diagnosis but had not taken him to surgery? If I had just thought, *Oh, it looks like cancer, so I'll send him for radiation and chemotherapy.*

Two disastrous results would have played out: (1) He would have received unnecessary, dangerous drugs and gamma rays that wouldn't have helped him and would most likely have hurt him, and (2) his infection would have worsened, and he probably would have died from it.

A good physician (and self–brain surgeon) never treats a patient without evidence that they're doing the right thing. In other words:

The biopsy squares up *what I think* I know with *what is true.*

And for most of us, our recurring thoughts about our most negative experiences in life are simply not true.

Here are some of the thoughts I had in the months following Mitch's death, thoughts that I still struggle with. See if any of them sound familiar to you:

- *I did something wrong, or he would have been home with me that night.*
- *Not protecting Mitch means I've failed as a father.*
- *What credibility do I have to try to advise my other kids when I couldn't even keep their brother alive?*
- *Nothing matters now.*
- *God abandoned me, doesn't love me, or maybe isn't real.*

If I let any of those thoughts go unchallenged, here's what will happen: I'll turn on "Beautiful Things," descend the dark mental staircase toward the door I'm too much of a coward to open, and sit on the bottom stair—letting my brain (or maybe the Enemy?) tell me all the ways I failed. I believe that it's hopeless, that my last name dies with Mitch since Josh is not my biological son, that I am a failure and Lisa will eventually figure this out and leave me, and that my other kids and everyone who reads my work or listens to my podcast can see right through me. They'll know that I am a loser who failed at the most important job a parent has. God obviously has abandoned me because he doesn't want to hang out with someone who couldn't even save his own kid.

I will wake up with more of a broken heart than I started with (another one of those impossible possible things) and—theoretically—covered in orange dust from the seventeen empty Cheetos bags around me, with nothing figured out and more convinced than ever that this is how the rest of my life will be.

But when Clyde turned out not to have cancer, I was finally able to visualize the fact that I was wrong when I'd felt sure I'd seen the end of him, and that what corrected my thinking was the biopsy. That thought expanded in my brain and flowed into my heart, and then it dawned on me that I'd been allowing myself to generalize a host of negative thoughts that, once examined properly, *simply were not true.*

> The biopsy squares up *what I think* I know with *what is true.*

My thought process transformed as follows:

- *Most people with solitary, round, enhancing lesions on brain MRI have cancer.*
- *Most people with primary brain cancer have GBM.*
- *On average, people with GBM die within twelve to fifteen months from their time of diagnosis.*
- *Clyde has a solitary, round, enhancing lesion.*
- *Clyde has GBM.*
- *Clyde is going to die.*
- Biopsy shows pus instead of tumor fluid.
- *Clyde does not have GBM.*
- *Clyde is not going to die.*
- *Not everyone with a solitary, round, enhancing lesion has GBM.*

This breakthrough changed my thinking dramatically. I first shared this thought process with Lisa, and then I began to share it more widely—on my podcast and in my weekly newsletter to people all over the world.

In neurosurgical training, one of the first operations residents are allowed to perform by themselves is a tumor biopsy. The procedure is elegant but relatively simple and safe. If you follow a good plan and are careful and diligent with the technical aspects, then you can reliably expect to get good tissue for the pathologists and not harm your patient with the procedure.

And once you've mastered the simple biopsy technique to *diagnose* your patient's problem, you're ready to move on to learning bigger and more complex operations to actually *treat* the problem.

When you've decided to draw a border around TMT, to attack it and push it back into being *a* thing so you can get your life back, then you're ready to become your own patient.

You've figured out that TMT was "the door of despair"[1] you went through that got you here. You're cognitively aware that TMT was real and devastating, but you now know you have to move it from being *the* thing that happened to *a* thing that happened so that you can find some hope of living again. You've become trauma-informed about yourself.

It's time to understand your thoughts about your TMT—the labels you've accepted, your regrets, shame, self-blame, fears, doubts, and grief.

It's time to learn the bad-thought biopsy. The biopsy will allow you to critically examine a thought, make the correct diagnosis, and form an appropriate treatment plan to take care of the problem.

Here's how it works for me when I have thoughts like I shared with you earlier:

THOUGHT: *I did something wrong, or he would have been home with me that night.*
BIOPSY: Is the thought true or false?

RESULT: It is objectively false.

TREATMENT REQUIRED: Thought transplant: *You didn't have any opportunity or possibility of changing where Mitch was that evening. He lived in another city and was an adult. You can't change it, and it doesn't help you now to ruminate on it.*

This technique helps me create space between the initial negative thought and my reaction to it. That space allows me to then *choose an appropriate response* to the thought, which limits self-inflicted secondary injuries and promotes better outcomes through wiser choices.

But as I have gained experience with the bad-thought biopsy over the years, I've discovered two surprising additional benefits to the procedure. First, I noticed that the more diligent I became at challenging negative thinking, the more vigilant I became at it in all areas of my life. By consistently applying the biopsy filter to my thoughts, it became almost automatic, which dramatically improved my mood and overall outlook on things. My hope began to grow as I realized that many of my thoughts simply were not true.

The second benefit I hadn't anticipated is that I now have a stream of preemptive positive thoughts in my head most of the time, which seem to buffer the negative ones. I get better at the procedure, which shortens the time I find myself dealing with those intrusive thoughts each time.

As usual, I found the Bible to be way ahead of me. In Psalm 116, David noted this type of running-thought optimism despite hard circumstances: "I trusted in the LORD when I said, 'I am greatly afflicted'; in my alarm I said, 'Everyone is a liar.'"[2]

Do you see that? His brain was saying, *I'm afflicted, and everyone is lying,* but at the same time it was telling him to trust the Lord.

Normally, my negative thoughts said: *I'm hosed, everyone's doing me wrong, and I'm on my own.*

But with the thought-biopsy prehab preparation, I now think more like this: *Yes, people are liars and it's causing me trouble, but God is with me and it's going to be okay.*

And it's not just David. Paul said it even more explicitly in 2 Corinthians 10:5 when he wrote, "We take captive every thought to make it obedient to Christ." This is biblical self–brain surgery, friend, and it starts with the bad-thought biopsy. David and Paul were aware of their baseline negative thinking, and they preemptively decided to *develop a discipline of thinking about their thinking* as a defense.

This discovery reminded me of Lucky Chuck's wife, Wanda, when she implored him to decide what he believed about God before the biopsy result came back. As a preventative measure to negative thinking, I had preloaded my brain with truths—from conversations and Bible study—and this served as prehab, to ready me for the next time invasive thinking appeared.

A final note about this powerful self–brain surgery tool: *Sometimes the negative thoughts are true.* But engaging the thought biopsy allows us to recognize the truth, and, as Jesus said, the truth will set us free.[3] Using the biopsy to *take captive* and manage every thought puts us in the *responding and not reacting* mode and gives us back some control. We're not victims to the negative thoughts anymore; we're surgeons with a good plan to act on the information the biopsy reveals.

Here's an example:

THOUGHT: *Your son is dead, and you will always be sad about that.*
BIOPSY: Is the thought true or false?
RESULT: It is objectively true.
TREATMENT REQUIRED: Self-care to transform your
　　thought process. Don't generalize a host of negative, untrue
　　thoughts around an objectively true reality:

- *You will always be sad about losing your son because you're normal.*
- *But Jesus said that in this hard world you'll have trouble* and *that he came to give you abundant life.*
- *Your sadness will never go away,* and *you can have an abundant life amid the hardest things because Jesus is not a liar.*
- *You have lost Mitch,* and *you have a beautiful family who loves you.*

- *You can think of a thousand ways in which having nineteen years with Mitch was better than having a lifetime without him.*
- *This gratitude makes the sadness a thing in your life, not the thing.*
- *You believe that you will see Mitch again, which means your sadness does not have the final word. There is more to this story.*

Learning the bad-thought biopsy technique and practicing it enough to make it a habit allowed me to form a new type of automatic thought. Now, whenever an intrusive thought shows up, my first reaction is to question it, because I've changed my mind.

28

Surgery and Rehab Will Change Your Life

Stop imitating the ideals and opinions of the culture
around you, but be inwardly transformed by the Holy
Spirit through a total reformation of how you think.

—Romans 12:2, TPT

Many of us have heard the saying "History doesn't repeat itself, but it
often rhymes."[1]

This is, perhaps, the reason that neurosurgical training takes approximately seven hundred million years. It takes so long because, even
though there are only a handful of basic surgical techniques to master,
our professors need us to see enough different situations to know when
and how to apply the right combination of those procedures to a particular problem. Over the course of a residency program, the young
neurosurgeon sees the most common issues over and over, and we encounter enough variants and rarer things that eventually we develop
the wisdom and discernment to practice safely on our own.

There's not a lot of difference, for example, in the techniques I use to
drain an abscess like Clyde's and what I would do to drain a cyst in
someone else's brain. The positioning, the approach, the instruments I
use, and the procedure itself are virtually identical.

But it takes years to learn when a cyst needs to be removed or when
it can be safely treated with observation, or to discern which cysts are
congenital and benign and which are filled with cancer or are growing

because of parasites in the brain. Similarly, some abscesses require drainage, and some can be cured with antibiotics alone. And during the surgery, we handle the contents differently if there is a risk of spreading the infection to other parts of the patient's brain or even to ourselves or staff members.

The same principle holds for other surgeries: those to remove tumors, to drain blood clots and reduce swelling, for seizure control, and for fluid buildup problems. There is only a small set of procedures but an almost infinite number of diagnostic, management, procedural, and postoperative nuances that separate a lesser surgeon from a great one.

Training long enough to have performed all these basic procedures hundreds of times and making appropriate decisions thousands of times gives us confidence that we can safely apply our experience to our own practice.

But there is another benefit to the eternal training process that I did not appreciate until I was in the extreme environment of a tent combat hospital in the Iraq War.

As a resident in Pittsburgh, I never encountered a bunch of patients arriving at the same time after a bomb exploded. Before I arrived in Iraq, I had not seen a canister filled with ball bearings, rocks, wires, D-cell batteries, and feces detonated and blasted into a person's frontal lobe.

The first time I encountered these devastating, unfamiliar injuries in young soldiers and Iraqi civilians, I was almost overwhelmed. My brain said, *Lee, you don't know what to do! The whole scalp is missing, and there's a* battery *in this kid's head! There's too much bleeding, too much swelling! You've never seen this before!*

But each time, Chris Voss's words I shared with you earlier proved to be true. I didn't rise up and become someone I wasn't. I didn't become a super-surgeon who knew all the answers. I just applied my training, and I talked back to my fears.

No, I haven't seen a battery in the head before or this much swelling in someone's brain. But I do *know how to treat brain swelling. I* do *know how to stop bleeding. So I'll do that.*

Over and over, my colleagues and I would encounter a new and horrifying situation, and we would fall back on our training and apply little bits of things we'd seen in other situations. And we saved lives. It was a little like the breakthrough I'd felt in college when calculus seemed so impossible until the day it dawned on me that you learn to solve huge problems by breaking them up into a bunch of easier, smaller problems; problems you've seen before that are more easily managed.

It's the same for learning to operate on the various maladies TMT will bring you.

I become a better surgeon over time by treating thousands of patients with variations of a set of problems that begin to rhyme as the years pass, by applying nuanced versions of several core procedures I learned over years of training.

As a self–brain surgeon, you treat one patient (yourself) for your whole life. But as I discussed before, though TMT cannot be cured, it can be managed. Thus, you will always have recurrent issues that are revealed over and over by the biopsies you learn to perform. For example, my current struggle with paralyzing doubt that losing one son disqualifies me from being a good dad will inevitably recur when I wonder if I should advise my grandkids, since I wasn't able to save their uncle Mitch.

But look what happens when I implement the prehab of loading my brain and heart with the truth, learn to biopsy and challenge the negative thought, and then carry out thought surgery to drain my paralyzing doubts and replace them with more solid thinking: *I have learned so much over the years, and I can see so clearly ways my other kids still need me and value my help. My grandkids need me to give them another perspective and be a safe person to talk to as they grow up. I can help them!*

Armed with the awareness that my initial thought was untrue, that my doubts were unfounded, I can draw on previous experience of handling other doubts and apply the procedure I need to begin to heal and get stronger and more prepared for the next time TMT rears its head:

- When I didn't think I would survive those mortar attacks, God protected me, and I *did* survive.

- When I thought I was unlovable and would always be alone, Lisa saw me and loved me.
- David, Asaph, and the Lamenter all thought they were beyond help, but God helped them, and they made it.
- Every time I've been through something hard and felt hopeless, somehow God showed me the light again.
- That means there's a legitimate basis for me to believe God can still use me, that he still loves me, even though losing Mitch hurts so much.

Just like performing a craniotomy to drain the pus from Clyde's abscess, I can biopsy my thoughts and identify the problem not as an unalterable truth but rather as a paralyzing, lying doubt that is a side effect of my TMT. Knowing this allows me to not only drain the doubt but also to fill up my faith since God has done it before and can be trusted to do it again.

When I was in Iraq, faced with having to figure out on the spot something like how to extract a twisted ball of baling wire from someone's sphenoid sinus, I would talk with other surgeons. We would break down the injuries we'd seen and compare notes on what worked well and what didn't. In doing so, we got better and became more agile each day. I spent less time freaking out in my head when I saw a horrifying CT scan—*What in the world is that? How am I going to save this person?*—and more time thinking about what I'd seen the day before and how this was a little bit like that.

Similarly, over time we become more experienced self–brain surgeons, and we develop a set of go-to techniques we can apply as TMT-related wounds revisit us. I remember how comforting it was for me the first time a horribly injured soldier came in with something I knew a civilian surgeon would have no idea how to treat, and I thought, *This reminds me of that Syrian insurgent we saved last week after he was too close to the bomb when it detonated. I'll be able to use the same technique here.*

Mark Vroegop wrote, "Hope springs from truth rehearsed,"[2] which is another way of phrasing what I told you before: Hope is a verb. Prehab is the art of flexing the components of hope—memory and movement—to build up a set of muscles that are sufficiently strong enough to hold on to hope no matter what TMT does to us. The thought biopsy then allows us to challenge our programmed negative thinking and learn to change our minds.

And, just as I learned in Iraq every day, TMT throws things at us that seem on the surface to be completely unique and impossible, until we fall back on our training and remember that *this situation almost rhymes with something we've faced before.* I'd never lost a son until Mitch died, and it was devastating and soul-crushing. But like a good trauma surgeon comes to realize over time, I remembered that my prior experiences had taught me lessons I could use to manage this one.

———— // ————

In medical school, the first time a patient you're taking care of dies, the resident physicians teach you how to fill out a death certificate. These are required by the state to document the way someone dies and to help determine whether there is a need for an autopsy or legal action.

I remember how hard it was to understand the difference between *cause of death* and *mechanism of death.*

When someone has a massive heart attack, a blocked artery in the heart robs the cardiac muscle of oxygen, leading to infarction—death of the muscle tissue—that subsequently causes the heart to be unable to pump blood effectively enough to keep the rest of the body alive. This can lead to respiratory arrest—when the lungs and the brain fail due to the lack of oxygen. The patient dies when they stop breathing— the mechanism is respiratory arrest—but the cause of death was the blocked artery.

As a student, I found it hard to parse out the differences between cause and mechanism, especially when a person had multiple things wrong with them. When the death happens from kidney failure but the patient was also obese, diabetic, a heavy smoker, and had a liver transplant due to alcoholism, what do I write down for cause of death?

I've come to understand over the years that the same is true for how we proceed after our exposure to TMT. The event—me losing my son, you going through your troubles—isn't what destroys our happiness. What does that is *how we think about TMT.*

Recall that the Lamenter *changed his mind in the middle of the problem.* Changing his mind did not make the problem go away, and it did not magically relieve his pain or reset everything to how it had been before—you can't have that, remember? No, changing his mind put the problem in the proper perspective and cleared his mind enough to help him decide that he had to keep moving in his life.

In Iraq, once we'd stabilized the patients enough to ensure they weren't going to die from their wounds, *then* we could move on to trying to maximize their outcome.

Once we realize that TMT hasn't killed us (even if our TMT is a fatal diagnosis, we still have to live the rest of our lives, right?), *then we have to apply the treatment plan to give us the best life possible going forward.*

> The event isn't what destroys our happiness. What does that is *how we think about TMT.*

The Lamenter remembered that God had delivered the people many times before—out of slavery in Egypt, through the Red Sea and the desert, into the Promised Land with all its battles—and thus God could be trusted to deliver them again. "Hope springs from truth rehearsed."

For me, once the primary injury settled down enough, I realized that even with my shingles, broken teeth, gray hair, and fibrillating heart, God was apparently not going to actually kill me with my grief, so I then had to make a decision: Was I going to fall down the staircase and sit in the darkness for the rest of my life? Or was I going to fight for hope and try to help my family and myself make it back to the light again?

And so, if we die of our TMT-related trauma, if we crash and go down to the pit with David before he flexed for hope, then we fill out our death certificates with *TMT* as cause and *hopelessness* as mechanism.

In Iraq, the exploding bombs created the brain injuries, but if the tissue damage was too great to repair, then the deaths occurred from bleeding, swelling, or projectile trauma. If I was able to stop the bleeding, manage the swelling, and remove the fragments, sometimes we could save the patient. This would not erase the fact that the bomb had done horrible damage, but it would turn it into *a thing* that happened instead of the *cause of death*.

So, too, with our responses to TMT.

———————————//———————————

As I type these words, my shoulder is on fire with my post-herpetic neuralgia, and my jaw hurts from grinding my teeth all night, likely because as I slept, my brain was tossing around the words I would write to you this morning. I carry these pains and wounds with me in my post-TMT life, but I did not die from them, not even in my heart. And the reason I did not die was that I made the choice to perform self–brain surgery and learn to change my mind so I could change my life after the devastating injury of losing my son.

I decided that losing Mitch will not be the cause of my death.

But to make that choice, the first thing I had to do was remember: I'd seen God get my brother through losing his son, I had survived a divorce and the horrors of war and had seen God keep his promises through all that pain, and I'd lived through enough other hard things to know that somehow God always showed up and I hadn't died yet.

This got me to my lamenter moment: "But this I call to mind, and therefore I have hope."[3]

Engaging the prehab by calling to mind the truth in the face of all those negative thoughts allowed me to hear the rhymes of other times I'd made it through, all the times I'd seen others—like David and Asaph and the Lamenter—make it through. Then all I had to do was choose the best procedure to handle whatever malady I was suffering from each time my TMT metastasized to another part of my heart.

Because I realized it wasn't TMT that was killing me. It was how I thought about it, and that was within my power to improve. And each time I apply a self–brain surgery procedure, I develop another muscle I can engage to tighten my core and heal more completely, as my patients do in rehab after surgery.

Every day in my practice, I converse with people who have had prior surgeries. I remind each of them that they not only survived but they also learned what to expect, and they can use that knowledge and experience to help them get ready for this one—prehab. I encourage them to practice what the physical therapists taught them, improve their diet, and cut down on anything that might hinder their recovery, like excessive amounts of alcohol or pain medication. I'm convincing them to flex the muscles of memory and movement to help them be more hopeful about their upcoming surgery, because I know that their mindset will have a huge impact on their outcome.

Hope, it's been said, is the belief that "you can get there from here."[4] This is the message I encourage my patients to believe in before they have surgery, and it's based on the question all of us ask ourselves when we're trying to decide if we can survive and live again after TMT: *Can I get there from here?*

Losing my son made me doubt for a long time whether it was possible to feel anything like happiness again, or whether I even wanted to try. I know you understand, because TMT happens to all of us. Once I understood that *hope* is a verb and that I could take action to find it again, I began to believe I could get there from here. And that little spark was enough to get me to sign up for surgery.

The treatment plan was stunningly simple: I had to make an operation out of it.

But understanding it and doing it are two different things.

29

Thoughts Become Things

I'd rather have a bottle in front of me than a frontal
lobotomy.

—Unclear origin (variously attributed to Dorothy Parker,
W. C. Fields, and others)

My phone rang one Monday evening while I was driving home from
work. It was Jack Phillips, a man I hadn't spoken with for a couple of
years.

Jack's son, Robbie, died at the age of five from liver failure, about six
months after we lost Mitch. A former GBM patient of mine, Eli Bai-
ley, had asked me to speak to Jack, to encourage him since I understood
some of what he was going through in losing a son. Jack is Eli's brother-
in-law.

Eli has turned out to be the longest survivor of GBM I've ever cared
for, more than ten years so far. The last time I saw him in Alabama, he
was symptom-free and doing great.

Jack and I have spoken face-to-face only once, and I did not think I
helped him much.

He had looked me dead in the eyes and said, "The worst part is that
Cindy and her family keep telling me God has a plan in all of this, that
it will all work out somehow, that I need to hold on to my faith. But to
be honest, I wasn't really sure how much of that I believed before Robbie died, and I definitely don't believe it now. Look around the world,

Doc. We're on our own. God's not out there making things happy for any of us. Robbie was a good kid. He didn't deserve being born with a bad liver and all he had to go through. It's not right. And even if God's real, I'm not letting him off the hook for taking my boy by saying it's part of some plan. If that's the plan, then I don't agree with it."

My problem was that I completely agreed with him. I was trying to encourage him and bolster his faith, but I found myself wanting to say, "You're right."

Still, I had tried to sound faithful and solid, and my answer was particularly lame. I said, "I don't agree with it either, Jack, but somehow I still believe he cares and he'll get you through it."

Jack had countered with, "He might care. But I'm not sure if I care whether he does or not. Tomorrow's my birthday. I'll turn another year older, but I realized this morning that Robbie will always be five. That's going to happen to you, too, Doc. Someday you'll be an old man, but your boy will still be nineteen. You tell me how we can reconcile that with God caring about us, and maybe we can talk again."[1]

I've only heard from him twice since then. The first time, he sent me a picture of Robbie's grave and a dark, hopeless text about how his son was cold in the ground and he had decided for sure that he no longer believed in God. The second time I received a cryptic and more positive text:

I feel a little better today.

Jack never responded to my replies, so this call was surprising to me. On the third ring, I answered.

"Hello, this is Lee."

A long pause. I could hear Jack breathing into the phone, and then he said quietly, "Eli died last night."

"Oh, Jack. I'm so sorry," I said.

His breath stuttered. "He was grateful to you, for giving him his life back. All of us were—are. He really believed he was cured."

"I know. I did too."

"You know he got married a couple years ago, right?"

"Yes," I said. "He told me that he was engaged the last time I saw him."

"Kristin," Jack said. "Beautiful young girl. Auburn grad, imagine that."

I laughed. "That's pretty amazing. Eli was a huge Alabama fan."

Jack sniffed again. "And now Kris is a widow, and my Cindy has lost a son and a brother and she's only thirty-five. Where's God in all that, *where*? I feel like he—if he's even real, somehow Cindy still believes he is—has singled out our family to hurt. It's just not acceptable."

He was audibly crying now, and so was I.

I tried to find words to encourage him because he was right—it's *not acceptable.* But I'd learned my lessons, both in reeling from the well-intentioned but unhelpful things people said to us after Mitch died and in watching Jack reel from the stupid Christian-y things I'd said to him. So I took a lesson from Pastor Jon and just said again, more quietly, "I'm so sorry."

"It's just scary, you know?"

"What's scary, Jack?"

"Everything. Kids dying, cancer coming to tear young couples apart. Before we lost Robbie, I was such a happy guy. But for the last several years, I've spent a huge amount of time just being angry and afraid about what might happen next. And then Eli's cancer recently came roaring back and killed him in two months. It's like an avalanche—nothing feels safe."

I instantly felt the pain in my jaw and shoulder and noticed the familiar acidic taste crawling up my throat. I remembered all those times after Mitch died when my body told me I was in physical danger, just like when I'd been in an actual war and terrorists were mortaring us. One of the many books given to me in those days was *A Grief Observed* by C. S. Lewis. When I finally got around to reading it, I'd nodded my head along with the author when he wrote, "No one ever told me that grief felt so like fear."[2]

"I understand," I told Jack. "I felt so scared when Mitch died too. Like if my son could die, then none of us could be certain of anything."

I heard him swallow. "Exactly. But there's something I can't figure out."

"What's that?"

Jack said, "Cindy and Eli's family, like yours, I think, are all in with God. Cindy's always talking about how we'll get to see Robbie again. I want so badly for that to be true, but I just can't make myself believe it most of the time. Eli's response, when his doctor told him that the tumor was back and there was nothing they could do, was that he was okay. Eli said he knew where he was going, he had peace that Kristin would be okay, and he would say hi to Robbie for me. I don't know if he was *strong* or *delusional* or what, but what he said was inspiring. I want that strength, that peace. I want to be there for Cindy like she's been there for me, but instead I'm just so angry, all over again."

I took a deep breath. So many people had walked into moments like this with me and just butchered the operation I desperately needed. Instead of giving me the encouraging words I needed, they said something like, "God must have needed Mitch more than you did." I wasn't going to commit that kind of malpractice on this vulnerable, hurting man.

"Jack, I know what you mean. But I think that even pondering all this is a sign that your heart is coming around to knowing you need faith to get you through. When you sent me the picture of Robbie's grave, you said you didn't believe he was anywhere but in that hole in the ground. And then later you said you felt a little better. What about now?"

There was a long pause. "I actually prayed this morning, which surprised me. But I'm not proud of what I prayed about."

"What do you mean?" I asked.

"It's just, I mean, I want God to tell me *why* I lost my son, but I'm not getting any answers. And it feels like the longer I don't have answers, then *the* answer is that I'm just supposed to be okay with it. So I'm in this box of needing God to be real so I can see Robbie again but also not believing he's real or I'd still have my boy. Am I crazy?"

"If you are, then we both are," I said. "You just articulated what Lisa and I feel all the time, and I think what everyone feels when they lose a child—or, really, when anything bad happens—if we tie God's *realness* to his *performance*. But after all this time for me, I'm starting to think there's a middle path."

"What's that?"

"I've decided that if God is the only one who can deliver me from this pain and someday set all this right *and* since I know that hard things naturally rekindle doubt in my heart, then I need to learn to aggressively doubt the doubts instead of doubting the Deliverer."

He took a deep breath and was quiet for a few seconds. Then he said, "You're doing it again. Does that actually work for you?"

Jack was right. Despite my good intentions, I *was* doing it again. I said, "I know; I'm sorry. That sounded trite. Let me say it this way: Sometimes I believe, and then I doubt, and I doubt myself and my faith for doubting so much, and then I land on faith and hope again, pretty much in a constant loop."

I heard him swallow. He said, "That actually makes sense to me. And it sounds more honest than when you try to Christian it up. Here's what happens to me: My boy hits some genetic anti-lottery, is born with a bad liver, and dies. I'm completely wrecked and almost lose my marriage, but we somehow survive. Some time goes by, and I think I'm getting better. But then Eli dies, and it's like I'm all the way back to the day after Robbie passed. It's infuriating. I just wish you could tell me that someday I will be okay again, that my faith will eventually just be solid, and I will be able to handle things like Eli dying without going all the way back to ground zero."

> Sometimes I believe, and then I doubt, and I doubt myself
> and my faith for doubting so much, and then
> I land on faith and hope again.

I thought for a beat. "You said it perfectly, and if I did tell you that, I'd be lying. I can't tell you that you'll be okay again if that means you'll feel like you used to. I guess what I'm learning is that 'okay' might mean something different than we thought it did."

He was quiet for so long that I looked at my phone to make sure the call hadn't dropped. Then he said, "Look, Doc, I need to go. I'm sorry to dump all this on you; you've got your own stuff to deal with."

"It's okay, Jack. Praying for you all. We can talk anytime."

He let out a long sigh. "I don't know. Maybe. Just needed to tell you about Eli."

Jack hung up before I could say anything else.

———*//*———

There is a hallway at Wyoming Medical Center that looks out over a cemetery across the street. I was walking down that hall the morning after I talked to Jack when I noticed a colleague looking out one of the windows.

"Hello, Carl," I said. He turned to face me, and I noticed how red his eyes were. "You okay?"

He blinked hard and said, "My little girl's buried out there. Today's her birthday. I was just thinking I'm glad it's warm today. I hate the winter; I worry about her being cold out there."

I squeezed his shoulder. "I'm so sorry. I didn't know. What happened?"

He sniffed. "Fell off a horse, got kicked in the head. She was only eight. Happened right in front of me. I did CPR all the way to the hospital, but she never took another breath."

"That's so hard. I'm sorry."

"I heard you've lost one too," Carl said.

I nodded. "Yes, our son Mitch, in 2013."

He turned his head and looked back out the window.

"It never stops, just so you know," he said. "That's the day I became an old man, but I was only thirty-five."

I could see in his eyes and his body language that those twenty years had not softened the edges of grief for Carl, and a black hole formed inside me. I'd been trying for almost four years to narrow the gap between *against* and *hope,* but seeing this suffering man worried about his daughter being cold in the ground was a gut punch.

Maybe it wasn't possible to close the gap after all?

———— *//* ————

The rest of that week lasted a month. I didn't feel well, and the phone never stopped ringing with Jonna and the other emergency physicians calling to inform me of the various ways people in Wyoming manage to get themselves hurt as summer winds down. I was exhausted, and as my father-in-law, Dennis, says, I hurt all over more than anyplace else.

I was about to leave for work on Friday when Lisa gave me a hug and a kiss goodbye. "I love you, Lee. Have a great day!"

"Doubt it," I said. "I've got to make rounds on all those trauma patients, then I have three boring meetings."

"Well, at least you have tomorrow off. And college football starts in two weeks!"

I shook my head. "Auburn is going to be terrible this year."

That was too much for Lisa. She shook her finger at me and said, "Hey, Grumpy McGrumperson, you got up on the wrong side of the bed again today."

"Me? No, I didn't! It's just been a hard week."

Her face softened and she wrapped her arms around my neck. "Honey, has it been different from any other week? You've seemed so frustrated and down these past few days. It's not like you."

I started to argue with her, but I've learned over the years to trust my insightful wife when she points out some aspect of my behavior. And, as always, she was right.

When I thought back through the week, I realized that everything had irritated me. Patients were *whiny,* all my surgeries were *hard,* board meetings were *eternal,* and I got a *stupid speeding ticket* on my way to a Bible study, which I was *too busy for anyway.* It was getting cold outside, we never had time to do anything because I was always on call, and I was just generally miserable.

I relaxed into Lisa's hug. "You're right. Nothing in particular has been bad this week. I don't know why I'm acting this way. I didn't even realize it until you pointed it out. I'm sorry."

Lisa held on tighter. "It's okay. And it's August 12, so maybe sub-consciously, you're already thinking about next week. I've been thinking about it every time I talk to Caity and Scarlett on the phone—how it's been almost four years."

Since Mitch died, we'd both feel a general malaise in the days ap-proaching big events: his birthday on February 9, holidays, August 20 (the day he died), and August 23 (the day we said goodbye). It was beyond random chance how one or both of us would have a cold or a stomachache or some other physical malady we couldn't quite identify before we realized what was happening.

As I sat through my meetings that morning, I decided to practice what I'd been preaching to myself.

I biopsied my thoughts and tried to understand why I felt the way I did. I held up to the light my feelings that everything was hard and frustrating, and it was obvious that hearing about my old patient Eli, talking again to Jack about his son's death, and seeing Carl carrying his pain so heavily after twenty years had somehow connected in my brain with the upcoming anniversary of Mitch's death. Nothing was actually happening to me, and this week had been no better or worse than any other recently.

The diagnosis was clear: I had a lousy attitude, and its root cause was a sick synapse.

Inside your head is the world's fastest supercomputer. It's composed of hundreds of millions of neurons and supporting cells. The actual num-ber of cells is quite controversial, with estimates ranging from one hun-dred billion to one trillion,[3] but suffice it to say, there are as many cells in between your ears as there are stars in our galaxy (cue Monty Py-thon's "Galaxy Song" here, but Clint Black's version is better than the original).

But all those cells would be useless if they could not communicate with one another. What makes the brain so amazing is its vast network of trillions of cellular connections called synapses.

Synapses are specialized connections between two or more cells. They allow cells to talk among themselves, to coordinate functions and automate tasks. They build networks and create little computer programs that make many important things happen in our bodies without us having to think about them every time, like how we automatically keep breathing even when we're asleep.

But synapses also trigger memories, drive emotional responses, and create physiological reactions to situations in our lives.

Healthy synapses keep your nervous system functioning as designed, meaning they control everything you do, think, and feel. Every organ in your body is influenced by synapses between cells. Synapses trigger a happy feeling when you get a good review at work, or perhaps a good grade, and can even help program you to try as hard the next time to receive the same reward.

But synapses can also make you sick, and they can hurt your life.

In recent years, synaptic dysfunction has been postulated as a cause or component of many neurodegenerative and psychiatric disorders, including Alzheimer's, Parkinson's disease, autism, and schizophrenia.[4] Neuromuscular diseases such as myasthenia gravis and Lambert-Eaton syndrome produce weakness and fatigue and are caused by a problem of the specialized synapses between nerves and muscles, the neuromuscular junction.

———//———

That Friday morning during my meeting, when I critically examined my thinking, I realized I had formed emotional synapses that fired memories of how Jack's and Carl's stories intertwined with mine and brought all that grief and loss together.

This time, though, I had not been pushed back down the staircase into the darkness. Instead, I was being insufferably irritable and negative, and I hadn't even realized it.

In epilepsy surgery, when we identify damaged brain tissue that is triggering synaptic connections, causing seizure activity to spread to other areas, we cut the tissue out or sever those sick connections. And in trauma cases in which a portion of the brain is so damaged that its very presence threatens to kill the patient by swelling and compressing the healthy brain nearby, we sometimes aggressively remove the whole lobe—a lobotomy—to allow the rest of the brain to survive.

When the problem area endangers the rest of the brain, and we can safely eliminate it, we perform these radical surgeries and sacrifice a small part to save the whole.

And that morning, as I listened to a consultant drone on about improving our customer service scores by implementing his proprietary staff checklists, I had a major breakthrough: I realized that sick synapses and lousy attitudes are the Two Dudes of TMT.

You're minding your own business, just like Anthony Walker, and the Two Dudes come out of nowhere to knock you out and leave you drunk and hammered. I had been having a good day until Jack Phillips told me about Eli and dragged me back into our mutual pain. And that phone call became the conduit for me to refire all those connections and wind up with a terrible attitude that had nothing to do with anything happening in my world at the time.

But good brain surgeons do not allow sick synapses and diseased lobes to kill their patients. Once I saw my attitude for what it was—lousy—I had to make a choice. Did I want to stay in the status epilepticus of being negative and grumpy and miserable, which would have the effect of making everyone else around me more unhappy, or did I want to feel better?

And during that meeting, I saw clearly that I *did* have a choice.

We can't control the firing of a sick synapse. Certain events around us will inevitably trigger us to remember and feel the echoes and ongoing realities of our TMTs. It is impossible for me to hear another bereaved parent tell their story without thinking of losing Mitch.

> Sick synapses and lousy attitudes are
> the Two Dudes of TMT.

I mentally checked out of the meeting, checked in for self–brain surgery, and went to work. *Lee, you're not having a bad week; you're just sad because it's close to the day you lost your son.*

Once we identify the result of that sick synapse—my lousy attitude, for example—then we must choose to either wallow in its aftermath or fix it. *Hearing Jack tell you about Eli and that he's still hurting from losing Robbie, as well as seeing Carl so torn up, naturally made you feel all those things again. That's normal. But you don't have to stew in the negative neurochemistry and let it change how you behave.*

I remembered part of a Bible verse about suffering and hope, and when the consultant wasn't looking my way, I googled it under the table on my phone: "We also glory in our sufferings, because we know that suffering produces perseverance; perseverance, character; and character, hope."[5]

For the past few days, I'd been focusing on the suffering part of this passage and had let my past, present, and future pain (which is real) create a synaptic connection (sick and false) to Jack's and Carl's (real) pain. Rather than appropriately empathizing with them and acknowledging to myself that remembering Jack, Eli, and Robbie and learning Carl's story made me (naturally) think about losing Mitch, I instead let it turn *feelings* of sadness into *real issues* with my own attitude and behavior.

I had proven in my own life that thoughts become things.[6]

Now that the diagnosis was obvious, the treatment was also. I needed to perform two types of thought surgery to sever the sick synapses I'd allowed to connect Jack's and Carl's troubles with mine, and to give myself a lousy-attitude lobotomy.

I started by reminding myself again that feelings are not facts but rather neurochemical events that can be challenged, but left unchecked they reliably produce a set of thoughts and behaviors that we program into our muscle memory over time: When I feel *this*, I think that, eat this, drink that, buy this, do that, say this, call that person, blame this person, etc. Thoughts become things.

Then I acknowledged that I needed to learn to empathize with others, like Jack and Carl, but also to be aware of my tendency to let other people's stories trigger the emotional responses that lead me down into the abyss of my grief. Learning that danger will help me in the future to recognize the triggers (talking to parents of lost children produces powerful synapses for me, apparently) and be more cognizant of my reactions to them.

Finally, I looked back over time to call this to mind, like the Lamenter, to take hope by engaging memory and movement:[7] Lisa and I and our whole family had absorbed a huge blow when we lost Mitch, *and* God had been there with us. He had been faithful and had given us the strength to persevere. We had survived. And as the swelling and initial trauma receded, we had been able to run our business, manage our family, rekindle our faith, move to Wyoming, and develop character as people who could mine their troubles to help others, like I had tried to do with Jack and then had done with my podcast and books. And in all that time of suffering, perseverance, and developing character, we had indeed found hope again: in Scarlett and our new grandson, George, in learning to see God's hand at work in our darkest hours, in still holding each other's hand and knowing that we were walking this road together.

The meeting was wrapping up, and I straightened in my chair as I realized I'd been lost in thought the whole time. I could hear my dad in my head saying, *"Turn that frown upside down!"* And I smiled a little. The consultant smiled back and said, "I'm so glad my message is helping you!"

I actually *had* found help, but not from the consultant. I let him take the win, but it was self–brain surgery that made me better because I had severed sick synapses and lobotomized my lousy attitude.

But to make it stick, I would need some rehab.

30

The Hard Work of Wellness

This is going to feel like it is going to kill me, I think,
reasonably. But all I have to do is step into it, right now.
And then I will not die.

—Jayson Greene, *Once More We Saw Stars: A Memoir of*
Life and Love After Unimaginable Loss

I was in my office one morning a few weeks later when my nurse Samantha knocked on my door. "Doc, your first patient's here, Marcus Green."

"Thanks, Sam," I said. "I've been wondering how he is."

"I was a little confused," she said. "Your last note from the hospital said he was basically paralyzed, but he came in here this morning using a walker. He looks pretty good."

We went down the hall, and I knocked on the door of the exam room. Marcus sat on the table, his wife, Doris, and daughter Susie in chairs across from him. He was wearing the cervical collar I'd put on him after the surgery I performed to take the pressure off his spinal cord and give him a chance to heal.

"Good morning," I said.

He looked up, smiled, and extended his right hand to shake mine. His grip was strong, dramatically more so than the last time I'd seen him.

"Hi," I said. "You look great."

"Thanks to you and those good folks at Elkhorn," he said. "I had a rough time there for a couple of weeks."

Elkhorn Valley Rehabilitation Hospital is a specialized inpatient rehabilitation facility in Casper, Wyoming. They have a full range of occupational, physical, and speech therapy programs to help people recover from strokes, brain and spinal cord injuries, and surgery.

"It was more than a 'rough time,'" Doris said. "He's downplaying how close he came to dying."

"That's right, Dad," Susie said. "You didn't mention the bedsores, the pneumonia, the urinary tract infection, and how you almost gave up."

Marcus's smile faded, and he looked down for a moment. When he looked up at me, his eyes were glassy. He said, "Yes. I was so tired and in so much pain. After surgery, when the numbness in my arms and legs started to improve, I could feel *everything, all the time.* It was like my whole body was on fire, and even a little touch on my skin felt so intense I could hardly stand it."

"That's called hyperesthesia, and it's pretty common after spinal cord injury," I said.

"I know, the therapists explained it to me. When I got pneumonia, they sent me back to the hospital. I told them that if my lungs failed, I didn't want to go back on the breathing machine. But I guess the antibiotics worked because I recovered from that. By the time I got back to Elkhorn, I was exhausted. The pain was unbearable, and I really didn't think I could take it anymore."

"I'm sorry you've had to go through all this," I said. "What happened next?"

Doris moved next to him and took his hand. "He almost gave up, didn't you, Marcus? Tell the doctor what happened."

Marcus nodded and said, "Yes, almost. One day, a physical therapist named Josh came in and told me I had to get up. I said it hurt too much, and I wanted to wait until the next day when I would feel better. He left, and a few minutes later the case manager came in and said if I couldn't do four hours of therapy a day, they would have to send me to a nursing home. I knew that would be the end of me, and I decided that afternoon to just go there and die. I'd heard about this so-called comfort care I could get once there was nothing else that could be done to help me, and at that point, it sounded pretty good."

Susie said, "But then the most amazing thing happened."

"What?" I asked.

Marcus smiled and said, "The next thing I knew, there was a knock on the door, and Josh had brought the whole therapy team in. The occupational therapist Kala; a huge physical therapist named Jake who was a coast guard veteran—imagine a Coastie in Wyoming; Viki, the speech therapist; and a psychiatrist named David."

"It was an intervention," Doris said.

He huffed and said, "More like a kidnapping. They basically told me that they were not going to allow me to give up on myself. Jake said, 'Dr. Warren fixed your neck, and God can fix your spinal cord. We're here to help you get stronger, and you're not letting us. You can't wait for the pain to go away before you start moving, because it never goes away. Every day you don't move, the pain will just get worse, and you'll eventually prove yourself right that it's hopeless. You have to get after it, and you have to start today.'"

"And it worked," Susie said.

"Yes," Marcus said. "Every day after that they stretched me and dragged me around that place. They put me through so much that eventually I realized that I could lie there in bed and hurt, or I could work hard and hurt, too, but that every time I worked hard, I seemed to have a little less pain and a little more hope."

He looked at Doris and then at Susie before he continued. "Then I saw the choice was really between participating in my own demise by doing nothing or pursuing my own recovery by going through rehab. And I decided that if my family and my therapy team refused to give up on me, then I owed it to them and God to not give up on myself either."

Doris said, "I'll never give up on you, Marcus Green." She leaned down and kissed the top of his head. At that point, there must have been some dust in the air or something, because my eyes were watering.

Marcus said, "I know. Doc, after several days of those folks ganging up on me like that, one morning it was like a light switch was thrown.

My legs started holding me up, and I was able to hold a spoon in my hand. I kept getting stronger, and they taught me all kinds of ways to relearn how to take care of myself. And I had to unlearn things that didn't work anymore and make new habits to help me in the future. It's a miracle, Doc. The night I met you I couldn't move anything, and I didn't think I would survive it. But now I can feed myself again. And on the last day at Elkhorn, I was able to make a loop around the nurses' station on my walker with Josh and Jake just walking alongside me."

We talked for a few more minutes, and I showed them Marcus's X-rays. The hardware in his neck looked great, and I felt it was safe to remove his collar.

"That feels better," he said as he slowly moved his neck around without the collar on for the first time. "But we better get going. I'm supposed to be at Elkhorn for outpatient therapy with Jake soon."

Sam scheduled another follow-up appointment for Marcus, we all said goodbye, and he left with his family. I went to see other patients, but for the rest of that day, I couldn't stop thinking about Marcus and his rehab story. His outcome so far was amazing, and he had beaten the odds to even survive, much less walk again.

One thing he'd said stuck with me because it paralleled what I'd figured out in trying to heal from TMT of losing Mitch: "You can't wait for the pain to go away before you start moving, because it never goes away. Every day you don't move, the pain will just get worse, and you'll eventually prove yourself right that it's hopeless."

Marcus never would have gotten better without surgery, but he also never would have recovered without rehab. And a crucial component of his rehab was the team of people who refused to let him sit and wallow in the pain. They helped him change his mind about it, and they convinced him to push through the pain and the fear to move again. Without that community of people who came alongside him, he would have died.

But the most important decision he made was when he decided to relentlessly refuse to participate in his own demise.

"You can't wait for the pain to go away before you start moving, because it never goes away. Every day you don't move, the pain will just get worse, and you'll eventually prove yourself right that it's hopeless."

He had to learn some new techniques to care for himself, to overcome some muscles that didn't work well and take advantage of others the occupational therapists taught him to use. He had to unlearn habits that would no longer work and would only frustrate him and use different approaches to accomplish his goal of regaining independence. His team was vital to his success and his survival.

Tina Tisdale thought she needed her pain to go away completely before she could live again. Once she lost hope of finding a simple fix for her pain, she killed herself.

King David pretended like all was well after his infant son died, and he tried to carry on with his life as if nothing had happened. He did not face his grief head-on or properly manage it with self–brain surgery or appropriate rehab, even though he had a group of advisers and friends around him to help.

I could see a clear contrast between these two and how Dennis and Patty had handled the loss of two of their children: Lisa's sister, Rebecca, and her brother, James. They embraced each other, their church community, and their faith. Patty had told me, "We knew we'd go insane or completely lose ourselves if we didn't find a context to put our pain into, some meaning or purpose for it. So Dennis became a chaplain to minister to other hurting people, and I started teaching the little ones about Jesus, and I found out who Jesus was by trying to show him to others. I learned more than I taught. And over time, we figured out that we hadn't died. We came alive again by deciding to live."

And that, I realized, was the rehab part of the treatment plan:

- We cannot wait to be pain-free before we decide to fight for life again, because life is never pain-free, and some things never stop hurting.

- We must believe that the pain of moving forward will produce improvement and healing, while the slow failure of staying put will lead only to more, and eventually inescapable, agony.
- We need the context of community to help us see that others have managed to hold on to or rediscover hope and faith again after they suffered TMT.
- We have to change our minds about what "okay" and "normal" mean going forward.
- We must, like Marcus Green did, be able to see how badly others in our lives still need and want us to stay in the fight.
- We must unlearn some things we believed we had to have to be happy, accepting the realities of where our TMTs left us so we can embrace the possibilities still available in our post-TMT lives.
- We must learn new skills to give our pain meaning and purpose despite our loss—like I've learned the joy in helping others whose pain is still in the primary injury phase to see that it is possible to keep going.

Every step Marcus Green takes for the rest of his life will be uncomfortable. He'll need to hold on to that walker, as his balance isn't what it was before his fall. He will sometimes need help, as some tasks are difficult with his residual spasticity and weakness. And he'll have to give up some things he used to do easily, as they will prove too challenging in his post-spinal-cord-injury life.

But every step he takes will be a step that would have been impossible if he had been unwilling to go through the hard work of rehab.

> We must relentlessly refuse to participate
> in our own demise.

And I realized it was true for me too. I first found community in the Bible stories of the Lamenter, David, and Asaph as they taught me the prehab procedure to combat hopelessness in my thinking and fight to build the muscles of faith. Then, with Lisa's help and the team of Pastor Jon, Dennis, Patty, and our family at my side, I learned the art of self–brain surgery to challenge negative thinking and regain control of my mind when it wanted me to believe that every feeling was a fact.

I knew that losing Mitch would never stop hurting and that it had and would continue to change my life—all of our lives—in many ways. Like Marcus Green, I *feel everything* since I've become afflicted by the hyperesthesia of TMT. But I still have a life to live, and I needed to get stronger so I could learn to have happiness in my post-TMT life and be prepared for whatever life brings next.

This is true for you as well, friend. Marcus needed his family and his team to help him become healthier, feel better, and be happier. You will too. But the most important aspect of his recovery was in his own head. He decided to take hope no matter how much it hurt or how scary it was.

Refusing to press in to the pain would have led to his death. But pursuing his recovery helped him regain as much of his former life as possible, accept his new limitations, maximize his abilities going forward, and become stronger to face whatever else came along in his life.

Inspired by Marcus, I made a decision: I will relentlessly refuse to participate in my own demise.

And I will press in to my recovery because rehab is the hard work of wellness.

31

No Old Beaches

"We will get there, won't we, Nuri?"

"Of course we will," I said, though I didn't really believe it then.

—Christy Lefteri, *The Beekeeper of Aleppo*

DECEMBER 2020
KIAWAH ISLAND, SOUTH CAROLINA

"All this and Jesus too," Dennis said. "It really is stunning, even on FaceTime."

"Yes," I said. I moved my phone so Dennis could see the ocean more clearly. "I love this place. Remember when you caught that starfish right here?"

We watched for a while as the sun began to set on the Atlantic coast, and Lisa held on to me tightly to keep warm as the temperature dropped quickly. "Dad, do you remember that day when Mom and Mitch found all those sand dollars together? We still have a bunch of them in our jar of memories."

Dennis looked down for a second, then slowly nodded. "That was a special trip. I remember all of it. Patty loved it there."

"I wish you were here," I said.

I held my phone a little higher, and Lisa and I turned to show Dennis the beach one more time before it was too dark.

He wiped his eyes and said, "I know. I just couldn't. I hope you find what you're looking for, though. I love you."

We clicked the red button to end our FaceTime call with Lisa's dad, who was in San Antonio.

I put my arm around Lisa, and we walked away from the ocean toward the boardwalk that would lead us back to our rental house. A young man jogged by, about the age Mitch would be now, leaving a trail of footprints in the sand behind him. I stopped to watch him for a moment, but I was ten years in the past.

A few seconds later, Lisa said, "Honey, it's getting cold. Let's go watch a movie with the kids."

I stared down the beach for a moment, pulled Lisa closer, and walked back into Christmas Eve.

———————— // ————————

The Atlantic coast is my favorite. I love the wild surf, great sand, plentiful shells, and perfect sunrises and sunsets. The Pacific is beautiful, but the water's colder. The Sea of Cortés in Cabo San Lucas takes my breath away, but the riptide is so strong it's not safe to get in the water most of the time. And the Gulf has warm water and great sand but lots of stinging jellyfish and tons of seaweed. The other oceans I've seen were from the air or on the way to or from the war, in Bahrain or some such spot.

But the water and the beach aren't why the Atlantic is my favorite. I love it because in 2010 we had one of our best family vacations there, on Kiawah Island in South Carolina. All but one of our kids went with us (Caity had to work) since this was before anyone was married and long before grandkids came along. Lisa's parents, Dennis and Patty, also came, and we rented a beautiful house on the water. It was an amazing time, and it turned out to be the last time we traveled anywhere with both Mitch and Patty.

Mitch died in 2013, and we lost Lisa's mom, Patty, in January of 2018.

Of course, it's not uncommon for seventy-six-year-old people to pass away, but Patty was no ordinary seventy-six-year-old. She and

Dennis had moved from Auburn to San Antonio in the spring of 2017 to live across the yard from Caity, Nate, Scarlett, and Georgie.

So they moved, and for several months it was almost magical. Nannie and Tata (here are those grandparent names again) spent hours every day with the kids. We went to visit in July, and Lisa and Patty planted rosebushes in their garden while I set up the internet and televisions, a job that always falls to me as our family's designated Geek Squad representative.

Everything seemed perfect, until Nannie fell.

Dennis called me from the emergency department of a local hospital early one morning in August to tell me that she had fallen in the bathroom and cut herself badly. Over the next few weeks, the story began to come out: She'd hidden it well, but Patty had been struggling with balance problems, coordination issues, swallowing, and intermittent confusion for several months. It came on slowly enough that each "little" thing was easily dismissed until the big fall made it clear that something was very wrong.

By September, it was unsafe to leave her alone. Lisa flew to San Antonio and brought Dennis and Patty to Casper because Patty insisted that I help take care of her. When I met them at the airport, I was shocked.

Patty's ever-present, beautiful smile was gone, replaced by an almost-frozen, grimace-like face. She could not stand unassisted, so Lisa was pushing her in a wheelchair through the airport. We got her into the car and then our house, but it was obvious that she needed to be in a hospital.

The next morning, she was unable to swallow enough to have breakfast, and the only words my mother-in-law said to me coherently were, "Fix me."

This was one of the last times I heard her speak clearly.

We had multiple neurologists and other specialists, including me, examine Patty. She had numerous MRI scans and other tests. Everything pointed to a rare brain stem disorder called progressive supranuclear palsy, or PSP. It mimics parkinsonism, but without tremors and with a much more rapid progression.

Patty spent weeks in the hospital, and we even sent her to Elkhorn, where Josh and company had done so much for Marcus Green, to see if aggressive therapy could help her. But she kept retreating into herself, stopped talking, and became totally unable to stand, hold on to anything, or communicate by the end of November.

The last words she spoke that were comprehensible were when she said through her rigidly clenched teeth, "Go home." Patty wanted to go home.

Lisa's sister Jessica had friends in San Antonio who offered us the use of their private plane, and Jessica flew up and took Patty and Dennis back to Texas. Home healthcare nurses determined that Patty was too sick to be at home, and she spent December in a nursing home with constant care.

Patty had made a pot of her famous gumbo and planted flowers in July, but she couldn't hold a spoon or open her mouth by the end of the year.

By January, she went to home hospice at Jessica's house, and then she was gone.

TMT was back.

Dennis had lost his wife of fifty-six years. Lisa and Jessica added losing a parent to having already lost their two siblings. My precious wife had now experienced almost all types of human grief—losing a parent, sibling, and child, but not yet a spouse—and I wrote the eulogy of a loved one for the second time in less than five years. Here's part of it:

> Patty grew up in South Texas. She loved the beaches of Port Aransas and gained local fame for her talent and beauty as Miss Shrimporee while in high school. She met Dennis McDonald at a mutual friend's wedding, and Dennis said she was the prettiest girl he had ever seen. But flattery wasn't enough to impress Patty; Dennis had to ask her out four times before she relented.
>
> Patty and Dennis were married on June 30, 1961, in the same church where they'd met. Fifty-six years later, her faithful partnership with Dennis is a wonderful example of a godly mar-

riage. She leaves behind a legacy of beauty, love, and a life well-lived. . . .

"Miss Patty" taught elementary school Bible classes to a countless number of children. Generations of Christ followers remember how she encouraged them in their faith and loved them well.

Losing Patty unanchored us for a while. It wasn't so much that we lost a parent; you expect that in life. But Patty had no medical problems, took no medications, and seemed completely well until this devastating neurological disorder—if GBM is the "I've seen the end of you" diagnosis for neurosurgeons, then surely PSP is one for neurologists—swept into her life and ripped her from us within six months. It was brutal to watch someone so vital and alive, someone who encouraged our faith and loved us well, taken from us in such a dramatic fashion.

If twenty-one paragraphs seem like a quick way to describe the path from healthy to gone of a seventy-six-year-long human life, imagine how it felt to us in real time.

And Patty never asked me for anything but love, until she asked me to fix her.

But I could not.

———— // ————

When we left Alabama for Wyoming, we thought the change of scenery and routine would help us heal after losing Mitch. And I already shared with you the two edges of that sword: trading a place where he was *everywhere* for one in which he was *nowhere* assuaged some pains, but it caused some new ones.

It did help, though, for a while.

I spent the early morning hours writing my book, which I finished in late 2017. But the rest of the time, I worked. Like most things that sound too good to be true, the recruiter's email about how "an exciting neurosurgery opportunity in the Rocky Mountains offers world-class medicine in a scenic setting. Established surgeon needs a partner to join him in the state's busiest trauma center" proved true-ish.

The day I started my new job, literally moments after I saw my first patient in the clinic, the *established surgeon* who needed a partner walked into my office and told me he was leaving. By the end of the day, it was clear that the only two people at Wyoming Medical Center who hadn't known this was coming were Lisa and me. It was literally *Tag, you're It!* And I was It.

For the next three years, I was the only neurosurgeon doing trauma surgery for a referral area that served almost half a million people. I was on call every day that I was in Casper, with only rare opportunities to go visit the kids when we could arrange to have a traveling *locum tenens* surgeon give me a break.

Lisa and I fell into a routine of working all day and then crashing into each other in the evenings. And each morning I would get up super early to work on my book. We enjoyed the *scenic setting*, but we mostly saw it through windows.

Still, we loved Casper and the good, hardworking people of Wyoming, and we gave it our all. We made lifelong friends, and we planned to stay there forever.

All the while, I was trying desperately to sew myself up spiritually and emotionally after TMT had taken my son. I had learned the prehab of how to stop some of the intrusive thoughts, the self–brain surgery of learning to biopsy and change my thinking, and I'd managed to reestablish a hopeful soul and believe it would be okay again someday, which felt much more possible since I had a great rehab community in Lisa, our kids, Dennis, and Patty to help make it so.

But losing Patty so quickly opened our eyes to what was happening around us, and both Lisa and I realized that our lives were terribly out of balance.

Needing something to do since she wasn't running our practice anymore, other than to miss our son and wait for me to get home, Lisa quickly became a juggernaut at raising money for the hospital's charitable foundation and served on their board of directors. I was on the hospital board and multiple committees, and we were passing each other coming and going. We'd displaced our grief with busyness, and even as we had managed to discover the plan and path of healing, we had also found ourselves buried, as Stephen Covey wrote, "in the thick of thin things."[1]

This isn't a book about work-life balance or the story of how an organization will grind its employees to dust until there's nothing left of them and then send out a flyer, hire a new person, and swap them out like car parts. But it can serve as a cautionary tale about the fact that there is no end, as Solomon said, to "hard work and chasing the wind."[2]

And after Patty died, I think our grief finally pulled the blindfolds off both our faces. We realized that since we moved to Wyoming, we had made emotional and intellectual progress on our healing journey back to "okayness." But even though we understood the plan and were implementing it in our brains, we were still using work as our preferred method of anesthesia to keep from feeling, as Marcus Green said, "everything, all the time."

Losing Lisa's mom was a new wound, like second impact syndrome, which magnifies the damage done when a concussion patient takes another hit before the brain swelling has healed. We were better equipped to treat ourselves, but now I can see that it was the beginning of the end of our time in Wyoming.

———— // ————

I told you earlier that my books always seem to leave out a big part of my story. *No Place to Hide* came out after Mitch died but doesn't talk about it. *I've Seen the End of You* was mostly written in Wyoming but doesn't discuss us moving there from Alabama.

So to keep from doing that again, I need to tell you almost two years' worth of a story in just a few paragraphs. Like Patty's decline from healthy in July to gone in January, this is Lisa and me working hard in Wyoming, the hospital being sold to a massive corporation I had no interest in working for, and us moving to Nebraska to start a new practice in a place that had never had a neurosurgeon, all in the span of a few months.

The whole story is probably for another time, but I'm sharing it here to give you a sense of how fast it felt for us.

Dennis came to live with us in Casper after the worst of winter had faded, as he was feeling the *everywhere* of Patty in their house in San Antonio and he needed to huddle up with us to sort things out for a while.

He stayed with us in Casper until the cold weather came again. Thirty below with two feet of snow and seventy-mile-an-hour wind is a little too much for an eighty-year-old from South Texas, but it's just a Tuesday in October in Wyoming. So Dennis went back to San Antonio, but there was too much trauma and emptiness in that house where Patty had planted roses and hung pictures and fallen and stopped talking.

He moved to a condo on the golf course close to Jessica's house and made a new routine of working out, encouraging people in the community, and playing golf. But he was spending so much time alone in a place where Patty was *nowhere,* and we all knew that wasn't healthy.

Meanwhile in Wyoming, Lisa and I were practicing the treatment plan for ourselves, trying to trust God to help us process the dramatic loss of Patty and to trust that he would help Dennis heal. Lisa stood up to the loss of her mother like she'd done when Mitch died, showing me over and over how to walk out our faith in life's hardest moments.

But something was broken, and we realized over time that the rehab part of our plan needed to include Dennis living with us. He needed us, and we needed him, as Marcus had needed the community of his therapy team and his family to help him get well. But it could not happen in Wyoming.

At the same time, as 2019 played out, it became clear that our hospital was going to be sold to a large corporation after one hundred years as an independent facility taking care of anyone in need within the state. I loved that aspect of working there, and the thought of being a cog in the giant machine of a multistate healthcare conglomerate was unappealing to me.

Our grandson Jase was born to Kimber and Bryce in May 2019, and we now had family in North Carolina, Alabama, and Texas. Our oldest son, Josh, had moved to Wyoming to go to welding school, and he loved living there as much as we loved having him close by. But when he moved back to Texas to marry Amber, we had nothing to tie us to Casper.

My book came out in January 2020, and we went to New York City for the book launch. It was exciting, and we had so much hope for that year.

But we came home sick, with a virus that would soon be known by everyone in the world. And just at the start of the global pandemic, my contract was up for renewal at Wyoming Medical Center. A few days after we got home from New York, I was informed by the chief medical officer that he was only offering me a one-year contract since the hospital sale was going through and part of the deal was that the new company only had to honor existing contracts for one year.

We had thirty days to sign the new contract.

I made a phone call to the recruiter who had previously told me about the "exciting neurosurgery opportunity in the Rocky Mountains" and told him that we were open to moving.

"Ty," I said, "if we go somewhere, it has to be the last move. We have to find a place with a better climate for our aging parents if they need to live with us, where maybe some of our kids would want to live someday, and where I can have a better balance between work and life for the rest of my career. But I want to make a difference, to go somewhere that really needs me."

The next day Ty called me back and said, "How do you feel about Nebraska? This hospital has never had a neurosurgeon, but they really need one."

On February 21, 2020, my fifty-first birthday, we walked into the hospital in North Platte, Nebraska. The lady in the lobby asked if we needed help finding something, and I introduced myself as Dr. Warren, a neurosurgeon.

"Neurosurgeon?" she said.

"Yes, I'm interviewing for a job."

"My daughter died in this hospital, waiting on a helicopter to take her to Omaha. She had a brain tumor. We really need you here," she said.

By the end of the day, we had met four people whose loved ones had been transferred elsewhere for neurosurgery or who had died waiting. We met with a broker, Amy, who took us out into the country to a place called Moon River Ranch. It's a beautiful spot on the North Platte River. On the way, Amy told us that the people who owned the place, Dale and Jo Margritz, had lost their son to glioblastoma a few years before. Like we did after losing Mitch, they moved to a different state so they could start over in a place where TMT was less omnipresent.

We stood in the backyard of the house, and a bald eagle flew down the river about fifty feet in front of us. Lisa and I held hands and breathed the oxygen-rich air at half the altitude of Casper, in a very comfortable temperature despite it being the middle of winter. And we felt at home.

Back in Casper, we met with Al and Kristin Genatone. A bronze star Army Ranger who had served in Afghanistan, Al worked with me in the OR. These people had become our best friends in Wyoming, and we felt like they should know we were thinking of making a move.

They listened to our stories about North Platte and then looked at each other and smiled. Al said, "We've been feeling like we were supposed to move, but we didn't know why. Starting a new practice is going to be hard. We'll go with you to help."

That night, Lisa and I sat on the couch in front of the fire and looked out over Casper Mountain. We held hands and I laid my head on her shoulder. We talked for hours and prayed about it.

Then Lisa said, "I think we have one more adventure left in our story. And those people need us. Let's do it."

———— // ————

We moved to Nebraska in June of 2020. The hospital hired Lisa as a consultant to set up the new brain and spine clinic since they had never had a neurosurgeon and she had run our practice for all those years in Alabama.

I did my first surgery in July. Helicopters started bringing neurosurgery patients *into* North Platte instead of *away*, and we saved some people who would not have survived long enough to be transported to another place.

Dennis came to live with us in October, and we adopted two puppies, Harvey and Louis, to roam these three hundred acres and help us scare off the coyotes.

As the year's end approached, we had performed almost two hundred surgeries in our new hospital. We weren't just out of gas or running on fumes, we were running on the memory of there having been fumes at some point in the distant past.

We needed a vacation.

––––––– // –––––––

The last truly happy time I could remember, before TMT showed up in its first form when Mitch died, was when we all went to Kiawah Island together in the summer of 2010.

We were doing well in Nebraska, but we needed to take a breath. We'd moved four times in four years—from our house in Auburn to the apartment in Casper, then a rental house, and then a house we built just a year before we decided to go to Nebraska. And all that moving and restarting had taken a toll, the mini-TMTs serving as secondary injuries in the midst of losing two of our people.

Lisa looked up from her iPad one evening and said, "It's a miracle. The same house we stayed in at Kiawah is available for Christmas week."

We reserved the house and then called the kids to tell them about it, but life got in the way again. Only half our kids could come.

Josh and Amber were expecting their first baby, and Amber's doctor told her she shouldn't travel. Nate had work issues, so he and Caity, Scarlett, and George couldn't come either. Kimber, Bryce, and Jase were all in as Kiawah was a short drive from North Carolina, and Kalyn was on break from grad school at Auburn, so she would come, as would her boyfriend, Noah, but he could stay only one night.

I went into the other room where Dennis was reading and sat down in the chair across from him.

"Hey, Dad," I said. "Remember the house we rented that week at Kiawah?"

He smiled and said, "Yes, one of the best weeks we ever had."

"Well, we're going back for Christmas! Lisa just booked it online!"

Dennis's face fell and he was quiet for a while. "Lee, I don't think I can go."

"Why not?"

"Well, she was so happy there, and we had so much fun," he said. "I think I need to leave that memory intact."

"I understand, but that's one of the reasons I *want* to go. It's the last time I remember Mitch being completely happy, even acting silly. Remember all the things we did? How he and Nannie spent so much time together?"

"Yes, I do. And those memories help me when harder ones try to force themselves on me. I need to keep them."

—— *//* ——

We flew to Kiawah, and Dennis went to San Antonio to see our family there.

We pulled into the driveway after dark. Kimber, Bryce, and Jase had already arrived, and Kalyn was a few hours behind us.

We had the same huge house but only half the people.

Everywhere around the house, I could see and hear moments from the past—*Here's where Mitch, Josh, and I wrestled; here's where Patty showed us all the seashells she'd found; there on the deck is where we took that crazy picture in the pool.*

The next morning, we walked down to the beach, and Jase saw the ocean for the first time.

The week was amazing and poignant, as Kimber and Kalyn also experienced the nostalgia and the pain of walking the ground Mitch and Nannie had walked in the pre-TMT world.

Then something remarkable happened as we walked the beach late one day toward the end of the week: I implemented my thought biopsy technique, and I decided to think *about* my memories instead of just remembering them. I again realized something I've pondered a lot in the years since Mitch died: *Memories often paint an imprecise picture of the past.*

The truth is that the real events we remember are rarely exactly as we recall them. We tend to glorify and make perfect our good memories, and we magnify and sharpen our bad ones. Memories become like fishermen's and preachers' stories over time, optimized to tell the emotional tale we want or need them to tell. This has to do with the neuroscience around how memories are stored, with painful things having a more powerful impact over pleasant things. There's a survival advantage to it, but it can make life hard to enjoy.

> Memories often paint an imprecise picture of the past.

Why? Because, unless we're aware of it, we often either continually compare today to some perfect, idealized past we can never match, or we constantly miss out on new opportunities for fear of something happening that we remember and don't want to feel again.

I'd find myself staring into the ocean, and along with the gulls' cries and the waves crashing, I'd hear the kids laughing a decade before and see Mitch running down the beach, Dennis finding a live starfish, and all of us having such a great time. The ocean is a playground!

Lisa and I would walk on the beach with the kids, but amid all the laughter and fun, there was pain too. Here's the spot where Dennis cut his foot on a conch shell; there's where Mitch got caught in the riptide. The ocean is dangerous!

It's all about perspective. You can't navigate your life by trying to make every moment match some magical time in the past or by being too afraid to live it because of something that happened before.

I realized as we walked that evening that I *thought* I was walking where I'd been with Mitch, but that sand and that water have turned over countless times in the years since we were there together. And it all finally became clear to me: You can't find closure by touching a beach or being in a place or reliving some experience; you have to change your mind about it.

But the opposite is also true. You can't find happiness *or* avoid more pain by refusing to revisit the sand you walked on before your TMT.

With that clarity in my thinking, I took a deep breath of the salty air and admitted to myself that I'd come to Kiawah to try to reconnect to some previous version of my life when Mitch was happy and Patty was healthy, but neither one of them was there.

I sent Dennis a text message:

> Dad, I figured something out. I thought coming here would heal a wound, and you thought it would open one. We were both wrong, because there are no old beaches. They refresh themselves with each high tide.

The treatment plan had come through for me. It allowed me to change my mind about The Massive Thing of losing Mitch, which would then allow for healing and moving forward in a healthy way. I was better prepared for the TMT of losing Patty than I would have been without the prehab, surgery, and rehab I went through before I knew that my son's death would always be *a* thing in my life, but it could not be *the* thing. And I could see how to square Jesus's seemingly irreconcilable John 16:33 promise about life being hard with his John 10:10 insistence that he came here to give us an abundant life.

They square up because of hope.

Hope says even though it's dark, it'll be light again soon. That even though life will pull the yellow handle again, the parachute will open just in time.

The treatment plan allows me to believe I can close the gap between *against* and *hope,* which is where faith lies, and it teaches me the self–brain surgery to change my mind so I can change my life.

> Hope says even though it's dark, it'll be light again soon.

Once I can close the gap, I'm able to believe I can get there from here, and that day on the beach was when I finally saw the path.

Turns out, Lisa showed it to me.

The wind picked up and I pulled her close. She laid her head on my shoulder, and we turned back toward the house. Suddenly, Lisa straightened and pointed to the sand in front of us. She said, "Look! There's Jase's little footprints heading up to the boardwalk."

It was getting dark, but I could clearly see for the first time in years. There are no old beaches. Mitch's footprints were all washed away from Kiawah Island, and yet we could still see Jase's.

We don't have to live in "but" as long as we can hold on to "and."

That's how we can find the new "okay," and that's how we can grab on to life again.

We stepped onto the boardwalk to go to the house where the kids were waiting to watch a movie with us.

I took one last look back at the beach, and I was able to breathe in the air of how grateful I was to have had time with Mitch here in this hallowed place and for the thousands of other beautiful moments we shared in his tragically short life. And for the first time since Mitch died, I felt truly happy that evening as the sun set over South Carolina.

You can, too, my friend. And you have to, because the stakes are so high.

Epilogue

The High Stakes of Happiness

And yet, this tale about despair becomes a story against despair.

—Elie Wiesel, *Dawn*

I started this book with a story about what happens when life pulls the yellow handle and launches us into the unknown of TMT. Along the way, we've met people like Tina Tisdale, who couldn't accept the "you can't have that" when she wanted a pain-free life, and Lucky Chuck Hobson, who stared into his own illness in the context of having watched his wife, Wanda, during hers and said, "Seems easier to die."

Earlier, I told you what I was going to tell you: that TMT can either be *a* thing that happens in your life or *the* thing that happens in your life, and that the difference lies in how you see and respond to it. Then in the pages that followed, I've shared how the treatment plan can help you put TMT into its proper place—as a devastating event, not the omnipresent and all-consuming furnace of suffering from which you can never come out.

I left you on the beach at Kiawah, where I was feeling happy for the first time in years. I had finally accepted the "and" of losing Mitch, and I felt grateful for still having a beautiful family, having Jase's footsteps to follow, and, hopefully, having a lot of life left to live.

But now it's time to tell you what I told you, so here's the punch line:

Of all the stories I've told in this book, perhaps the most important is that of Anthony Walker. He's the young man who was minding his own business when the Two Dudes hammered him, crushed his facial nerve, and left him unable to close his eye or smile.

Why is that the most important story?

Because it shows us the high stakes of happiness.

I recently heard through a colleague in Denver that Anthony's face has improved significantly. He can close his eye almost all the way and can manage an almost-normal smile now. The deficits are much more subtle than they were the day of the crush injury because of surgery, rehab, and the tincture of time.

He had been in grave danger of going blind because of the inability to close his right eye. If he had chosen not to have surgery, his eye would have dried out, and his cornea would have become progressively more scarred and eventually opaque, unable to allow light in.

And so, too, for us, my friend.

TMT becomes the only thing we can see when the yellow handle is pulled and we're crashing toward our doom and realize there's not enough altitude or time for the chute to open. This is where Jenny got stuck, going to the support group over and over for fifteen years but not letting them take her eyes off her pain and onto a treatment plan so she could see hope again.

If you can't blink your eye and shift your focus away from TMT and onto the plan, you'll soon find that the dark void of hopelessness is the only thing you can see. And once the scar forms, the pain becomes *the* thing in your life, the last thing you remember seeing.

I told you that hope was the first dose of the treatment plan. And I don't want you to confuse hope and faith; they're different. I've met a lot of Crashers (and I spent years with them at the bottom of the curve), and the surprising thing is that many of them still have faith. They believe in God, and they believe in heaven. They just forgot to have hope, so they believe they have to gut the rest of their lives out and maybe someday God will take them to a better place.

But the Bible says that faith is the evidence that the things we hope for are really true.[1] And hope is the light on the path back to happiness so that we can still live while we're waiting to *get there from here*. It's not an accident that I started this book with Ephesians 5:14: "Awake, O sleeper, and arise from the dead, and Christ will shine on you" (ESV).

TMT leaves us hammered, comatose, and with our nerves crushed.

The treatment plan can bring us back.

And hope is the first dose.

I wrote the first chapters of this book in April 2021, sitting by the fire while Harvey and Louis, then seven-month-old puppies, slept. It's now December, and here I am again. They're older now, but they still love to sleep by the fire while I write.

Both of our dogs have been struggling with an upset stomach lately, no doubt because they ate something nasty as they roam around on these three hundred beautiful acres. And in a few minutes, I'll mix some medicine into their food, since that's the prescription Dr. Susan, our amazing vet, gave us to make them better.

But I can't slip what you need into your food. You must choose the treatment plan, just like Anthony and Clyde and Marcus Green did when they signed the consent forms for their surgeries. And just like the Lamenter and Asaph and David did when they chose to engage the muscles of hope.

My colleague showed me the before-and-after pictures of Anthony Walker's face. And Anthony's facial reanimation is remarkable. But if you look close enough, you can see the little scar in front of his right ear and notice slight asymmetry of the right corner of his mouth. He'll have to live with those persistent reminders of his injury, but he can smile when he feels like it.

And so can you.

My shoulder is hurting this morning, the most consistent reminder of my TMT of losing Mitch. You have scars too.

But the scars mean your body healed, that you survived. And you can learn again, using the treatment plan, to smile when you feel like it.

In the operating room, my hands are rock steady. Through training and years of practice, I've learned to calm my anxiety and not make an operation out of everything.

But I'm writing this to you with the trembling hands of a once-broken and always-bereaved dad who lost his little boy. I'm holding out the treatment plan that has brought "and" to my life, to Lisa's life again.

I want you to become healthier, feel better, and be happier. That's what hope will do for you.

Lucky Chuck Hobson was right—it is easier to die. But it's usually not best.

I want you to live again. TMT doesn't have to be the only thing you can see.

You just have to follow the treatment plan.

And you have to start today.

Keep your feet off them pedals, though.

Acknowledgments

God keeps his promises. When I sat down to acknowledge those who have helped to make this book possible, I knew I had to start with him. *Father, thank you for giving us Mitchell and for showing us that he's not behind that door at the bottom of the staircase. He never was, because he's safe with you. Thank you for giving us the treatment plan and for infusing us with enough hope that we could see the steps we had to take to get there from here. Amen.*

Every word of this story was lived with and next to Lisa Warren. She demanded that I write it, supported me in every way while I did so, and opened her heart to allow me to show you how we, with weeping and gnashing of teeth, have learned to live again after TMT left us crushed.

I didn't share as many stories about Lisa here as I have in my previous books. That was intentional, born of the corollary to Warren's Law of Suffering I shared with you earlier: We may suffer together, but we grieve alone. She has her own stories, those of choosing a son to love as her own and then falling hard for him and having him ripped from her life by TMT. Of helping her husband and our other children learn to stand under TMT's weight and still be who we're called to be. Of losing her mother and two siblings and still having enough hope in her heart to share some with me. And of how to keep Mitch's memory alive so that he's real to Scarlett, George, Jase, and Ryker, his niece and nephews.

Lisa, I love you more than I can express with words. I know who I was before you, and that man could not have survived what TMT did to him without you. I am forever yours and so grateful. The first time I saw your eyes, I said, "Wow." I've said that every day since.

Dennis and Patty McDonald walked this whole story with us as well. Patty never failed to call or come over on August 20 and 23 and February 9. And when she went to heaven in 2018, Dennis told us he wanted to be wherever we are. You don't get to choose the family you're born with, but you get to choose who you do life with. Since you moved here, Dad, it's been a master class on grieving well. You taught me to shake my fist, but not at God, and that's everything.

All of our children have responded to losing their brother differently, but all in ways that honor him. Josh moved to Wyoming so he could put his arms around us just when we needed him most. And he moved back to Texas for Amber, our only daughter-in-law and the one we were rooting for since they met. Caity and Nate named their first son George Keaton Vanepps, giving him Mitch's middle name. Kimber and Bryce gave Jase the middle name Warren so our family name goes on after I'm gone. And Kalyn is becoming a therapist, using what she learned in the school of pain to help others. Each of you have my heart, and I'm so proud of you all.

Kathy Helmers called me when I emailed her the idea for this project. I told her that Lisa and I wanted to do this with her as our agent and guide again, and after she read the first chapter, she cried and said, "This is the book the world needs after *I've Seen the End of You*. And it's the book I need too." Kathy, you've been more than an agent. You're a guide, coach, editor, mentor, and friend. And so much of this book has the salt and pepper you added as its sous chef. Thank you.

And to my podcast listeners and newsletter subscribers all over the world, thank you for letting me bounce so much of this off you as over the years we've learned together how to survive and live again after TMT.

I love you, my friends.

W. Lee Warren, MD
Moon River Ranch, Nebraska

Notes

CHAPTER 1: Where on Earth Is Hope?

1. John 10:10; 16:33.
2. Aeschylus wrote these words in his play *Agamemnon*. In *Three Greek Plays: Prometheus Bound, Agamemnon, The Trojan Women, trans.* Edith Hamilton (New York: W. W. Norton & Company, Inc., 1937), 169–70.
3. See Psalm 40:2, AMP.

CHAPTER 2: Un-Holy Week

1. Genesis 1:5.

CHAPTER 3: What Color Is Today?

1. Matthew 27:46.
2. Genesis 1:8.

CHAPTER 4: Can It Get Any Worse?

1. Genesis 1:13.

CHAPTER 5: A Test Dose

1. Genesis 1:16.
2. Genesis 1:17–18.
3. Genesis 1:19.

CHAPTER 6: Holding the Light, Feeling the Darkness

1. "Never shall I forget that night, the first night in camp, which has turned my life into one long night." Elie Wiesel, *Night,* trans. Stella Rodway (New York: Bantam Books, 1982), 32.

CHAPTER 7: The Apogee of Hopelessness

1. Lamentations 3:4.
2. You can get my "weekly prescriptions" email for free at www.wleewarrenmd.com /newsletter.
3. Dennis Prager, *Happiness Is a Serious Problem: A Human Nature Repair Manual* (New York: ReganBooks, 1998), 56.
4. Lamentations 3:16.
5. Christopher Sirk, "Diffusion of Innovation: How Adoption of New Tech Spreads," CRM.org, August 21, 2020, https://crm.org/articles/diffusion-of-innovations.

CHAPTER 8: The Best-Laid Plans

1. "Why do you see the speck that is in your brother's eye, but do not notice the log that is in your own eye? Or how can you say to your brother, 'Let me take the speck out of your eye,' when there is the log in your own eye?" (Matthew 7:3–4, ESV).
2. "A person standing alone can be attacked and defeated, but two can stand back-to-back and conquer. Three are even better, for a triple-braided cord is not easily broken" (Ecclesiastes 4:12, NLT).

CHAPTER 9: Extraordinarily Ordinary

1. Chris Voss, *Never Split the Difference: Negotiating As If Your Life Depended on It* (New York: Harper Business, 2016), 211.
2. "Claiming to be wise, they instead became utter fools" (Romans 1:22, NLT).
3. The story of God giving the people the Ten Commandments and carving them into stone tablets is told in Exodus 20; 32; 34.

CHAPTER 10: Origami Golden Calf

1. Rudyard Kipling, "If," Poetry Foundation, accessed November 1, 2022, www.poetry foundation.org/poems/46473/if---.

CHAPTER 11: A Little Bit Like Hope

1. Psalm 139:14.
2. Philippians 4:8–9, TPT.

CHAPTER 12: Seems Easier to Die

1. "The remarkable thing about fearing God is that when you fear God you fear nothing else, whereas if you do not fear God you fear everything else." Oswald Chambers, *The Pilgrim's Song Book*.
2. My newsletter reaches forty-plus countries each week and can be found at www .wleewarrenmd.com/newsletter. My podcast, *The Dr. Lee Warren Podcast*, is heard all over the world three times a week and can be found anywhere podcasts are available. https://drleewarren.substack.com/podcast.
3. Isaiah 38:15.
4. Jennie Allen, *Anything: The Prayer That Unlocked My God and My Soul* (Nashville: Thomas Nelson, 2015).
5. Katelyn N. G. Long et al., "The Role of Hope in Subsequent Health and Well-Being for Older Adults: An Outcome-Wide Longitudinal Approach," *Global Epidemiology* 2 (November 2020): 100041, https://doi.org/10.1016/j.gloepi.2020.100018.

CHAPTER 13: All in Your Head

1. Christopher Marlowe, "The Face That Launch'd a Thousand Ships," All Poetry, accessed November 3, 2022, https://allpoetry.com/The-Face-That-Launch%27d-A -Thousand-Ships.

CHAPTER 14: Data Stories

1. Bernie Siegel, *Love, Medicine and Miracles: Lessons Learned About Self-Healing from a Surgeon's Experience with Exceptional Patients*, 60th ed. (New York: William Morrow, 2011).
2. Daniel Amen, *Change Your Brain, Change Your Life: The Breakthrough Program for Conquering Anxiety, Depression, Obsessiveness, Lack of Focus, Anger, and Memory Problems*, rev ed. (New York: Harmony, 2015). You can find further information regarding SPECT imaging on Dr. Amen's website: www.amenclinics.com/approach /why-spect.
3. Tommy Walker, vocalist, "These Things Are True of You," by Tommy Walker and C.A. Worship Band, track 33 on *Anthology: 1991–2002*, Get Down Ministries, 2008.
4. "He was despised and rejected—a man of sorrows, acquainted with deepest grief. We turned our backs on him and looked the other way. He was despised, and we did not care" (Isaiah 53:3, NLT).
5. "In that same hour he rejoiced in the Holy Spirit" (Luke 10:21, ESV).

CHAPTER 16: Reanimation

1. "If only for this life we have hope in Christ, we are of all people most to be pitied" (1 Corinthians 15:19).

CHAPTER 17: Data Stories, Part 2: Gap Theory

1. *Merriam-Webster*, s.v. "visualize," accessed November 2, 2022, www.merriam-webster.com/dictionary/visualize.
2. "Therefore, it was necessary for him to be made in every respect like us, his brothers and sisters, so that he could be our merciful and faithful High Priest before God" (Hebrews 2:17, NLT).
3. John 10:10; 16:33.
4. See Genesis 32:22–31.
5. Paraphrase of John 20:27, inspired by Nicholas Wolterstorff in his book, *Lament for a Son* (Grand Rapids, Mich.: Eerdmans, 1987).
6. "Shadrach, Meshach, and Abednego replied, 'O Nebuchadnezzar, we do not need to defend ourselves before you. If we are thrown into the blazing furnace, the God whom we serve is able to save us. He will rescue us from your power, Your Majesty. But even if he doesn't, we want to make it clear to you, Your Majesty, that we will never serve your gods or worship the gold statue you have set up'" (Daniel 3:16–18, NLT).

CHAPTER 18: Hope Is a Verb

1. Lamentations 1:9.
2. Lamentations 1:16.
3. Lamentations 2:2.
4. Lamentations 2:11–12.
5. "'For I know the plans I have for you,' declares the LORD, 'plans to prosper you and not to harm you, plans to give you hope and a future'" (Jeremiah 29:11); "He has shown you, O mortal, what is good. And what does the LORD require of you? To act justly and to love mercy and to walk humbly with your God" (Micah 6:8).
6. Some biblical scholars believe the prophet Jeremiah is the author of Lamentations, although the book does not actually identify who wrote it. This is an interesting article on the topic: "Who Wrote Lamentations?" Stack Exchange: Biblical Hermeneutics, August 1, 2014, https://hermeneutics.stackexchange.com/questions/12897/who-wrote-lamentations.
7. Lamentations 3:1 (emphasis added).
8. Mark Vroegop, *Dark Clouds, Deep Mercy: Discovering the Grace of Lament* (Wheaton, Ill.: Crossway, 2019), 102.
9. Lamentations 3:17–20, NLT.
10. Lamentations 3:21, ESV.
11. Lamentations 3:21–26, NLT (emphasis added).
12. "The children cry for bread, but no one has any to give them" (Lamentations 4:4, NLT); "Joy has left our hearts; our dancing has turned to mourning" (Lamentations 5:15, NLT).
13. Lamentations 5:21–22, NLT.

14. Vroegop, *Dark Clouds, Deep Mercy,* 28.
15. Lamentations 3:22, NLT.

CHAPTER 19: Memory, Movement, and the Science of Happification

1. The Bible does, indeed, teach that God is happy and he wants us to be happy. The best exegesis of this I've ever read is Randy Alcorn's book *Happiness* (Carol Stream, Ill.: Tyndale, 2015). I cannot do a better job than he did, so please read it.
2. Psalm 77:1–2.
3. Psalm 143:3–4.
4. Psalm 77:3–12.
5. Psalm 143:1–4.
6. Psalm 143:5–8.

CHAPTER 20: The Happification of Hopeful Souls

1. "When the members of the Sanhedrin heard this, they were furious and gnashed their teeth at him. But Stephen, full of the Holy Spirit, looked up to heaven and saw the glory of God, and Jesus standing at the right hand of God. 'Look,' he said, 'I see heaven open and the Son of Man standing at the right hand of God.' At this they covered their ears and, yelling at the top of their voices, they all rushed at him, dragged him out of the city and began to stone him. Meanwhile, the witnesses laid their coats at the feet of a young man named Saul. While they were stoning him, Stephen prayed, 'Lord Jesus, receive my spirit.' Then he fell on his knees and cried out, 'Lord, do not hold this sin against them.' When he had said this, he fell asleep" (Acts 7:54–60).
2. Tom Waits, vocalist, "Come On Up to the House," by Kathleen Brennan and Thomas Alan Waits, track 16 on *Mule Variations,* ANTI-, 1999. (I added my name to the lyrics.)
3. "When he [Thales] was asked what was very difficult, he said, 'To know one's self.' And what was easy, 'To advise another.'" Diogenes Laërtius, *The Lives and Opinions of Eminent Philosophers,* trans. C. D. Yonge (London: G. Bell and Sons, 1915; Project Gutenberg, 2018), https://gutenberg.org/cache/epub/57342/pg57342-images.html, 19.
4. Psalm 28:1, Voice.
5. In the previous chapter, I quoted Psalm 143:7, "Answer me quickly, LORD; my spirit fails. Do not hide your face from me or I will be like those who go down to the pit." I'd missed this before—when David lets TMT speak to him, he identifies the pit as a place God doesn't go.
6. Psalm 139:7–8, Voice.
7. Psalm 28:1, ESV (emphasis added).

CHAPTER 21: Lucky Chuck's Last Ride

1. Thomas Aquinas, *Summa Theologiae* I–II, Q. 40, Art. 2, in *Summa Theologiae of St. Thomas Aquinas*, 2nd and rev. ed., 1920, quoted in Karen Swallow Prior, *On Reading Well: Finding the Good Life Through Great Books* (Grand Rapids, Mich.: Brazos, 2018), 123.

CHAPTER 22: The Punch Line

1. When I was older and began to show interest in public speaking, Dad shared that this model—"Tell 'em what you're gonna tell 'em, then tell 'em, etc."—is actually widely known and was not his original thought. Its origins are unclear, but it seems to go back mostly to old preachers or possibly even the philosopher Aristotle. See "Tell 'Em What You're Going To Tell 'Em; Next, Tell 'Em; Next, Tell 'Em What You Told 'Em," Quote Investigator, August 15, 2017, https://quoteinvestigator.com /2017/08/15/tell-em/.
2. W. Lee Warren, *I've Seen the End of You* (Colorado Springs: Waterbrook, 2015), 247.
3. Warren, *I've Seen*, 254.

CHAPTER 23: Choosing Your Treatment Plan

1. Habakkuk 1:2.

CHAPTER 24: A Controlled Form of Trauma

1. Thomas Hobson was a stable owner in England who gave customers the choice of renting the horse in the stall closest to the door or renting none at all. From Hobson's business model came the phrase "take it or leave it." See *Merriam-Webster*, s.v. "Hobson's choice (*n.*)," accessed September 22, 2022, www.merriam-webster.com /dictionary/Hobson%27s%20choice.
2. Tom Inglis et al., "In-Hospital Mortality for the Elderly with Acute Traumatic Spinal Cord Injury," *Journal of Neurotrauma* 37, no. 21 (October 15, 2020): 2332–42, https://doi.org/10.1089/neu.2019.6912.

CHAPTER 25: There's No Failure in Prehab

1. 2 Samuel 12:20, MSG.
2. 2 Samuel 12:21–23.
3. 2 Samuel 13:21.
4. See 2 Samuel 13:38–39.
5. 2 Samuel 12:10.
6. Per Rotbøll Nielsen et al., "Prehabilitation and Early Rehabilitation After Spinal Surgery: Randomized Clinical Trial," *Clinical Rehabilitation* 24, no. 2 (January 26, 2010): 137–48, https://doi.org/10.1177/0269215509347432.
7. "Eleanor Rigby by the Beatles," Songfacts, accessed November 5, 2022, www .songfacts.com/facts/the-beatles/eleanor-rigby.

8. "Who shut up the sea behind doors when it burst forth from the womb, . . . when I fixed limits for it and set its doors and bars in place, when I said, 'This far you may come and no farther; here is where your proud waves halt'?" (Job 38:8–12).

CHAPTER 26: Understanding Your Brain on TMT

1. John Ortberg, *Know Doubt: The Importance of Embracing Uncertainty in Your Faith* (Grand Rapids, Mich.: Zondervan, 2008), 85.
2. W. Lee Warren, *I've Seen the End of You* (Colorado Springs: Waterbrook, 2020), 251.
3. "This Is Your Brain . . . This Is Your Brain On Drugs: 80s Partnership for a Drug-Free America," YouTube video, :30, posted by Anthony Kalamut, March 21, 2010, https://youtu.be/GOnENVylxPI.
4. I learned the phrase "Think about your thinking" from my friend Dr. Daniel Amen. His work has helped millions of people learn to love their brains and improve their lives. He can help you too. www.amenclinics.com.

CHAPTER 27: The Biopsy Will Change Your Mind

1. Dane Ortlund says, "Fallen human beings enter into joy only through the door of despair." Dane C. Ortlund, *Deeper: Real Change for Real Sinners* (Wheaton, Ill.: Crossway, 2021), 38.
2. Psalm 116:10–11.
3. "Then you will know the truth, and the truth will set you free" (John 8:32).

CHAPTER 28: Surgery and Rehab Will Change Your Life

1. This saying is thought to have originated in a 1965 essay by Theodor Reik: "It has been said that history repeats itself. This is perhaps not quite correct; it merely rhymes." But it is frequently attributed to Mark Twain. See "History Does Not Repeat Itself, but It Rhymes," Quote Investigator, January 12, 2014, https://quoteinvestigator.com/2014/01/12/history-rhymes.
2. Mark Vroegop, *Dark Clouds, Deep Mercy: Discovering the Grace of Lament* (Wheaton, Ill.: Crossway, 2019), 105.
3. Lamentations 3:21, ESV.
4. Casey Gwinn and Chan Hellman, *Hope Rising: How the Science of Hope Can Change Your Life* (New York: Morgan James Publishing, 2018), 11.

CHAPTER 29: Thoughts Become Things

1. W. Lee Warren, *I've Seen the End of You* (Colorado Springs: WaterBrook, 2020), 228.
2. C. S. Lewis, *A Grief Observed* (New York: HarperOne, 1994), 3.
3. Jennifer Welsh, "Human Brain Loses Billions of Neurons in New Analysis," Live Science, February 29, 2012, www.livescience.com/18749-human-brain-cell-number.html.

4. Katarzyna Lepeta et al., "Synaptopathies: Synaptic Dysfunction in Neurological Disorders—A Review from Students to Students," *Journal of Neurochemistry* 138, no. 6 (June 2016): 785–805, https://doi.org/10.1111/jnc.13713.
5. Romans 5:3–4.
6. I discovered this phrase when I saw it on a T-shirt. In bold black letters it simply said, "Thoughts Become Things." I searched it and found this phrase has been used in countless book titles, blog posts, metaphysics lectures, and even a movie.
7. Lamentations 3:21.

CHAPTER 31: No Old Beaches

1. Stephen R. Covey, *The 7 Habits of Highly Effective People: Powerful Lessons in Personal Change* (New York: Simon & Schuster, 2020), 182.
2. Ecclesiastes 4:6, NLT.

EPILOGUE: The High Stakes of Happiness

1. My paraphrase of Hebrews 11:1.

W. LEE WARREN, MD, is a practicing neurosurgeon and the award-winning author of *A Peek Under the Hood, No Place to Hide,* and *I've Seen the End of You.* He talks to thousands of his closest friends daily about faith, doubt, and neuroscience on *The Dr. Lee Warren Podcast* and at his website, www.wleewarrenmd.com. His wife, Lisa, is way out of his league, and his four grandkids have him completely wrapped around their little fingers.

He lives on the banks of the North Platte River in Nebraska with Lisa; his father-in-law and sidekick, Dennis; and two overprivileged dogs, Harvey and Louis.

ABOUT THE TYPE

This book was set in Caslon, a typeface first designed in 1722 by William Caslon (1692–1766). Its widespread use by most English printers in the early eighteenth century soon supplanted the Dutch typefaces that had formerly prevailed. The roman is considered a "workhorse" typeface due to its pleasant, open appearance, while the italic is exceedingly decorative.

"In beautiful, haunting, powerful prose, *I've Seen the End of You* will inspire you, make you cry, and ultimately help you see God and suffering in a new way."

—DANIEL G. AMEN, physician and bestselling author

I've Seen the End of You provides a page-turning, raw, honest look at how we can remain on solid ground in our darkest moments. Get your copy today.

WATERBROOK

Available wherever books are sold

Neurosurgeon and author Dr. W. Lee Warren
delivers prescriptions for how to lead a healthier, better,
happier life on daily episodes of his podcast.

Through engaging conversation with guests like Max Lucado,
Philip Yancey, and John Bevere, Dr. Warren aims to leave you
encouraged with each episode.

Listen to *The Dr. Lee Warren Podcast*
on Your Favorite Podcast App